PELICAN BOOKS

A356

ARCHAEOLOGY FROM THE EARTH

SIR MORTIMER WHEELER

Sir Mortimer Wheeler, who has been Director of the National Museum of Wales and Keeper of the London Museum, was the first Director of the Institute of Archaeology in the University of London, and later Director-General of Archaeology in India and Adviser in Archaeology to the Government of Pakistan. In the intervals of war service, during which he attained the rank of Brigadier in the Eighth Army, he excavated Roman forts in Wales, the Roman city of Verulamium, the famous prehistoric fortress-town of Maiden Castle in Dorset, and other sites both in this country and in northern France. Whilst in India, he discovered the site of a Roman trading-station on the coast of the Bay of Bengal and carried out a series of excavations on prehistoric and early historic sites, including those of the Indus Civilization of the third millennium B.C. In addition to his more academic work, he has broadcast widely on archaeological subjects.

ARCHAEOLOGY
FROM THE EARTH

SIR MORTIMER WHEELER

PENGUIN BOOKS

Penguin Books Ltd, Harmondsworth, Middlesex, England
Penguin Books Inc., 3300 Clipper Mill Road, Baltimore 11, Md, U.S.A.
Penguin Books Pty Ltd, Ringwood, Victoria, Australia

—

First published 1954
Published in Penguin Books 1956
Reprinted 1961, 1964, 1966

—

—

Made and printed in Great Britain
by Cox & Wyman Ltd
London, Reading and Fakenham
Collogravure plates by Harrison & Sons Ltd
Set in Monotype Bembo

'Quand le sol aura été interrogé, il répondra'.

L'ABBÉ COCHET

CONTENTS

PLATES

TEXT FIGURES

PREFACE

IT is something like a quarter of a century since I first undertook to write this book. I now know less than I did then, and will probably in the following pages more often recommend what *not* to do than what to do. That is perhaps as it should be. It cannot be affirmed too often that bad scholarship in the field generally involves the fruitless and final obliteration of evidence, and bad scholarship is still all too prevalent there. On the positive side, I have described certain methods and principles, which, on the basis of trial and much error, I have found less harmful than others that have been employed. Many of the selected methods and principles are derived from those of the greatest of all archaeological excavators, General Pitt Rivers. Others I have learned from colleagues and from the workmen whom I have employed in various parts of the world. A few may be of my own devising. They are offered, not as laws, but as the notes and reminiscences of a lengthy and varied archaeological experience. For the most part I have refrained from discussing aspects of field-archaeology of which I myself have no considerable first-hand knowledge. The repeated use of the first personal pronoun is a reminder to the reader that some at least of the limitations of this essay are appreciated by the author.

If there be a connecting theme in the following pages, it is this: an insistence that the archaeologist is digging up, not *things*, but *people*. Unless the bits and pieces with which he deals be alive to him, unless he have himself the common touch, he had better seek out other disciplines for his exercise. Of this more will be said in the first and last chapters, but I would make it clear at once that here is an earthy book, inapt to clerkly hands. Not for an instant, of course, is it pretended that the spade is mightier than the pen; they are twin instruments; but, in this matter of digging, the controlling mind must have in a developed degree that robust three-dimensional quality which is less immediately essential to some other inquiries. In a simple direct sense, archaeology is a science that must be lived, must be 'seasoned with humanity'. Dead archaeology is the driest dust that blows.

The substance of this book constituted the Rhind Lectures for 1951.

In its preparation I must isolate two acknowledgements: to Miss Kathleen Kenyon, my colleague and merciless critic for many years, and to Miss Theodora Newbould who has relentlessly urged me from chapter to chapter and cannot disown all responsibility for the result. For permission to reproduce illustrations thanks are due to the Society of Antiquaries of London, the Louvre Museum, the Prehistoric Society, the editor of *Antiquity*, the British School of Egyptian Archaeology, the Oriental Institute of the University of Chicago, and the American Schools of Oriental Research.

R. E. M. W.

INSTITUTE OF ARCHAEOLOGY
UNIVERSITY OF LONDON
1956

CHAPTER I

Introductory

THERE is no right way of digging, but there are many wrong ways. Amongst the latter our successors will no doubt include ways which we regard to-day as relatively right, in accordance with the natural principle whereby every generation is liable to belittle the achievement of its predecessors. This attitude is often enough unjust. Before heaping scorn too promiscuously upon our untutored forebears, it is at least only fair to classify their shortcomings and to differentiate between culpability and immaturity. It is unprofitable to blame Xerxes for omitting to deploy torpedo-boats at Salamis, or Napoleon for attacking the British squares with cavalry instead of machine-guns. Nor, by the same token, can we honourably blame an Early Victorian barrow-digger for omitting to record by the three-dimensional method. But there is much, far too much, in more recent archaeological excavation that falls short of the highest available standards and therefore deserves the lash. At the best, excavation is destruction; and destruction unmitigated by all the resources of contemporary knowledge and accumulated experience cannot be too rigorously impugned. In the following pages attention will be drawn from time to time to the crimes no less than to the virtues of contemporaries and forebears, in the full awareness that, as a fellow-practitioner, the author is himself a vulnerable target.

And when in these pages certain methods are suggested as preferable to others in certain contexts, I would at once make it clear that I am indulging in reminiscence, not laying down laws. For thirty years it has been my occupation to dig up antiquity in a variety of countries and circumstances, and I have sought to profit from experience and criticism. But there is no term to either, and I have no doubt that, as I write, further experience and criticism are building up or eliminating what I have written. Who would have it otherwise? πάντα ῥεῖ. We cannot twice descend into the same stream, said the philosopher.

To-day it is indeed no easy matter to preserve a just balance between aim and method in this business of digging up the past. Developing technique is liable to obscure the objective; at the best a sort of leap-frog progress ensues. Attempts of a semi-philosophic kind to adjust the priorities are not always very helpful. What in fact is Archaeology? I do not myself really know. Theses have been written to demonstrate that it is This or That or not the Other Thing; for example, I may refer the reader, if he will, to a laborious analysis with a bibliography of 612 works which was produced in 1948 by an American exponent.[1] It may be doubted whether all this matters very much to us in our daily application. We may be content to see that the grass is green without understanding the mysteries of chlorophyll or attempting to distinguish too cleverly between botany and chemistry; we may appreciate the Unfinished Symphony without a profound knowledge of the physics of the vibratory disturbance which we call sound. I do not even know whether Archaeology is to be described as an art or as a science; more will be said of this in the concluding chapter. But it is at least abundantly clear that Archaeology is increasingly dependent on a multitude of sciences and is itself increasingly adopting the methodology of a natural science. It draws to-day upon physics, chemistry, geology, biology, economics, political science, sociology, climatology, botany, and I know not what else. As a science, it is pre-eminently a synthetic process; and if we prefer to regard it as an art, or even as a philosophy, we must still affirm that it is an integration of scientifically observed and dissected phenomena relating to man; it is still a synthesis. These are not definitions, they are merely description, and incomplete at that. It will not help us forward to our main objective, the study of human cultures, to spend time and ingenuity upon the academic niceties of definition.

But there is one guiding condition of our work which I would emphasize at the outset. We belong, some of us, to a generation which has been involved actively in two wars. Military similes are therefore not entirely alien to us. And I would accordingly urge that in one vital respect at least there is an analogy between archaeological and military field-work that is recurrent and illuminating. The analogy rests – strangely enough as between the dead and the deadly – in the under-

1. Walter W. Taylor, 'A Study of Archaeology', *American Anthropologist*, 1, Memoir no. 69 (Indiana University, 1948).

lying *humanity* of both disciplines. The soldier, for his part, is fighting not against a block of coloured squares on a war-map; he is fighting against a fellow-being, with different but discoverable idiosyncrasies which must be understood and allowed for in every reaction and manoeuvre. Equally, as has been urged in the preface, the archaeological excavator is not digging up *things*, he is digging up *people*; however much he may analyse and tabulate and desiccate his discoveries in the laboratory, the ultimate appeal across the ages, whether the time-interval be 500 or 500,000 years, is from mind to intelligent mind, from man to sentient man. Our graphs and schedules mean nothing if they do not ultimately mean that. Of our scraps and pieces we may say, with Mark Antony in the market-place, 'You are not wood, you are not stones, but men'. It is a truism of which I constantly find it necessary to remind the student and indeed myself: that the life of the past and the present are diverse but indivisible; that Archaeology, in so far as it is a science, is a science which must be extended into the living and must indeed itself be lived if it is to partake of a proper vitality.

Let me for a moment amplify this matter. I have said that we cannot properly understand the past unless we have a living sympathy with the human stuff which its relics represent. We cannot understand, for example, the structural mechanism of an ancient burial-mound unless we can bring to bear upon its details a rational imagination capable of comprehending and vitalizing them. If we fail to do that, we are not humanists but mere collectors of disjected minutiae, signifying almost nothing. We would be better employed collecting bus-tickets, an occupation which at least involves no damage to scientific evidence. And since I have mentioned burial-mounds, let me carry my example a stage further. No one has done more to vivify the mumbo-jumbo of our Bronze Age burials than has Sir Cyril Fox during a long series of excavations as Director of the National Museum of Wales. One example in particular recurs to my mind. Many years ago, Fox and I were trudging across a desolate Welsh moorland and came upon a small barrow set within an earthen circle. Offa's Dyke came steadfastly up to the lip of the circle and then on the other side started off again with equal determination on a new alignment. The whole scene stirred Fox's ready enthusiasm, and a week or two later he had dug himself well into the landscape.

The mound had by now vanished, and Fox stood, in the spirit, amongst its makers. He was almost physically present at the living ritual, the actual procedure of burial. I quote his own words:

> Under the centre of the mound was a deep and large grave-pit on the floor of which lay the skeleton of a full-grown man. To enable this grave to be entered with ease and dignity a sloping passage from ground-level had been cut on the north side. Surrounding the grave-area was a circular trench, which also had a sloping entrance, and on the same side. *But it had no exit*: the area round the grave was isolated. The con-clusions drawn from these facts were that the dead man's home was on the north side of the site chosen for his burial; that he had been cere-monially borne by friends or kinsfolk up to, and into, the trench: that those who carried him were not allowed to enter the consecrated area round the grave, but that the persons charged with the performance of the burial rites were awaiting the bearers beyond the trench. The body was handed over, and these persons descended with it into the grave.[1]

What matters to us here and now is not, of course, the particular episode which I have cited but the creative act of reasoned imagina-tion that has gone to the making or remaking of it. Fox's interpreta-tion may not be correct in all its details; in any event the objective facts upon which it is based are fully recorded, and the interpretation of them can be reshaped in the light of fuller knowledge. The great thing is that those facts are infused with a rational intelligence; they emerge from Fox's brain as three-dimensional entities. Contrast the ordinary excavation-report. Year after year, individual after indi-vidual, learned society after learned society, we are prosaically reveal-ing and cataloguing our discoveries. Too often we dig up mere things, unrepentantly forgetful that our proper aim is to dig up people.

So too with ancient fortifications. It is no accident that leaders in their interpretation have so often been soldiers: General Roy, for example, in the eighteenth century; General Pitt Rivers, Napoleon III's colleagues, and the distinguished officers who manned the Ger-man *Limes* Commission in the nineteenth. Our hill-forts, as Leland long ago remarked, are the works of 'men of warre'; and their study demands the virile spark of the mind militant. It is no mere by-

1. C. Fox and Bruce Dickins, *The Early Cultures of North-west Europe* (Cam-bridge, 1950), p. 54.

product of the study of culture-creeps and ceramic crosswords: both, be it added, admirable and indeed essential preoccupations, and lovable after their fashion.

Enough, now, of these general matters of approach. Some pains have been taken to emphasize initially the vital principle because so much of the substance of the following chapters is concerned with the dry bones, with procedures, with the extraction of evidence rather than with its interpretation. It is to be hoped that, even so, their contents may be of some slight interest beyond the limited range of archaeological practitioners. To-day, we can scarcely touch history without touching archaeology; and for the greater part of human existence we cannot touch history at all. Prehistory is a hundred times as long as history, in the isolationist usage of the terms. The proper study of mankind involves therefore a disproportionate amount of archaeology; and, unless the reader have more faith in the professors than I have, he will demand, and very properly demand, to know something of their credentials. How does archaeology *work*? We know that the historian goes to his documents and his epigraphs. On what does the prehistorian depend? An attempt will be made in these chapters to indicate, mainly from personal experience, some part of the rather complicated machinery with which he wrings his evidence from the earth.

CHAPTER 2

Historical

FIRST it may be useful to see something of the upgrowth of the technique of archaeological excavation during the past century, and so to establish, however summarily, a perspective for our subject. It would be of little profit to carry the matter further back behind the Victorian era, and to follow others in a general discussion of the evolution of conscious antiquarian thought from the time of the Renaissance or earlier. We are concerned here with methodical digging for systematic information, not with the upturning of earth in a hunt for the bones of saints and giants or the armoury of heroes, or just plainly for treasure. It is of no importance to us that, as long ago as the twelfth century, the monks of St Albans were digging up, recording, and sanctifying the remains of some poor Saxon in Hertfordshire; nor even are the early probings of the curious into sites such as Pompeii or Herculaneum strictly relevant to the theme, although they no doubt played their part as a stimulus to subterranean research *in partibus*. True – a truth stranger than fiction – as early as 1784 a future President of the United States of America, of all people, was already carrying out an excavation on surprisingly modern lines in Virginia – the first scientific excavation in the history of archaeology. This astonishing episode will be described in a future chapter (p. 58). It was unique, not only in its age but for long afterwards, and it were better to begin here with an incident of more normal kind.

The chosen incident occurred in those forties of the nineteenth century which were more fruitful than any other decade, whether in Britain or abroad, in the foundation of new institutions for the furtherance of our science. On all hands new antiquarian societies were being established in England and Wales. The close of the decade was marked by the transfer of the collections of the Society of Antiquaries of Scotland to the Crown, and by the establishment of a separate section of British and Medieval Antiquities in the British Museum. 'Within no very distant period', wrote a contemporary observer, 'the study of antiquities has passed, in popular esteem, from contempt

20

to comparative honour.'[1] And it was in accordance with the new spirit of the times that on an August day of 1844, on an obscure hill in Kent above the vale of Maidstone, there assembled a top-hatted gathering of the local nobility and gentry, reinforced by some twelve or fourteen labourers who proceeded to hew a great gash through a tall Romano-British barrow.

It was the labour of four long days [the contemporary account informs us] to cut entirely through the barrow, but we who were not absolutely diggers contrived to pass our time to the full satisfaction of all the party.... A plentiful supply of provisions had been procured for picnicking on the hill, and we remained by the barrow all day, watching and directing the operations. ... We contrived to pass our time, at intervals between digging and picnicking, in games of various descriptions ... and in other amusements. The season was fortunately exquisitely fine, and it was only once or twice that we were visited with a heavy shower from the south-west, when the only shelter was afforded by the hole we had ourselves dug ... in which we managed to interlace parasols and umbrellas – much as the Roman soldiers are said to have joined together their shields when advancing to the attack of a fortress – so as to form a tolerably impenetrable roof over our heads. ...[2]

The woodcuts (Pl. 1) speak for themselves.

Such was the sense of light-hearted adventure that stirred our great-grandparents in the dawn of a popular interest in archaeological field-work. That spirit is not to be scorned. These gentry were, of course, the veriest amateurs (blessed word!) or merely curious spectators. But their curiosity was the chrysalis of cultivated opinion from which, in the fullness of time, modern archaeology was to emerge and take wing. Of the same ilk were the ladies and gentlemen who a little later flocked in their carriages to watch Canon Greenwell dig a barrow on the Yorkshire wolds. A very notable man, the Canon; at the age of 97 he could still land his salmon, and those of us who have the good sense to be fishermen are careless of our best interests if we cannot find a 'Greenwell's Glory' somewhere in our fly-books. But it is as the author of *British Barrows* that for the moment he recurs

1. 'Introductory Address' by E. Oldfield to the (Royal) Archaeological Institute (itself founded in 1844), *Arch. Journ.* ix (1852, 1).

2. *Gentleman's Magazine*, Dec. 1852, p. 569.

to us. The apocryphal history has it that on one occasion an elegant and admiring assembly clustered round him whilst, with the intuition of the inspired connoisseur, he chose his barrow from a series within range and turned his labourers on to it. In due course, a handsome burial-urn began to emerge from the excoriation, amidst the manly gasps and ladylike cries of the spectators. As always, the dear and wonderful Canon was infallible! The workmen gingerly lifted the urn – exposing beneath it a copy of the previous day's *Times*!

Such were the methods of a less finicky age. Nevertheless, a procedure which was still justifiable in Kent in 1844 or on the wolds a few years later was in fact rendered obsolete by a young army officer working in his spare moments in central India as long ago as 1851. These dates are worth emphasizing because the work of Captain Meadows Taylor, though limited in scope and scarcely noticed at the time, marked or should have marked the beginning of a new epoch in technical method and scientific observation. It did not, of course, stop or even check picnic-party excavation. But the fact remains that, after 1851, digging such as that described above, or such as normally indeed persisted until far more recent times, was for ever obsolete and culpable. Let us pause for a moment to examine this innovation more nearly.

The basis of scientific excavation is the accurately observed and adequately recorded section. More will be said of this matter in a later chapter. Here it will suffice to premise that the successive accumulations of construction and debris on a buried occupation-site have much the same validity as the successive pages of a book, and, to be understood, must be comprehended in their proper sequence, like the pages of a book. In a haphazard excavation such as that of the Kentish barrow it is scarcely necessary to observe that such accumulations or strata as may have been present are not merely torn ruthlessly from their context but are not even postulated by the carefree excavator. The whole mechanism of the 'book' is ignored or misunderstood. If we set aside the eighteenth-century American statesman of whom mention has been made, Meadows Taylor was the first man, so far as I know, to hint implicitly at the true function of the excavator and recorder in this vital matter. He was an officer and highly successful administrator in the relatively obscure service of the Nizam of Hyderabad State. He is known to fame, if at all, as the author of *The Confessions of a Thug*; but of his work as an amateur archaeologist the *Dictionary of National Biography* says nothing. For that we have to turn to three papers published in the *Journal of the Bombay Branch of the Royal Asiatic Society*, iii (1851), 179–93, and iv (1852), 380–429; and, unexpectedly, in the *Transactions of the Royal Irish Academy*, xxiv, pt. iii, *Antiquities* (1862), 329–62. These three papers show an acuteness of perception and a technical competence far in advance of the time. Meadows Taylor dug into a number of the megalithic tombs characteristic of central and southern India, and drew and described sections which preserve an informative and convincing record of what he found, with differentiated strata (Fig. 1). When one recalls that only seven or eight years divide the work of the Kentish party from that of the lone fever-stricken Englishman in native India, the latter's achievement stands out as a landmark in the annals of archaeology. Unfortunately, British archaeology in India was not destined to maintain this pre-eminence.

During the following decades much pick-and-shovel work of a spectacular kind drew increasing attention to the possibilities of the craft. Troy and Mycenae set Homer and Schliemann firmly upon their feet. In France, under the eagle of Napoleon III, the admirable Colonel Stoffel ran Julius Caesar to earth with a considerable measure of success, combining military manoeuvre with a certain rudimentary technical skill. He realized, for example, the significant fact that soil, once disturbed, rarely quite resumes its original compactness, and that in particular the ditches of Caesar's camps, now utterly levelled, could still be detected in section. His method of search, reasonably enough, was to attack his buried fortifications with massed formation of trial-trenches.

I placed the workmen [he wrote] with picks and shovels in several files, in a direction perpendicular to one of the presumed sides of the [buried] camp, the workmen in each file 20 or 30 metres from one another. Each of them was ordered to remove the layer of *humus* to a width of 2 feet. If, after having removed this layer to a depth of 70 centimetres, they felt that their picks were striking a resistant soil, the inference was that this soil had never been removed and that there was *no* Roman ditch. The workmen then continued to advance so long as nothing different was encountered. But when they arrived, beyond doubt, at the ditch, the difference was at once apparent.

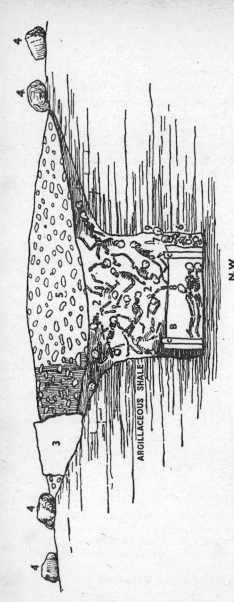

ARGILLACEOUS SHALE

Section of Cairn D

2. Space filled with grey earth, and skeletons irregularly thrown in.
3. Entrance stones, limestone slabs, 2 ft. apart.
4. Outside circle stones.
5. Loose stones and earth.
6. Space filled with small urns.
7. Single skull on top of urns.
8. Single skull on top of skeletons.
9. Single skull on ledge of shale over urns.

Cairn D. Ground Plan of Cist

A, A. Slabs of limestone for floor.
B, B. Upright slabs for side.
C, C. Head and foot slabs.
D, D. Two skeletons.
E, E. Place filled with urns.

Fig. 1. Section through a megalithic grave in Hyderabad State, India. By Meadows Taylor, 1851

It may be added that the Colonel's regimented enthusiasm was shared by his Emperor who, at Gergovia, 'was so wonder-struck on seeing the profiles [of the Caesarian ditches thus revealed in section] that he thought of buying the hill to preserve them. He abandoned this idea when he learned that the inhabitants did not desire to be dispossessed, and he ordered me to fill in my trenches and to restore everything to its former state.'[1] The path of science never did run smooth!

But it was left to another soldier, a Briton, to make the first substantive advance in the technique of excavation and recording. In the year 1880, General Lane Fox by a surprising series of chances succeeded to the Rivers estate situated in Wiltshire and eastern Dorset, and under the terms of the will assumed the name Pitt Rivers. He had already varied a military career by a study of artifacts along evolutionary lines, and had been admitted to the Royal Society for his anthropological work. The principle of the evolution of human institutions was no new concept. It had indeed found expression as far back as 1786, when Sir William Jones in Calcutta had enunciated the evolutionary relationship of certain languages – Sanskrit, Greek, Latin, Persian, Celtic, and 'Gothick' – another example of British pioneer scholarship *in partibus*. But the dramatic development of that principle in relation to natural species during the fifth and sixth decades of the nineteenth century had given a new impetus to its application in the humanistic field. And now the General, in the course of his musketry, had found the same basic principle in the development of fire-arms, and had extended it to other human instruments. His whole approach to archaeology was thus from a modern angle, and for twenty years he explored the ancient sites on or adjoining his estate with a science and scholarship that half a century of subsequent work has supplemented rather than superseded.

Above all, the General's constant plea was for 'greater precision and detail in excavation'.[2]

It will, perhaps, be thought by some [he remarks] that I have recorded the excavations . . . with unnecessary fullness, and I am sure that I have done it in greater detail than has been customary, but my experience as

1. T. Rice Holmes, *Caesar's Conquest of Gaul* (Oxford, 1911), pp. xxv ff.
2. *Excavations in Cranborne Chase*, i (1887), pp. xvi–xvii.

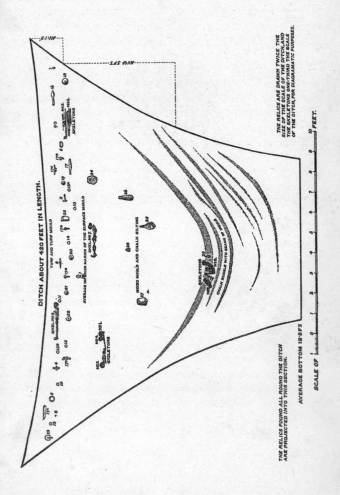

DITCH ABOUT 420 FEET IN LENGTH.

TURF AND TURF MOULD

AVERAGE INFERIOR MARGIN OF THE SURFACE MOULD

MIXED MOULD AND CHALK SILTING

CHALK RUBBLE WITH SEAMS OF MOULD

SKELTONS

AVERAGE BOTTOM 12·8 F²

SCALE OF   0 1 2 3 4 5 6 7 8 9 10 FEET.

THE RELICS FOUND ALL ROUND THE DITCH
ARE PROJECTED INTO THIS SECTION.

THE RELICS ARE DRAWN TWICE THE
SIZE OF THE SCALE OF THE DITCH, AND
THE SKELETONS ONE-THIRD THE SCALE
OF THE DITCH, FOR DIAGRAMMATIC PURPOSES.

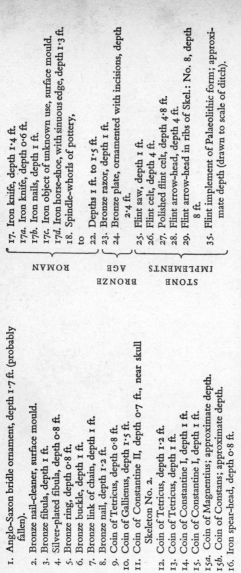

ROMAN

1. Anglo-Saxon bridle ornament, depth 1·7 ft. (probably fallen).
2. Bronze nail-cleaner, surface mould.
3. Bronze fibula, depth 1 ft.
4. Silver-plated fibula, depth 0·8 ft.
5. Bronze ring, depth 0·8 ft.
6. Bronze buckle, depth 1 ft.
7. Bronze link of chain, depth 1 ft.
8. Bronze nail, depth 1·2 ft.
9. Coin of Tetricus, depth 0·8 ft.
10. Coin of Gallienus, depth 1·5 ft.
11. Coin of Constantine II, depth 0·7 ft., near skull Skeleton No. 2.
12. Coin of Tetricus, depth 1·2 ft.
13. Coin of Tetricus, depth 1 ft.
14. Coin of Constantine I, depth 1 ft.
15. Coin of Constantine I, depth 1 ft.
15a. Coin of Magnentius; approximate depth.
15b. Coin of Constans; approximate depth.
16. Iron spear-head, depth 0·8 ft.

ROMAN

17. Iron knife, depth 1·4 ft.
17a. Iron knife, depth 0·6 ft.
17b. Iron nails, depth 1 ft.
17c. Iron object of unknown use, surface mould.
17d. Iron horse-shoe, with sinuous edge, depth 1·3 ft.
18. Spindle-whorls of pottery, to

BRONZE AGE

22. Depths 1 ft. to 1·5 ft.
23. Bronze razor, depth 1 ft.
24. Bronze plate, ornamented with incisions, depth 2·4 ft.

STONE IMPLEMENTS

25. Flint saw, depth 1 ft.
26. Flint celt, depth 4 ft.
27. Polished flint celt, depth 4·8 ft.
28. Flint arrow-head, depth 4 ft.
29. Flint arrow-head in ribs of Skel.: No. 8, depth 8 ft.
35. Flint implement of Palaeolithic form; approximate depth (drawn to scale of ditch).

Fig. 2. Section by Pitt Rivers across the ditch of Wor Barrow, Dorset, 1898, showing relics projected from a three-dimensional record

an excavator has led me to think that investigations of this nature are not generally sufficiently searching, and that much valuable evidence is lost by omitting to record them carefully. . . . Excavators, as a rule, record only those things which appear to them important at the time, but fresh problems in Archaeology and Anthropology are constantly arising, and it can hardly fail to have escaped the notice of anthropologists . . . that, on turning back to old accounts in search of evidence, the points which would have been most valuable have been passed over from being thought uninteresting at the time. Every detail should, therefore, be recorded in the manner most conducive to facility of reference, and it ought at all times to be the chief object of an excavator to reduce his own personal equation to a minimum.

In practice, Pitt Rivers's method was to record every object in such a manner that it could be replaced accurately in its findspot on the recorded plan and section. That is the essence of three-dimensional recording, and three-dimensional recording is the essence of modern excavation. Since the time of Pitt Rivers we have in some respects elaborated his technical processes, and there is no doubt that the best records of the present day surpass the General's. It is salutary to reflect, however, what he might himself have done with another fifty years of experience behind him!

Let us glance for a further moment at the master's working principles. From the outset, he grasped the vital need of an adequate staff, a need which has since his time been too often neglected, with deplorable consequences. He at once

determined to organize a regular staff of assistants, and to train them to their respective functions after establishing a proper division of work. . . . The work of superintending the digging – though I never allowed it to be carried on in my absence, always visiting the excavations at least three times a day and arranging to be sent for whenever anything of importance was found – was more than I could undertake single-handed . . . and I had by ample experience been taught that no excavation ought ever to be permitted except under the immediate eye of a responsible and trustworthy superintendent.[1]

Or again:

The excavations in Winkelbury [a Wiltshire 'camp'] having been carried on before my assistants were sufficiently trained, I never left the

1. *Excavations in Cranborne Chase*, i, p. xviii.

ground during any great part of them. One or more of the assistants was always engaged in superintending the workmen upon the ground or in drawing the objects, in repairs to the skulls and the pots, and in forming the relic tables, by which means the records have been kept up to date, and it has been found important that, as far as possible, everything should be recorded whilst it was fresh in memory.[1]

The fruits of this irreproachable system are shown in the classic sections across the Dorset dykes or the ditches of Wor Barrow (Fig. 2), where every object found is projected carefully on to stratified sections in a fashion which has stood the test of constant back-reference by two generations of archaeologists.

I pass on to 1904, four years after the General's death. In that year, Flinders Petrie, whose genius will long outlive the occasional gibes of his successors, described his aims and methods in a classic monograph which is itself a curiosity. Typical, for example, both of the man and of the age in which he worked is his advocacy of the payment of labourers on a piece-work basis rather than by the day. 'Working by the piece saves all this trouble [i.e. of constant supervision], and if the men are well-trained, and the work is simple, it goes on automatically and takes the smallest amount of attention. In detached small sites men may even be left unvisited for two or three days, merely reporting each evening how they have worked.'[2] My pen melts as I transcribe those words. The almost complete absence of measured sections from Petrie's reports is the inevitable corollary of his 'method'. His great problem was to keep his labourers at work. An air of vigilant surprises had to be sustained. He devised sunken approaches to the scene of operations, so that he could come upon his diggers unawares and catch them out; and he supplemented this device by long-range snooping through a telescope, with results which he triumphantly retails.[3] The same spirit, with an alternative remedy, survived a quarter of a century later in a manual on field-work issued in 1929 by no less exalted a body than the French Prehistoric Society. There also it is the congenital 'dishonesty' of the workman rather than the scientific need for constant skilled supervision that constitutes the major problem; but the remedy, printed in italics and praiseworthy

1. *Excavations in Cranborne Chase*, ii (1888), p. xiv.
2. W. M. Flinders Petrie, *Methods and Aims in Archaeology*, p. 29.
3. Ibid., p. 28.

enough in itself, is: *The best way to ensure the honesty of your workmen is not to leave them a minute.*[1] That is by the way; to return to Petrie, it is only fair to add that I knew him well, and, like all who knew him, profoundly admired his untiring search for truth by such means as he understood. But it is abundantly apparent that, between the technical standards of Petrie and those of his older contemporary Pitt Rivers, there yawned a gulf into which two generations of Near Eastern archaeologists have in fact plunged to destruction. Petrie worked for more than the normal span and with more than the normal energy in a particularly spectacular field. His pupils were legion and his hold upon them was manifested in an unquestioning fidelity that was sufficiently intelligible and creditable but was itself a bar to progress. When I last visited him, on his deathbed in Jerusalem at the beginning of 1942, his restless brain was still hovering over a multitude of problems and possibilities which extended the smaller minds of his listeners, and I left him for the last time with a renewed sense of that devotion which he inspired in the hearts of his pupils and friends. It is almost with a feeling of guilt that I now, after considerable experience of his work and of the tradition which he established widely over the East, find myself compelled to deplore an influence which in much of its technique so long outlasted its scientific usefulness.

Thirty years after Petrie's ingenuous self-revelation, another archaeologist, arguing from experience in Palestine (where more sins have probably been committed in the name of archaeology than on any commensurate portion of the earth's surface), could still write as follows:

[the foreman] receives general instructions from the director for each day's work, picks men for special tasks, . . . sees to it that regulations are carried out, . . . [and] usually stands on some high point from which he can oversee the excavations. . . . *Of course, it would be very unwise for a director to leave him or any overseers of gangs to their own devices for long, since their understanding of methods is mechanical*[2] [italics mine].

The glimmerings of conscience are visible in that sentence, but the

---

1. *Manuel de recherches préhistoriques*, published by the Société Préhistorique Française (Paris, 1929), p. 23.

2. W. F. Badè, *A Manual of Excavation in the Near East* (Univ. of California Press, 1934), p. 20.

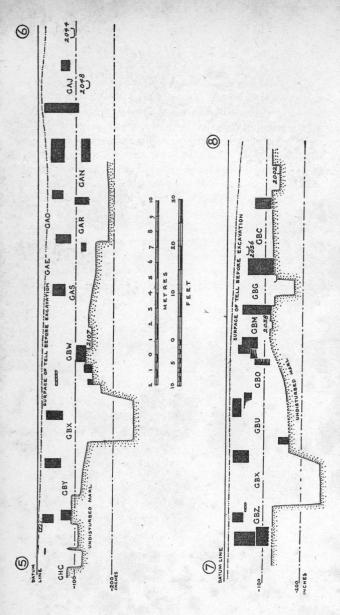

Fig. 3. Part of a section through Tell el Ajjūl, Palestine, 1938

old sin shows through. There is still no real understanding of the primary principle of all excavation, that no shovelful of earth shall be cut save under direct and skilled supervision. And those who have witnessed Palestinian excavation with a critical eye know all too well how widespread and enduring has been the technical irresponsibility of much of its direction throughout an active half-century.

Let us transfer our cautionary tale from precept to practice: not to stir more mud but to point the lesson, however negative it be. The sections (from Tell el Ajjūl in Palestine) reproduced in Fig. 3 represent a long and hard-worn tradition which dies hard and still awaits a *coup de grâce*. They were drawn in 1938 and published in 1952, so that they may be regarded as of comparatively modern date. Nevertheless, they belong technically to the infancy of archaeology and were, in fact, obsolete more than a century ago. Regard the absence of associated strata, the omission even of symbolical levels, so that the walls are suspended in section as in a vacuum. And that this sort of technical atavism is still international in its vogue is shown by a

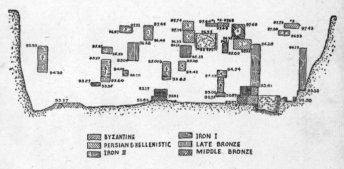

Fig. 4. Section through part of the site of Bethel, Palestine, 1939

section from another Palestinian site (Bethel), reproduced here from an authoritative American commentary published in 1939 (Fig. 4). Better far is a section through one of the mounds of Sialk, in central Iran, published in 1938 (Fig. 5): yet, even here, observation and record are scrappy, strata are unlabelled and are left incomplete and in mid-air, detailed reconstruction of the picture is impossible and the

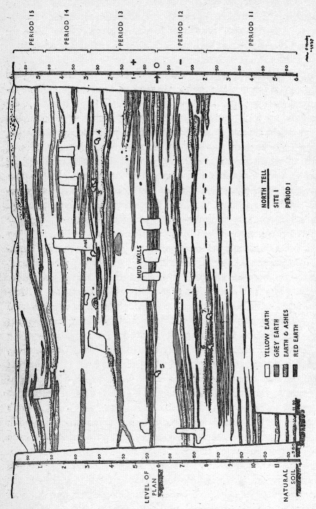

Fig. 5. Section through part of the mound of Sialk, Iran, 1938

PERIOD 15 PERIOD 14 PERIOD 13 PERIOD 12 PERIOD 11

NORTH TELL
SITE I
PERIOD I

☐ YELLOW EARTH
▨ GREY EARTH
▨ EARTH & ASHES
▮ RED EARTH

MUD WALLS

LEVEL OF PLAN

NATURAL SOIL

T – B

accurate projection of finds on to the section would be impracticable even were the necessary data tabulated. But for downright technical incompetence, the largest archaeological department in the world – the old Archaeological Survey of India – was unbeatable. Here the primary blame rests not with the Indians, who are quick and ready to learn, but with the successive British staffs responsible for the establishment and initial running of the department. It is almost beyond belief that as recently as 1940 the Survey could publish in monumental form 'sections' such as those here illustrated (Figs. 6 and 7): the one showing walls suspended, like those of Bethel, in a featureless profile of the site, with neither building-lines nor occupation strata, varied only by indications of the completely unmeaning piles of earth on which the excavator left some of his walls standing; the other showing the burials of two variant cultures floating like a rather disorderly balloon-barrage, without hint of the strata and the grave-lines which would have indicated their scientific inter-relationship. It is sad to compare these caricatures of science with the admirable sketch-records of Meadows Taylor, nearly a century earlier.

This circumstance is the more remarkable in that the average standard of field-archaeology in Great Britain itself during the past half-century has been unsurpassed, if approached, by that of any other country. That statement is made with no insular prejudice. In Holland, Dr van Giffen and others have evolved methods of excavation which mark a new standard of finesse, and certain of the German excavators, notably Dr Gerhard Bersu, need no commendation from me. Since its inauguration in 1890, the German *Limes* Commission, though often technically below the General Pitt Rivers standard, has produced admirably co-ordinated work, particularly valuable in its attention to small finds. But in the very limited area of the British Isles, rich in remains of differentiated cultures, with the General's example behind them, field-archaeologists have worked within close range of one another and under the fire of constant and even fierce mutual criticism. Bad work has been done, but rarely with impunity. Experience has been readily shared and a steady progress assured, from the days of J. P. Bushe-Fox in the first quarter of the century to those of Ian Richmond and Grahame Clark in the second.

In the face of this achievement at home, what has gone wrong with Eastern or Near Eastern field-archaeology? The question is worth asking if a remedy is to be found. The answer is not in fact difficult, and the remedy follows. The error has lain not in quantity but in quality. In the first place, few excavators who have gone East have in the past received adequate preliminary training under closely critical observation such as has been noted above from Britain. They have generally gone East as class-room or museum orientalists, with the bare knowledge of an ancient language or of more-or-less classified

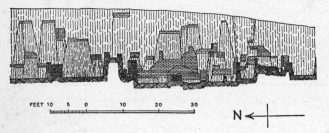

FEET 10   5   0   10   20   30   N

Fig. 6. Section of part of Harappā, Pakistan, 1940

exhibits and *disjecta* but without practical experience of the field-problem. And, once there, they are generally lost. An excavator may work for years on a remote Asiatic site without being able to discuss his methods and results *on the spot* with competent critics. In the second place, Eastern excavation has in the past tended to attract relatively liberal endowment, either through the natural lure of a Biblical context, or of association with famous and impressive civilizations, or of the general 'romance' of the Orient, or even of the East as a winter-tourist objective to wealthy Western benefactors. This liberal endowment, coupled with the relatively cheap cost of native labour, has encouraged wholesale mass-excavation, rewarded by extensive building-plans and ample finds which gratify the patron but are far beyond the capacity of anything approaching exact record. Indeed, cheap oriental labour has in the past been a constant snare (compare Pl. 4a). 'The maximum number of labourers employed at any one time was something over thirteen hundred', states the report of the excavation (in 1912–13) of an outstandingly important Eastern site where only one supervisor was present. In the third place, the common use of mud-brick for building and the impact of extreme weather-conditions have often (though not always) combined to deepen the strata on an Eastern site, so that their over-all depth may be at least five times as great as on a closely interleaved British site. It is understandable that these deep strata encourage proportionately drastic methods of excavation which tend to outpace supervision. A ruined mud-brick building will dissolve into several feet of almost uniform deposit; desert winds will cover it with a thick mantle of undifferentiated sand; torrential rains will transfer material in bulk and may artificially intermix and level it. I have indeed heard it

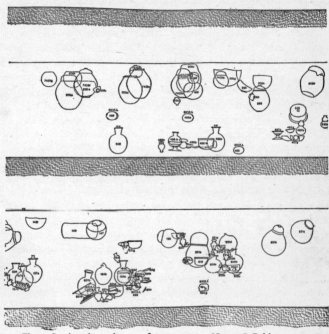

Fig. 7. Section through part of a cemetery at Harappā, Pakistan, 1940

stated that there is often no appreciable stratification on a sun-bleached, monsoon-swept Eastern site. The allegation is quite untrue. *There is no method proper to the excavation of a British site which is not applicable – nay, must be applied – to a site in Africa or Asia.*

The remedy therefore is that the oriental field-worker shall, as a matter of routine, have a preliminary and thorough grounding in the West, where critical control is at hand, and where strata are liable to be more concise and so to provide a more concentrated experience than an Eastern site can be expected to furnish. There is scarcely anything, be it repeated, in the work of Pitt Rivers or his accredited British successors that is not relevant to the excavation of a *tell* in Turkestan or a tomb in Syria. It is the more astonishing that those standards have so rarely penetrated to the further shores of the Mediterranean; east of Suez, they were until very recent years almost unknown.

It will thus, I hope, be appreciated that these remarks thinly veil an appeal – an appeal above all to the younger generation of archaeologists. I have, from experience, recommended elsewhere[1] the use of Roman Britain as a suitable basic training-ground for excavators of all periods and regions, by reason of its structural variety, its abundant stratigraphy, its productiveness, and its ready availability. There are many alternatives but the principle is the same: always that of precise and detailed training. We must give our recruits their Aldershot discipline before sending them out on to the battlefields of the world. In the past we have been unwisely casual in this matter.

In the present chapter an attempt has been made by way of introduction to do two things: first to sketch, very summarily, the main phases of technical development during the past century, and secondly to hint at a sustained and dangerous cleavage in technical standards between East and West. This cleavage will be reconsidered at a later stage; meanwhile, in the next two chapters something of a more positive and constructive kind must be said of the ordering of our field-evidence, and of its interpretation in terms of an absolute or relative chronology.

1. 'The Archaeology of the Roman Provinces, and Beyond', *Fifth Annual Report of the London University Institute of Archaeology*, 1948.

CHAPTER 3

Chronology

It is a truism that the backbone of history is an agreed chronology. Yet it sometimes seems that to-day chronology of the old rigid type is a trifle out of fashion in the routine of historical studies. To an older generation the mathematics of the business were important; the treasure-house could only be unlocked by combinations of integers painfully remembered often long after the treasure itself had passed into limbo. Now that is in some measure changed, doubtless on the whole for the better. Archaeology, not as a rule clogged with overmuch arithmetic, may be in part responsible for the shifting bias. It has begun to percolate through our universities to our schools, and sometimes forms innocuous pools of somewhat colourless knowledge – mostly a refined Darwinism – in which our kindergartens are encouraged to paddle. Ships and sealing-wax are beginning to rank almost with kings, dateless everyday things with calendared State secrets. The recentness and incompleteness of this emergence of archaeological as distinct from historical education is hard to realize until we recall, for example, that it is still possible to take a First in Greats at Oxford without even glancing at a Parthenon sculpture or an Attic vase. To-day, when the traditional precision of history has nevertheless been extensively supplemented by broadly based cultural studies, it may seem reactionary and perverse to reaffirm, as I do, at the beginning of a book on archaeology in the field that mere dates are still of primary and ultimate and unrelenting importance. And by dates I mean not simply those nebulous phases and sequences, those date-substitutes, with which archaeologists often enough try to bluff us. I mean time in hard figures. I mean Bradshaw.

The need for re-establishing the *relative* sequence of ancient cultures or cultural episodes, if we are to begin to understand their interactions and values, is self-evident, and stratigraphical excavation, of which more will be said in the next chapter, is a primary means to that end. The old comparison between the successive strata in the soil and the successive leaves in a book holds good: and is emphasized negatively by the fact that displacement in either case involves a *non sequitur* which confuses and frustrates and, in excavation, cannot be rectified. To that matter I shall recur. But even the most careful maintenance of correct succession and the postulation of a convincing culture-sequence are not in themselves enough. And for two reasons. First, without an absolute chronology cultures of different regions cannot accurately be compared, their inter-relationship cannot be assessed: in other words, the vital causative factors of human 'progress' cannot be authoritatively reconstructed, and may be widely misunderstood. Secondly, the fluctuating tempo of human achievement – itself an integral quality of that achievement – cannot be estimated: the lightning flash, for example, of Periclean Athens, or the glow of the slow-moving riverine civilizations. It is important but not enough to know that in the twentieth century A.D. an aeroplane flew from London to Singapore. It is almost equally important, in our estimate of human achievement, to know that in 1950 the aeroplane took 50 hours for the journey, and in 1999 only 50 minutes. Do not let us forget the significance of tempo; and that implies a time-table in the most literal sense, nothing less.

This question of tempo is worth a further moment's thought. It is at least as deserving of the attention of the archaeologist who is concerned with the evolution of human institutions as it is of the biologist who is concerned with the formal evolution of natural species and genera. In the language of the biologist, phases of 'increase', phases – expressive term – of 'explosive' evolution, 'stationary' or 'decline' phases, the whole rhythm of human as of animal life is itself an absorbing phenomenon, full of meaning, often full of mystery. I happen recently to have been making some slight study of one of the great civilizations of the ancient East, the Indus Valley Civilization of the third and second millennia B.C. in what used to be called India but is now Pakistan, and, though it is true that at present we know all too little about the beginnings of that civilization, the indications are that it flowered with an almost dramatic celerity, the sudden offspring of opportunity and genius. It was preceded by a miscellany of upland villages and cultures, set in the tumultuous eastern borderland of the great Iranian plateau. Such villages, grouped and confined by precipitous ranges, provide the optimum conditions for the earlier essays in communal life within the boundaries of a parochial self-sufficiency.

But for wider political horizons wider geographical horizons are a prior condition. Tentative moves from the highland zone down on to the great riverine plain must have drawn an immediate and compelling challenge. On the plain, the dangerous annual flood can only be constrained or utilized by combined effort on a large scale. On the plain, fertile soil resulting from that same flood is as abundant as mineral and other resources are scarce. With the added urgency of one cause and another, the river itself and its flanking lowlands facilitate and stimulate traffic, commercial or military, and at once enlarge human relations far beyond the precedent of the upland valley. The opportunities and difficulties implicit in civilization, in the full sense of the term, are at once present and insistent. The remaining postulate is that of a creative imagination sufficient to grasp the occasion. And without that creative imagination, no stretch of time could provide a substitute. A phase of increase, amounting even to 'explosive' evolution, may be assumed.

Many other significant examples of rapid evolution might readily be cited: an obvious one is the invention of the great windows, barred with a simplified perpendicular grid of tracery, wherewith the medieval builders illuminated the dim interiors of English churches in the latter part of the fourteenth century – sudden and triumphant answer to an insistent problem of engineering towards which earlier builders had merely groped. And on the other hand the patient 'stationary' evolution of Byzantine art is sufficiently familiar and significant to need no elaboration in the present context. Speed is a mighty factor in our evaluation of human achievement, and it is a mere truism to affirm that our appreciation of speed is contingent upon a nice chronology.

How then are we archaeologists, we fumblers in the earth, to attain this difficult degree of precision? For something like one-hundredth of the vast period with which modern archaeology is concerned, the historians have given us a framework in the Old World. Let us be grateful to them and take them into the fullest partnership. In a region which has a history, the archaeologist must know the framework of that history from A to Z (not merely the miserable fraction of it in which he happens to be interested) before ever he enters the field. The day is gone by when the Egyptologist, intent upon the Pharaonic period, may cast the Greek and the Roman, the Arab and the Chinaman, carelessly upon his tip-heap. But that is by the way. The important thing is that the archaeologist must know his dates and how to use them: recorded dates where they are valid, and unwritten dates where geological or physical or chemical or botanical science can win them from the earth. And year by year the objective sciences are coming more and more to the rescue of that subjective science, the study of man.

Chronology was once a simple enough matter. In a notorious pronouncement, Archbishop Ussher, properly styled *ad miraculum doctus*, affirmed that the world was created in the year 4004 B.C. A more sceptical age has been content, until quite recently, to postulate 4241 B.C. as the earliest calendar-date. It was believed – and the textbooks still have it – that the Egyptians, having observed the approximate coincidence of the reappearance (just before dawn) of Sirius or Sothis, the Dog Star, after a period of invisibility, with the beginning of the Nile flood, chose the date on which this phenomenon occurred in that year (July 19th of the Julian Calendar) as their calendrical New Year's Day. The initial date was inferred backwards from A.D. 139, when the synchronization again occurred, by a logical computation which was generally accepted. The Egyptian calendar, recognizing the incompatibility of the lunar months with the solar year, divided the latter into artificial calendar-months each of thirty days, and added five feast-days in an attempt to make up the required total. These intercalary periods, however, still fell short of the Sothic year (approximately the same length as the solar year) by one day in four years (hence our Leap Year); with the result that the synchronization was exact only once in 1,460 years. But it seemed likely that the calendar was already in use in the time of the Pyramid-builders of the Egyptian IVth dynasty, who were computed on the basis of native annals to have lived before 2775 B.C.; which took the calendar back to an initial Sothic synchronism not later than 2781 B.C. and more probably not later than 4241 B.C. So much for the long-established view. In recent years this view has been modified; on cultural grounds (the absence of writing) so early a date as 4241 is now regarded as impossible. It is now argued that, although the Egyptians at an early period were able by their observations of the heliacal rising of Sothis to check the position of their 365-day calendar in the Solar year, they never had a Sothic calendar. But on the generally accepted assumption that the 365-day calendar operated continuously from early

Dynastic times, combined with the contemporary records which have survived of heliacal risings of Sothis in terms of that calendar and the lengths of reigns given in ancient King Lists, Egyptian history – the oldest history in the world – can still be carried back continuously, if not to 4241 B.C., at least to the last centuries of the fourth millennium B.C.

It would be irrelevant here to develop the far-reaching implications of this Egyptian calendar. It underlies the whole of our pre-classical chronology in so far as that stands on a historical basis. Slightly modified, we still use it. But it is more to our purpose to consider parallel and supplementary methods of calculation, and, by way of transition, reference may first be made to an ingenious theory propounded in 1949 by Dr Claude Schaeffer.[1]

At Ras Shamra, on the coast of Syria, Dr Schaeffer has for many years excavated the Bronze Age metropolis of Ugarit, and has there determined five main successive layers. Of these the last, marking the end of the Late Bronze Age, shows evidence of destruction by a violent earthquake which dislocated the buildings at ground-level. Contemporary sites in Syria, Palestine, and Asia Minor have yielded similar evidence of violence; on dating now superseded, the fallen walls of Jericho were witness to it; and Dr Schaeffer ascribes the widespread disaster to c. 1365 B.C. when, according to a Tell el Amarna letter, 'Ugarit has been destroyed by fire; half the city has been burnt, the other half has ceased to be'. If this basis be accepted – and it is not perhaps quite as clear as Schaeffer maintains – a definite phase in all the cities in question is dated with an insignificant margin of error. Nor need this line of research end there. Another catastrophic earthquake seems to have centred upon Asia Minor at the beginning of the Middle Bronze Age, between 2100 and 2000 B.C., and may be thought to tie together the whole or partial destruction of Troy and Tarsus, Alaja Hüyük on the Anatolian plateau, Chagar Bazar and Tel Brak, Tepe Gawra north-east of Mosul, and a series of Syro-Palestine cities, once more including Ugarit itself. And yet other earthquakes, between 2400 and 2300 B.C. and about 1730 B.C., provide further chronological bonds. It all seems too good to be true, but is not on that ground false. Schaeffer was not indeed the first to recognize something of the

1. C. F. A. Schaeffer, *Stratigraphie comparée et chronologie de l'Asie occidental* (IIIᵉ et IIᵉ millénaires), Oxford, 1948.

archaeological potentiality of earthquakes. In 1926 Sir Arthur Evans wrote a description of a violent earthquake shock which he had just experienced at Knossos in Crete, and added:

> The archaeological *sequitur* of this is very important. When in the great Palace of Knossos, we find evidence of a series of overthrows, some of them on a scale that could hardly be the work of man, there seems real reason for tracing the cause to the same seismic agencies that we have certainly to deal with in the case described above. It may be possible even to fix approximately the date of seven earthquakes, four of them of great severity, between the last century of the third millennium and the beginning of the 14th century B.C.[1]

Therein lies a germ of the Schaeffer scheme, though not the scheme itself. The general suggestion is indeed a serious one, and archaeology may take a cautious cognizance of it, with the neutralizing proviso that the earthquake synthesis is used only where other evidence has already established contemporaneity. In other words, we must in fact regretfully admit that earthquakes, in view of our limited knowledge of their incidence and frequency in ancient times, are a shaky basis on which to build a precise chronology. But the theory is of interest.

In another context, geology has given us a surer and now very familiar footing. The recognition of the clearly stratified varved or laminated clays of Sweden (and elsewhere) as the annual deposits of the retreating ice, and as the time-table therefore of a related human phase, is now notorious. By counting these annual deposits in a series of sections from the south of Sweden to recent deposits in north-central Sweden, the Swedish geologist de Geer and some of his colleagues calculated 6839 B.C. as the beginning of the post-glacial period in their country and as the beginning, therefore, of potential human life there.[2] Others prefer a slightly earlier date, but the principle is the same. On this basis, a series of changes in the Scandinavian coast-line, climate and vegetation have been given approximate dates which can now claim a value approaching the absolute and are fundamental for the mesolithic of northern and north-western Europe.[3]

1. Cited by Joan Evans, *Time and Chance* (London, 1943), p. 382.
2. Summary by F. E. Zeuner, *Dating the Past* (2nd ed., London, 1950), pp. 20 ff.
3. Ibid., pp. 46 ff.

43

Incidentally, it follows that a proportionate chronological value is thereby attached to the identification of pollen and the reconstruction of vegetation on mesolithic sites.[1]

Geological stratification further plays an important part in the chronology of the palaeolithic cultures. Artifacts belonging to the Old Stone Age are frequently found in the gravels of river terraces, in brick-earths, in cave sediments and so forth, under conditions which enable the Pleistocene geologist to determine the age of these artifacts relative to the sequence of climate-fluctuations that make up what is commonly called the Quaternary Ice Age. In particular the wind-borne loess deposits and solifluction layers formed in the cold phases and the fossil soils resulting from the weathering of ancient land-surfaces have contributed to the establishment of a relative chronology in an area ranging from northern France through Germany, Austria, Bohemia, and Hungary to the Ukraine. But there is more in it than that; for the attempt has repeatedly been made to convert this *relative* into an absolute time-scale. 'Time-gauges' are provided by the rates of weathering, of denudation and of sedimentation, calculated upon such evidence as that provided by varved clays and, more recently, for restricted periods by C14 (see below); so that if the geological results obtained by Penck and others are applied to the sequence of palaeolithic industries, the Abbevillian would appear to be about half a million years old, the middle Acheulian about a quarter of a million, and the Mousterian about a hundred thousand years.

When we leave geological stratification and turn to stratification derived mainly from human occupation, inference is less certain. It is impossible to lay down any law for the equation of man-made strata with an absolute time-scale. For example, at a site (Chandravalli) which I excavated in India, coins that were not, apparently, earlier than 50 B.C. or much later than A.D. 200 ranged through a vertical accumulation of 5 feet; the period thus represented was probably in fact not more than two centuries. In what is now Pakistan, at the famous site of Taxila (Sirkap), excavations in 1944-5 indicated that 6-9 feet of floors and debris were deposited during some two centuries of very intensive occupation. In an earlier phase of the same city, Taxila (Bhir Mound), an untidy site, 14-15 feet were ascribed to

1. *Dating the Past*, pp. 56 ff. and bibliography.

three centuries or a little more; but the masonry and building-methods were here of so unstable a character that the accumulation may well have been exceptionally rapid. In every instance a multitude of unknown and variable factors is involved, and objective calculation on the basis of depth is virtually impossible. Nevertheless, fortified by the seasonal regularity of the Nile valley, Petrie was greatly daring. 'Generally', he maintained, 'it is possible to date the latest date of a town by the potsherds lying on the surface; and to allow a rate of growth of 20 inches a century down to the visible level; if that gives a long period we may further carry down the certainly artificial level by 4 inches in a century for the Nile deposits when in cultivated ground' – and so on.[1] Such calculations have, if any, a purely academic or abstract interest. They make no allowance for the intermittencies and vagaries which, alike in human and in geological history, defy the confines of mathematical formulae.

Only on rare occasions can a chronological connotation in terms of calendar-years be attributed with plausibility to man-made strata. I will give two examples. My first comes from Scarborough in Yorkshire where, during the excavation of prehistoric pits of the fifth century B.C. underlying the Roman signal-station, Mr F. G. Simpson, always most scrupulous of excavators, observed that the human debris – sherds, bones, ash, etc. – in the pits was interleaved with layers of clean soil (Pl. 2a). He further observed, on returning to the site after a winter's absence, that an identical clean layer had accumulated in the re-excavated pits as a result of the rains and frosts of the preceding winter months. From this observation, two inferences were deducible: first, that each of the pits had only been used by the prehistoric inhabitants for some three or four years (represented by three successive ancient rainwash layers with interposed occupation-debris); and, secondly, that the site, on a stormy headland overlooking the North Sea, had been abandoned during the winter months, when the deposition of occupation-debris had ceased, and that the place was used only as a summer station.[2] Both these inferences are of importance in the chronological and sociological evaluation of the settlement.

1. *Aims and Methods in Archaeology*, pp. 10–11.
2. A. Rowntree, *History of Scarborough* (London, 1931), pp. 20 and 32, and fig. 6.

My second example comes from Iraq. At Khafājah, in the Diyala region north of Baghdad, a temple dedicated to the moon-god Sin was built and rebuilt ten times on the same site in the fourth and third millennia, and an elaborate attempt was made to construct an absolute chronology for the building, and hence for its dynastic or cultural background, upon certain structural evidences. It is not necessary here to reproduce the argument in all its more theoretical ramifications,[1] but its root is of interest. The seventh Sin temple showed two phases, with two floor-levels for the second (later) phase. Between these two secondary floor-levels, the temple-wall had been mud-plastered sixteen times, each plaster coat being applied to the surface of its predecessor (Pl. 2b). Now, to-day it is the custom in the Near East to plaster the surface of adobe (or mud) walls, such as those of the temple, every summer in preparation for the winter rains; and, since circumstances have not materially changed, it is a fair assumption that the sixteen plasterings represent in fact a lapse of sixteen years. But during that inferred sixteen years the ground-level at the entrance to the temple rose 12 cm. – the vertical distance between the two floors. Applying this ratio to the accumulation on the floor of the first phase, namely 75 cm., we may calculate the time represented by that accumulation at $16 \times \frac{75}{12} = 100$ years. To this we must add the 16 years already calculated for the interval between the two floors of the later phase, and we get a total of 116 years for the time-interval between the first and last floors or made-levels of Sin temple VII. There we will leave the computation, at a point beyond which inference becomes increasingly conjectural. But as far as we have carried it, the argument has considerable weight, and well represents the type of evidence for which the excavator in search of precision may usefully keep an open eye.

From vertical stratification we may turn for a moment to what is in effect horizontal stratification: a method of computation, simple in theory but full of pitfalls in practice, which has been disguised under the term Dendrochronology. The principles of Dendrochronology have been widely advertised, and a convenient summary will be

1. They will be found in Pinhas Delougaz and Seton Lloyd, *Pre-Sargonid Temples in the Diyala Region* (Univ. of Chicago Orient. Inst. Publications, lviii, 1942), pp. 125 ff. I am indebted to Professor M. E. L. Mallowan for drawing my attention to this.

found in Professor Zeuner's handbook.[1] It is a sufficiently familiar fact that a section across a tree grown in a climate with seasonal variations reveals more or less concentric growth-rings, usually representing annual accretions, which will differ with the age of the tree and the climate of the particular year. In years of drought the growth will naturally be less than in wet years, but a tendency for the rings to group in 11-year cycles, in conformity with the 11-year sun-spot cycle, has suggested that solar radiation is a further and independent factor. On the basis of the ring-sequence of long-lived trees in California, Dr A. E. Douglass and his associates were able to work out climatic curves for that part of North America for the last 3,000 years; but it is more important to us that variant features of individual rings or their grouping can be plotted and compared from long-lived trees to timbers cut in the same region as the type-specimens in ancient times. Thus in Arizona tree-ring analysis has been brought to the rescue of American prehistory with astonishing results. Here the correlation of the tree-rings of timbers from prehistoric (i.e. pre-sixteenth century) Indian houses with dated sequences enabled Douglass to determine, with a minute margin of error, dates at which the ancient timbers had been cut as far back as his material could take him, in fact to the eighth century A.D. and earlier. There always remains, of course, the imponderable factor of the date of construction relative to the date at which the component timbers were actually cut. Timbers were liable to be reused from building to successive building, and a particular structure may thus be as much as some centuries later than the tree-ring dating of one or more of its timbers would alone suggest. In other words, tree-ring analysis can only provide a *terminus postquem*.

Attempts have been made to apply the tree-ring method to material from Europe, but so far with limited success, although some value has been claimed on insecure evidence for tree-ring graphs prepared in this country from Roman and medieval timbers.[2] The absence of very ancient trees, however, and the much greater remoteness of European prehistory combine with a (usually) less discriminating climate to militate against success. Nor have attempts to project

1. *Dating the Past*, pp. 6 ff.
2. A. W. G. Lowther, 'Dendrochronology', *The Arch. News Letter* (London), March 1949.

American data across the Atlantic ('teleconnexion') met with wide acceptance. On the other hand Africa and Asia have not yet been adequately exploited by dendrochronologists and may in future add new laurels to a technique which has certainly been dramatically successful in the land of its origin.

The mention of solar radiation opens up wide vistas in the computation of geological time and the dating of remote men in their geological setting. It is not for a layman like myself to pretend to more than the most general understanding of the methods employed. It is, however, comforting to be told that ancient climatic fluctuations, deduced from the examination of loess-deposits and the analysis of river-gravels, agree closely with certain fluctuations of the intensity of solar radiation calculated on an astronomical basis; with the corollary that these fluctuations, with their related human phenomena, are approximately dated objectively. Thus it is calculated that in the open spaces of north-western Europe palaeolithic man began his Sisyphean task some 500,000 years ago, without any pedantic limitation within 30,000 or 40,000 years on either side: a date which is found to be in excellent agreement with that which I have already mentioned as obtained from the rates of weathering and denudation.[1] It may therefore be regarded for some time to come as sufficiently absolute in relation to an epoch when fashions in craftsmanship may have lasted for anything up to, or even beyond, a quarter of a million years.

I mention these calculations, merely to hurry on; like the measurement of geological time on the premise that the time-rate at which the disintegration of a radioactive mineral proceeds is constant and determinable,[2] I accept them calmly with other marvels of the age. But it is important to know what the geochronologists want for their alchemy, and to see that they get it. It is the duty of the field-archaeologist to supply them, for example, with classified gravel and loess and with related artifacts. They are gradually bringing order into our remoter prehistory, transforming the jellyfish of its chronology into something vertebrate. Their work is integral with ours, both in the laboratory and in the field.

The marvels of science as applied to archaeology would not be

1. F. E. Zeuner in *Proc. Linn. Soc. Lond.*, 162 (2), p. 125.
2. Again I refer to reader to Zeuner, *Dating the Past* (2nd ed., 1950), with bibliography.

fully catalogued, however, without a reference to two developments of another kind. The first is the so-called Fluorine Test. Since 1844 it has been recognized that buried bone absorbs an element known as fluorine from the moisture of the sand or gravel in which it lies. The process is a very slow one, and it varies quantitatively with the amount of fluorine which happens to be present in the ground-water of a particular site. This variability obviously robs fluorine-content of any value as an absolute time-indicator. On the other hand, as Dr Kenneth Oakley and his colleagues have demonstrated, it may be of use within very wide limits as an indicator of the approximate contemporaneity or otherwise of bones from the same locality, and one notable instance of this utility is already on record. A brief glance at it will suffice to indicate the potentialities of the method.[1]

The example relates to the much-discussed skeleton found in 1888 in the Galley Hill (north) gravel-pit at Swanscombe in Kent, 8 feet below the surface. The gravel in which the skeleton was found is of middle pleistocene or early palaeolithic age, and controversy has raged as to whether the skeleton, unmineralized and modern in character as it is, was (say) a quarter of a million years old or of relatively modern date. If the former it is obviously a remarkable proof of the antiquity of a modern skeletal type. The general problem has now been set at rest. A number of fossil bones, including the famous Swanscombe skull, has been collected from the same early palaeolithic gravel, and others from later palaeolithic deposits in neighbouring gravel-pits, together with some from local recent deposits, including part of an Anglo-Saxon skeleton. Analysis showed that the Swanscombe skull and other early palaeolithic bones contained about 2 per cent fluorine, the later palaeolithic about 1 per cent, and the recent bones 0·3 to 0·05 per cent. The Galley Hill skeleton was found to contain only 0·3 per cent, and its relatively modern date is thus apparent. It passes finally and inescapably out of the textbooks into limbo.

1. See Kenneth Oakley, 'Some Applications of the Fluorine Test', *The Archaeological News Letter*, Nov.–Dec. 1949, pp. 101 ff.; K. P. Oakley and M. F. Ashley Montagu, 'A Reconsideration of the Galley Hill Skeleton', *Bulletin of the British Museum (Nat. Hist.)*, i, no. 2 (1949); K. P. Oakley, 'Relative Dating of the Piltdown Skull', *The Advancement of Science*, vi, no. 24 (1950); K. P. Oakley and C. Randall Hoskins, 'New Evidence on the Antiquity of Piltdown Man', *Nature*, clxv (11 Mar. 1950), 379.

Similar fluorine tests have been applied to the much-discussed human or simian bones from the gravels of Piltdown in Sussex. The results, confirmed whilst this book was in the press, are dramatic in the extreme. The jaw and canine tooth, found subsequently to the skull-cap, are now demonstrably of modern date, altered and coloured by a forger and carefully 'planted' for discovery by distinguished visitors. The cranium found nearby by gravel-diggers, on the other hand, is genuine and of Upper Pleistocene date. In itself it presents no special problem, but the removal of all temptation to associate it with the jaw removes also a potential anomaly from the complex problem of skull-evolution. See *Bull. of the British Museum* (*Nat. Hist.*), vol. 2, no. 3 (1953), and J. S. Weiner, *The Piltdown Forgery* (Oxford, 1955).

At the best, however, the local and relative value of the fluorine test must not be forgotten; at the best, as Dr Oakley emphasizes,

it does not provide a means of *close* relative dating. A given bone or group of bones shows a certain range in fluorine content. Unless the difference in age between the bones which are being compared is considerable (e.g. 10,000 years), there is usually an overlap in the range of their fluorine-contents. For this reason it would probably be impossible by this method to differentiate clearly between say a Saxon and a neolithic skeleton; whereas it should enable one, for example, to distinguish bones of neolithic or later age from others of Acheulian age, when both occur under similar conditions at the same locality.

Potentially more sensitive is a new method of dating organic material by means of its radiocarbon content. This method, a by-product of atomic research, was announced in 1949 from America and, though still in the experimental stage, may eventually enable specimens up to 40,000 years old to be dated objectively. The method, known summarily as the 'Carbon 14' method, has been described by Professor W. F. Libby, Dr E. C. Anderson, and Dr R. J. Arnold, of the Institute of Nuclear Studies in the University of Chicago, who have tested it upon wood-samples from Egyptian tombs.[1] The possible error is at present appreciable but will probably be reduced, and it seems likely that for the mesolithic at any rate the new method, if made sufficiently accessible, will produce useful results.

1. *Science*, cix, no. 2827, 227–8 (4 Mar. 1949); *Science Today*, v, no. 125 (24 Mar. 1949); *Antiquity*, xxiii (1949), 113–14 and 229. See also Hallam L.

The principle of the method, if not its practice, is simple and logical enough and may be stated categorically and very summarily:

(i) Cosmic rays, which arrive from the outer space, produce radioactive carbon atoms of atomic weight 14 in the atmosphere. The C14 thus formed is an isotope of ordinary carbon of atomic weight 12 (C12); and both are contained in the carbon dioxide of the atmosphere in a proportion which is stable and corresponds with the rates of production and disintegration of C14.

(ii) Now this carbon dioxide is taken in by plants, and, since all animals derive their body-material ultimately from plants, it is universally incorporated in living organic matter. Therefore, the proportion of C14 to C12 in all living organic matter is the same as in the atmosphere.

(iii) But once an organism is *dead* (e.g. when a tree is cut down), it ceases to take up carbon from the atmosphere. On the contrary, the C14 content slowly diminishes, reverting to nitrogen at such a rate that after about 5,600 years (termed the 'half-life') only half the original amount of C14 is left. After twice that period, only half the residue – i.e. a quarter of the original quantity – is left, and so forth until all the C14 has disappeared.

(iv) In dead organic matter, therefore, the ratio of C14 to C12 decreases with time at a known rate. The proportion of C14 to C12 in a given organic specimen can be determined in the laboratory, and from it the time elapsed since the 'death' of this organic matter can be calculated.

That is the principle. The chief practical difficulty is that, at the best, the initial ratio of C14 to C12 is exceedingly small and therefore difficult to measure with precision. Some organic substances are indeed relatively easier than others to deal with; such are wood or charcoal, which contain much carbon. Bones, on the other hand, contain only small amounts of carbon, and it seems doubtful whether even

Movius ibid. xxiv. (1950), 99–101; report of Brit. Assoc. discussion in *Nature*, clxvi (4 Nov. 1950), 756 (J. V. P. Long, F. E. Zeuner, and K. P. Oakley); F. E. Zeuner in *Science Progress*, no. 154 (London, April 1951) pp. 225–38 (with bibliography); G. H. S. Bushnell in *Antiquity*, xxv (1951), 145–9; and especially 'Radiocarbon Dating' assembled by Frederick Johnson in *American Antiquity*, xvii (Soc. for Amer. Arch., Salt Lake City, Utah; July 1951), and W. F. Libby, *Radiocarbon Dating* (Univ. of Chicago, 1952).

very large quantities of them, with special 'boosting' superadded, will in fact yield the necessary concentration.[1] As a whole, the technique is still (1955) in the experimental stage, and a number of unresolved difficulties remain. For example, a specimen of ancient charcoal may have been contaminated by the absorption of substances containing charcoal of younger age; a particularly dangerous source of contamination is fungal and bacterial growth which, even when removed from the specimen, may have falsified (reduced) its apparent age. But, in spite of these and other complications, there is reason to hope that it may be possible to achieve an average accuracy of $\pm$ 200 years in the dating of charcoal and certain other categories of organic material ranging in date from the late palaeolithic to the beginning of the present era. Consistent accuracy within those limits would mark a formidable advance in the pursuit of prehistoric chronology.

A number of examples of the application of C14 analysis have now been released. Thus it has been announced that the last (Mankato) advance of the Wisconsin glaciation of North America passed over treetrunks the average age of which by the Carbon 14 method is about 11,400 years from the present day, less than half the age expected by geologists. It is shortly after that time that man is believed to have first appeared in North America. The oldest artifacts determined in America are several pairs of rope sandals covered by volcanic deposits in Oregon; the age indicated was about 9,050 years, i.e. about 7000 B.C. In the eastern United States, the earliest cultures are proving so far to be later than in the west. Carbon 14 dates suggest that man spread there under 5,000 years ago, but much verification is needed. Other C14 determinations are reported to confirm the beginning of the First Dynasty of Egypt at about 3000 B.C., and that primitive agriculture was already being practised in the Kurdish hills at about 4700 B.C. – charcoal and shells of land-mollusca from a village-site excavated by Mr R. J. Braidwood at Jarmo in northern Iraq have given the remarkably consistent C14 dates of 4757 B.C. $\pm$ 320 years, 4654 B.C. $\pm$ 330 years, and 4743 B.C. $\pm$ 360 years. Nearer home, Dr

1. In order to obtain the quantity of pure carbon required for a satisfactory determination based on several test runs, the following minimum quantities are recommended: 65 grammes of charcoal, 200 grammes of other types of vegetable remains (wood, grain, basket-work, &c.), and 700 grammes of molluscan shells. H. L. Movius in *Antiquity*, xxiv (1950), 99–101.

Grahame Clark's already-famous village of mesolithic food-gatherers at Seamer in east Yorkshire seems, by this method of diagnosis, to have flourished at about the acceptable date of 7000 B.C. But it is fair to repeat the emphatic affirmation of Dr Libby and his associates that all such results are at present tentative.

In this chapter nothing has been said of typology as a basis for chronology, nor do I propose to enter generally upon this thorny subject. The study of the systematic development of types or forms was long normal to biological studies before it became a recognized method in archaeology; indeed it scarcely entered into our discipline until Petrie based the relative chronology of his famous Diospolis Parva cemetery upon it in 1901.[1] Its virtues and its vices[2] now constitute a standard question in archaeological examination-papers, and it is not necessary here to attempt a model answer. But there are two points upon which a word may be said. Much work – and much able work – has been done in the European and in the Asiatic fields upon the comparative typology of industries, particularly of pottery. In this valuable endeavour may be observed the recurrence of two sources of doubt. The first is a tendency to give a diagnostic significance to types of pattern which are either insufficiently specialized or are at any rate repeated, without likelihood of contact, in widely disparate times and places. The second tendency, not unrelated to the first, is to devolve the comparative study of pottery into a pursuit more akin to philately than to archaeology: to compare line-illustrations of pattern with insufficient reference to other factors such as paste, method of manufacture, and firing. For a *reductio ad absurdum* of this abstract and theoretical procedure I may refer once more to that unfailing source of cautionary examples, Palestine. In a monumental report on Tell en-Nasbeh, the date of a series of tombs has been 'calculated' by an astonishing statistical method.

All parallels in form to a pot-type have been traced, including Middle Bronze ones, to a clearly Early Iron pot (differences in technique being

1. *Diospolis Parva* (Egypt Exploration Fund, 1901), pp. 4 ff.
2. For example, see G. Coffey, *Guide to the Celtic Antiquities of the Christian Period* ..., p. 4: 'It is not to be supposed that a series of progressive forms always correspond to a series of dates. After the final form has been reached, earlier steps may re-appear; the whole series forming a stock of ornament from which the artificer could draw.'

ignored). The result, as a graph of frequency, is plotted for the tomb, in combination with the frequency graphs of other forms (from the same tomb). This yields a series of peaks which more or less coincide, but gives the ludicrous result that the extremes of the graph stretch from the seventeenth to the second centuries B.C.! On the other hand, no account is taken of the appearance or non-appearance of diagnostic forms or techniques. . . .[1]

In other words, we have here a crude example of the impact of two-dimensional diagnosis upon three-dimensional material.

The other point which may be stressed is the risk inherent in the broadcast application of typological criteria which may in a majority of instances be perfectly sound in themselves within their proper and restricted context. For example, those antiquaries who are accustomed to deal with ancient building-construction are familiar enough with the potential time-values of evolving structural or ornamental features. Thus, students of medieval mouldings, of ancient styles of masonry, of ancient brickwork, of ancient staircases, window-frames, roof-constructions, have evolved criteria of a rule-of-thumb character which are more often correct than not, if cautiously used. 'Rusti-cated' masonry – ashlar with rough surface and drafted margins – is A.D. 1–50 in Rome.[2] Roman bricks and brick-joints vary in absolute and relative thickness in accordance with a time-scale.[3] Deeply invol-uted Gothic mouldings of the thirteenth century contrast with the plump mouldings of the fourteenth and the flatter mouldings of the fifteenth century. Queen-post roof-trusses begin in the time of Henry VIII. And so on. But in all these rules lurk hidden dangers. Thus out-side Rome, in Palestine for example, rusticated masonry may be at least as early as the ninth century B.C.;[4] the smooth chronology of Roman bricks has been established only for Rome itself, and there perhaps only for certain categories of building; the Gothic mouldings of Britain do not apply to Gothic France; most British queen-post roof-trusses are of the sixteenth century, but they occur occasionally

1. K. M. Kenyon in *Antiquity*, xxiv (1950), 200, commenting upon C. C. McCown, *Tell en-Nasbeh*, i (1947), with special reference to pp. 146–7.

2. G. T. Rivoira, *Roman Architecture* (Oxford, 1925), p. 70, ascribes it especi-ally to the Claudian period, but notes its earlier occurrence in Etruscan tombs.

3. Esther B. van Deeman, *American Journ. of Archaeology*, 2S., xvi (1912); &c.

4. G. A. Reisner and others, *Harvard Excavations at Samaria* (Harvard, 1924), p. 104 and pl. 27.

as early as the fourteenth.[1] Taken alone, therefore, almost any one of these and comparable criteria may trap the unwary. Their values are liable to be local rather than universal, and must be established afresh and objectively for every fresh locality. With that proviso, they may be of great use, but the proviso is an important one.

So much, then, for some of the principles or practices underlying archaeological chronology. Their importance is manifest; so much so that it is perhaps advisable to end on a note of warning. We must not allow chronology to monopolize our discipline. It is a means to an end, not an end in itself. Those of us who know the deep-seated satisfaction which accrues from the settlement of the chronology of a site know also something of the danger imminent in that satisfaction. What are we really out for? I began this chapter by describing chronology as the backbone of archaeology; and so it is, but the backbone is not the whole skeleton, still less is it the flesh and blood and spirit of our subject. Our objective is a reconstruction of human cultural achievement in all those aspects of life which are susceptible to material evidence. A chronologist is not an archaeologist. As an American writer has put it, 'Chronology is admittedly an important factor in any archaeological research, and the earliest and surest method of establishing it is to be commended. But after a sequence of periods has been established, if then the very culture of those periods is unknown, we may justifiably ask "so what?"'[2] Something will be said about 'so what?' in Chapter 17. Meanwhile, we must proceed to consider how in practice our cultural material may best be equated with our time-scale both in the digging and in our records of it.

1. Royal Commission on Historical Monuments (Eng.), *Essex*, ii, Central and S.W. (1921), p. 76, Gatehouse Farm.
2. W. W. Taylor, 'A Study of Archaeology', *American Anthropologist*, Indiana Univ., (1948), p. 62.

CHAPTER 4

Stratigraphy

In the last chapter reference was made to a number of ways, some of them very familiar ones, whereby an approximation to absolute chronology can sometimes be extracted from undocumented archaeological material. Such absolute chronology is essential alike to the appreciation of the varying *tempo* of human achievement, and, above all, to the establishment of the cultural inter-relationships which help to rationalize human 'progress'. But in much of our archaeology fixed time-points are intermittent and chancy. More usually, the archaeologist must be content to establish the *relative sequence* of his evidence, to ensure that, however ill-focused, his perspective is essentially correct. Therein lies his primary duty: to secure beyond doubt the orderly succession of the vestiges with which he deals, even though, in any given phase of research, he may be compelled to leave finer adjustment and interpretation to his successors. To come at once to the core of the matter, his first task as an excavator is with *stratification*.

In picturesque fashion, Mrs Jacquetta Hawkes has had something to say of the Law of Stratification. It is as simple, she remarks, as gravity, as falling down stairs, and is indeed rather like that. There follows a little fantasy which I abstract from her text.

If [she says] instead of one apple falling on the head of Sir Isaac Newton a heavenly orchard had let tumble a rain of fruit, one of the greatest of men would have been overwhelmed and then buried. Anyone examining the situation afterwards in a properly scientific spirit, clearing the apples layer by layer, would be able to deduce certain facts. He would be able to prove that the man was there before the apples. Furthermore, that the blushing Beauty of Bath found immediately over and round Sir Isaac fell longer ago than the small swarthy russets that lay above them. If, on top of all this, snow had fallen, then the observer, even if he came from Mars where they are not familiar with these things, would know that the apple time came before the snow time. Relative ages are not enough [Mrs Hawkes adds], the observer would want an absolute date, and that is where Sir Isaac comes in again. An examination of his clothes, the longskirted coat, the loose breeches and the negligent cut of his linen, the long square-toes pointing so forlornly up to the sky, would date the man to the seventeenth century. Here would be a clue to the age of the apples and the snow.[1]

In more prosaic sense, this term stratification has already appeared here and there in the previous chapters and will remain a recurrent theme. It was long understood by geologists before it became the commonplace of archaeology. The protagonist in the geological use of the term was William ('Strata') Smith who, in 1816, began the issue of a work entitled 'Strata Identified by Organized Fossils', and thereby opened up new geological profundities and successions. With so long and familiar a history behind it, it is unnecessary to enter here into any detailed exposition of the stratigraphical principle, but, for completeness's sake, I will briefly recall the nature of its application to archaeology.

In this context, its principles are – in theory, at any rate – simple enough. The human occupation of a site normally results in the accumulation of material of one kind or another on and about the area occupied. Objects are lost or discarded and become embedded in the earth. Floors are renewed and old ones buried. Buildings crumble and new ones are built upon the ruins. A flood may destroy a building or a town and deposit a layer of alluvium upon its debris; and later, when the flood has subsided, the levelled site may be re-occupied. Sometimes, the process is in the reverse direction: evidences of occupation may be removed, as in the deepening of an unsurfaced street by traffic, or the digging of a pit for the disposal of rubbish or for burial. At Sabratha in Tripolitania, a Roman temple was found in 1948 to have been rebuilt at a *lower* level than its predecessor on the same site, through an intentional lowering of the whole *temenos* at the time of rebuilding. In one way or another, the surface of an ancient town or village is constantly altering in response to human effort or neglect; and it is by interpreting rightly these evidences of alteration that we may hope to reconstruct something of the vicissitudes of the site and its occupants.

As it happens, the first recorded instance, so far as I am aware, of the observation of archaeological stratification related not to an

1. *A Land* (London, 1951), p. 26.

occupation-site but to a burial-mound. At the time when the episode occurred, the word *stratification*, in the sense in which I have just used it, was not yet in circulation, but the elements of the matter were precociously appreciated by that remarkable man, Thomas Jefferson, whose major title to fame is, I suppose, that he was third President of the United States and an author of the Declaration of American Independence. For us he may rank in the lesser but not negligible role of the first scientific digger. His sociological interests were wide; in particular, as governor of Virginia, he concerned himself with the problems of the Red Man and the Negro, and in the course of his studies he became interested incidentally in certain 'barrows of which many are to be found all over in this country' (i.e. Virginia). One of them, situated 'on the low grounds of the Rivanna, about two miles above its principal fork, and opposite to some hills, on which had been an Indian town', he opened in order to satisfy himself of the correctness of opinions and traditions relating to these mounds. His report is a testimony to his careful observation:

Appearances certainly indicate that it [the mound] has derived both origin and growth from the accustomary collection of bones, and the deposition of them together; that the first collection had been deposited on the common surface of the earth, a few stones put over it, and then a covering of earth, that the second had been laid on this, had covered more or less of it in proportion to the number of bones, and was then also covered with earth, and so on.

These facts caused him to reject two notions: first, that the mound covered only bones of those slain in battle (not a single weapon-wound was found); and secondly 'that it was the common sepulchre of a town, in which the bodies were placed upright, and touching each other'. He remarked that a few stones found in the mound were 'brought from a cliff a quarter of a mile off, and from the river, one-eighth of a mile off'. He also recorded that infants were buried there, since a rib of an infant, part of the jaw of a child which had not cut its teeth (the right half of the under jaw), etc., were discovered.[1]

All that, be it noted, was in 1784, and I have therefore thought it worth while to relate the episode at some length. Let us consider the

1. T. Jefferson, *Notes on Virginia* (8th ed., 1801), pp. 142–7; account here derived from A. F. Chamberlain in *The American Anthropologist*, ix (1907), 499 f.

contents of Jefferson's clear and concise report. He describes the situation of the mound in relation to natural features and evidences of human occupation. He detects components of geological interest in its materials and traces their sources. He indicates the stratigraphical stages in the construction of the mound. He records certain significant features of the skeletal remains. And he relates his evidence objectively to current theories. No mean achievement for a busy statesman in 1784!

Unfortunately, this seed of a new scientific skill fell upon infertile soil. For a century after Jefferson, mass-excavation remained the rule of the day. In Chapter 2 the successive layers in the soil, in other words stratification, were compared to the successive pages of a book. The analogy is essentially a true one, and includes the corollary: a prime condition of intelligibility is that the layers, like the pages, shall be brought to our eyes reasonably intact and in proper sequence. Of course, mass-excavation has not always been devoid of all merit. In a rudimentary stage of research, it may help to point the way and stimulate advance along it. We may be grateful to Schliemann for plunging his spade into Troy, Tiryns, and Mycenae in the seventies of the last century, because he showed us what a splendid book had in fact been buried there; but he tore it to pieces in snatching it from the earth, and it took us upwards of three-quarters of a century to stick it more or less together again and to read it aright, with the help of cribs from other places. On a smaller plane, I remember my gratitude in 1944 to certain ardent but highly unskilled French antiquaries at Pondicherry in south India for scraping up a heterogeneous mass of material from an ancient site because, although they knew it not, their spoliation showed that the site contained imported (and dated) Arretine pottery which subsequently, by more orthodox methods, enabled us to determine the first archaeological datum-line in pre-medieval south India. But the accidental benefits conferred on us by our Pondicherry friends, or even by Schliemann himself, are no longer a valid excuse for archaeological illiteracy. To-day, the digger must learn to read his sections, or he should be constrained from digging.

In practice, the identification and correlation of the strata or layers which represent the successive phases in the archaeological 'history' of a site is one of the principal tasks of the excavator and will occupy the major portion of his time. So important is this task that, at the risk of wearying the reader either with the excessively unfamiliar or, more likely, with the excessively familiar, it would be wrong to forbear from certain rather arid technical details. The task is one which involves clear and logical thinking reinforced by experience and infinite patience. Normally, the strata are differentiated by variations in colour or material or content. Not infrequently, however, these variations, particularly under the bleaching influences of an African or Asian sun, present difficulty even to the experienced eye: so much so that more than one archaeologist who ought to know better has denied the presence of stratigraphy (in the Western sense of the term) on Eastern sites. 'There was no clear stratification', writes a well-known American archaeologist with reference to a Palestinian site, 'during a good part of the period covered because there was no complete destruction and rebuilding at any one time.'[1] This, of course, is nonsense; by 'stratification' the writer quoted means merely 'continuous building-levels', oblivious of the no less important layers which on any site may be expected to supplement and interrelate phases of actual construction. The fact is that the observer had simply failed to observe. There are in practice various ways and means of dealing with the reluctant, sun-baked section of the Orient, or indeed with many sections in the West. Damping, and careful scraping with a knife or turf-cutter, will often provide the remedy by bringing out the more subtle variations of colour or material. Observation in different lights at different times of the day may help. In a difficult and important section, observation may be continued over a period of days before certainty is reached. And finally an attempt must be made to 'read' the section – to discriminate, without prejudice, between the more significant and the less significant differentiations of strata: for example, between a mere 'tip-line' in a continuous accumulation on the one hand and a substantive and emphatic occupation-level on the other. It is not enough to identify layers, although that is, of course, the essential first step; it is the task of the archaeologist to *interpret* them, to understand the sentence as well as to transliterate it.

On this all-important question of interpretation something more must be said, always with the proviso that the written word is no sort of substitute for field-experience. The most that the professor

1. C. C. McCown, *Tell en-Nasbeh, excavated under the direction of the late William Frederic Bade* (Am. Sch. of Or. Res., 1947), i. 10.

can do is to offer such hints or warnings as shall create in the mind of the student a healthy wariness and a proper regard for trifles. Let us take once more as our theme the first and universal question, of which something was said in the preceding chapter: What is the time-value of archaeological strata? How long did it take, say, 4 feet of stratified deposit to accumulate? A very searching and important question, well worthy of the most careful consideration: if we could always answer it, half our battle would be won.

Reference has already been made to a famous lead which geology has given us by the recognition of the varved clays of Sweden (and elsewhere) as the annual deposits of the retreating ice, and as the time-table, therefore, of a related human phase. But it is rarely, in all conscience, that geology deals with us so straightforwardly; whilst man-made strata are capable of every sort of perversity. Some of them, indeed, are of no chronological import whatsoever, and, as instructive disturbers of all faith, these nonentities shall be considered first.

It has been my practice, from time to time, to persuade my students towards the end of the day's work to cut a section through the dump which is the outcome of their digging. They normally discover, as is to be expected, that the section thus cut is replete with stratification – tip-lines, streaks of variant soil, a miscellany of the materials through which they have been working in the course of the day. Nothing is more calculated to disturb their faith in the time-significance of stratification. Here, in front of them, is the variegated accumulation of a few hours; how is that to be reconciled with the interpretation of the adjacent strata below ground in terms of centuries?

In theory the answer is difficult, in practice it is usually easy. It will often be found that certain of the strata cease towards one end or both, in such a fashion that the underlying and overlying layers unite to clasp them and hold them within a uniform mass, as it were in suspension – a sufficient proof of contemporaneity. A succession of layers may join up laterally, like fingers extended from the palm of the hand, essentially integral therefore with one another in substance and date. Very rarely do deposits of this sort consistently ape a prolonged and systematic accumulation. On the other hand, they present a warning: a selected portion of them may be found to simulate a consistent and logical sequence, and so serve to point the danger of argument from small sections. Fig. 8 shows a problem of this kind, solved on the right by an extension of the section. It should in any event be axiomatic that no chronological sequence can be regarded as established securely on the basis of a single section.

A good archaeological instance of the insignificance of stratification is provided by many of the storage-pits cut by Early Iron Age farmers round about their dwellings, particularly on the chalk-lands. After being used for a time for the storage of farm-produce, these pits were liable to 'turn sour' and were summarily filled up with any material

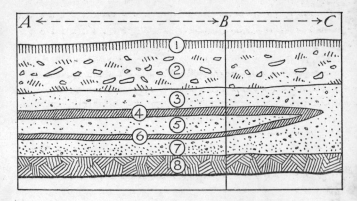

Fig. 8. Section illustrating (A-B) an apparent succession of strata (3-7), shown by an extension of the cutting (B-C) to have been deposited simultaneously

which happened to be nearby. The result is often a strikingly variegated filling, of which the stratification bears no relation to time-sequence. In other words, the first rule about stratification is that there is no invariable rule.

The opposite danger to the over-emphasis of what may be called 'accidental' and contemporary features is the under-emphasis of time-values: the assumption that a succession of strata have accumulated continuously whereas in fact they represent an intermittent growth, with one or more time-gaps. Thus the original excavator of Gezer in Palestine in 1902-9 hopelessly telescoped the Iron Age chronology of Palestine through a failure to recognize a gap of some five centuries in the occupation of his site. The mistake was gradually rectified, years later, by the evidence of other excavations, but for a time it

completely upset the dating of these centuries in Palestinian archaeology. How is a misjudgement of this sort to be prevented? This
question is manifestly important and deserves careful consideration.

There is no single answer to the question, but at least two criteria
are feasible, and either or both must be considered in the interpretation of a section illustrating more than one cultural phase.

The first criterion is the nature of the soil at the point of junction
between two cultures. An interruption in the occupation may here
be represented by a layer of wind-blown or water-borne sand, or by
the debris of turf or other vegetation. On a Dorset site, a dark layer
separated the Early Bronze Age from the Early Iron Age, and this
dark stratum was diagnosed on analysis as 'brown-earth soil developed on a subsoil rich in chalk. It evidently means a gap in the occupation and a covering of the hill with woods' – in fact, a gap of a
thousand years or more. A mere 4 or 5 inches of brown soil, compressed for more than twenty centuries beneath a rising canopy of
trampled earth tell us all that, and hint at changes of climate and water-
table which for a thousand years diverted family-life to more homely
lowlands. A subtler example comes from Hadrian's Wall, from the
filling found by Mr Gerald Simpson and Professor Ian Richmond
in the ditch of the Vallum where it was locally superseded by the
Roman fort at Birdoswald, in Cumberland. The problem was to
ascertain how long the Vallum ditch was open at this point before
the fort was built over it, and investigation was therefore made on a
vertical section of the material now filling the ditch. The result, as
reported by Dr Kathleen Blackburn, of the Department of Botany
in King's College, Newcastle upon Tyne, settled the matter and is
worth quoting. It is as follows:

Above the yellow silt of which the bottom (of the filling) was composed were deposits of peat, which varied in thickness in different sections and were obviously composed of lumps of peat put in by hand. . . .
An investigation of the material from the floor of the ditch showed little
organic matter, and no traces of the dark coloration which is the usual
product of organic decay. What little remains were present consisted
very largely of weed seeds: the majority of these were of the Knot-grass
(*Polyponum aviculera*), but examples were also found of Chickweed
(*Stella media*) and of a buttercup, which was probably *Ranunculus acris*.
These seeds were in perfect preservation, probably due to the preserving

action of the water draining from the peat immediately above. Such a flora as these seeds suggest is one which would only be found on newly-disturbed ground. From this, and from the absence of organic remains, I think we may assume that the ditch could only have been open a year or two before the re-filling with the peat.[1]

The ditch of the Vallum was therefore deliberately blotted out of existence here (for the accommodation or extension of the fort) almost immediately after its creation – a conclusion of revealing lucidity and of a notable importance in the historical diagnosis of the frontier-system. Similar evidence was recovered nearby from the ditch of the Turf Wall where it underlay the fort, showing that the fort was built across it with no appreciable intervening period – again a 'historical' inference of the highest value.

Even without analysis, careful observation under favourable conditions may reduce stratification to terms of a precise chronology, occasionally comparable with that of the famous varved clays. Two examples, one from England and one from Iraq, have been cited above (p. 45); and time-gaps and even time-spans may thus on occasion be identified in a number of ways, provided by the close observation of weather-worn or overgrown surfaces and, above all, by soil-analysis. But suitable phenomena or facilities are not always present – though the latter at least should be available to a modern excavation. There is, in any event, another approach to the problem, and the best way to describe it is by illustration.

In 1947 I was digging a town-site on the Mysore plateau in south India, in the vicinity of an undated Iron Age megalithic cemetery, with a view to the correlation of the culture of the cemetery with one or other of the phases of the town. In fact, the sections through the town-site revealed three successive and quite different cultures, of which the middle one was that of the cemetery. For the understanding of the sequel I must burden you with names. The topmost culture was known as 'Āndhra', from the name of a local kingdom, the middle culture as 'Megalithic', since it was also that of the local megalithic tombs, and the lowest as 'Stone Axe', from its characteristic product. Of the three, the only datable culture was the Āndhra, which

1. *Trans. Cumberland and Westmorland Ant. Soc.* (N.S.), xxix (Kendal, 1929), 308.

could be ascribed mainly to the first century A.D. The problem was to relate the other two cultures to this and so, for the first time, to obtain some sort of chronology for them.

For this purpose it was obviously of cardinal importance to ascertain whether the three cultures formed a continuous succession or whether they were divided from one another by time-gaps. Examination of the sections failed to reveal any intervening weathered or exposed surfaces; and indeed, had there been such surfaces, laboratory facilities for their analysis were not available in India. Accordingly, recourse was had to other types of data. In one instance, chance played happily into our hands: a pot-burial of the distinctive Stone Axe type was found inserted into the lowest overlying stratum of the megalithic culture, implying a co-occupation by the two cultures at this point. But even without so incontrovertible a demonstration of continuity, the matter was set at rest by what I may call the actuarial analysis of our sections. Such actuarial analyses should, in my view, be made more frequently than they are, and the Mysore example may therefore be described in some detail. Briefly, the method was this.

In an extensive cutting, chosen as free from complication in the form of intrusive pits or structures, a careful register was kept, layer by layer, of every potsherd found, and the results were tabulated (Figs. 9–10 and Pl. 3). Fortunately the fabric and technique used by the three cultures were so distinctive from one another that their classification was beyond doubt; the pottery of the Stone Axe people being coarse, hand-made stuff, that of the Megalithic folk being a polished and beautiful black and brown and turned slowly if at all, that of the Āndhra at the top being turned more mechanically on a fast wheel and otherwise elaborated with glaze and patterning. Now the table shows a substantial overlap, running through three successive layers, between the Stone Axe and the Megalithic series, followed by a similar overlap between the Megalithic and the Āndhra series. In estimating the significance of these very substantial overlaps, due allowance must be made for the fact that, from a variety of causes, the subsoil is always in a state of less or greater movement. Animal and vegetable life, and climate, are constantly at work in it. Relics of one stratum are always liable to find their way sporadically into another and to confuse our exact minds. But the thrusting-upwards respectively of 239 and 219 sherds from one culture into the next above it in this single section is not to be thus lightly dismissed. The only acceptable explanation is that on neither occasion did the arrival of the newer culture on the site involve the immediate extinction of

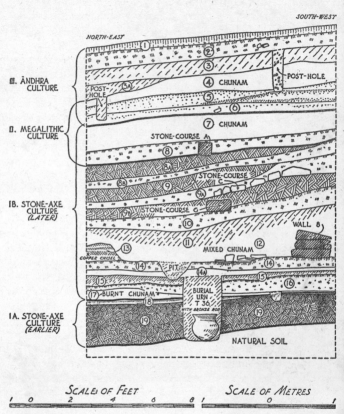

Fig. 9. Section from Brahmagiri, Mysore State, India, showing three cultural phases with overlaps

the older: in other words, that the cultural sequence was *continuous* and, in our estimate of its chronology in relation to the fixed point at the top, we can ignore the possibility of unknown factors arising

Layer	I. Stone Axe	II. Megalithic	III. Āndhra
1	..	..	52, including 1 yellow-painted sherd
2	..	..	384, including 10 yellow-painted sherds
3	..	..	480, including 68 yellow-painted and 1 rouletted sherd
3a	..	..	67
4	..	36	269, including 51 yellow-painted sherds
5	..	68	219, including 10 yellow-painted sherds[1]
6	26	115	405, including 7 yellow-painted sherds
7	63	407	..
8	150	199[2]	..
8a	36	..	..
8b	89	..	..
9	76	..	..
9a	196	..	..
10	46	..	..
11	33	..	..
12	23	..	..
13	26	..	..
14	48	..	..
14a	15	..	..
15	198	..	..
16	7	..	..
17	45	..	..
18	25	..	..
19	321[3]	..	..

1. In adjacent cuttings, layers equating with 5 and 6 of Br. 21, i.e. the lowest 'Āndhra' levels, produced 7 sherds of rouletted ware.

2. In an adjacent cutting, the layer equating with this contained an urn-burial of the 'Stone Axe' culture.

3. Including 18 'Early Painted' and 6 incised sherds of the IA culture, which this layer represents.

Fig. 10. Tabulation of sherds representing the three cultures at Brahmagiri
(See Fig. 9)

from interruptions in the occupation. We are here in no danger of repeating the disastrous oversight of the excavator of Gezer (p. 62). Details of this specific Mysore example do not concern us; it will suffice to observe that the overlap thus demonstrated between the megalithic culture and the overlying first-century culture proved that the megalithic tombs were there in use until the first century, and so provided the first firm date for this very abundant category of south Indian structures.

Well, there are examples of various kinds of stratigraphical evidence: of layers that are contemporary with one another, layers that are separated by greater or lesser time-intervals, layers that have accumulated in unbroken succession. The reading of a section is the reading of a language that can only be learned by demonstration and experience. A word of advice to the student. However practised, do not read too hastily. Be your own devil's advocate before passing judgement. And, wherever possible, discuss your diagnosis with others – with colleagues, with pupils, with your foreman. ('The testimony of one person is no testimony', declares Hywel Dda, the wise Welsh law-giver.) Be humble. Do not ignore the opinion of the uninstructed. 'Everyone knows as much as the savant. The walls of rude minds are scrawled all over with facts, with thoughts.' Emerson said so, and he was right. Even if you do not accept the views of those you question, the mere act of questioning is at the same time a restraint and a stimulus.

We turn now from interpretation to record. But first reference must be made to a method of recording that not long ago was widespread in the East and may in fact still survive there. If so, it is the survival of a fantastic and monstrous device evolved in the alluvial plains of the great river valleys of Egypt and Mesopotamia as a substitute for exact observation in ill-controlled 'mass excavations'. Its origin is probably to be found in Petrie's belief that on an Egyptian town-site it was possible to equate the accumulation of material with a specific time-scale (p. 45). The validity of this 'principle' was doubtful and dangerous enough in its original specialized context; it has no place whatsoever in the general technique of modern field-archaeology. Yet in India, for example, as recently as 1944 it was still the only method known.

Briefly, it consisted of the mechanical recording of every object and structure in relation to a fixed bench-level. Thus in the excavations at the great prehistoric city of Mohenjo-daro in the Indus valley, in 1927–31, the records were prepared from bench-levels, in one area '178·7 ft. above mean sea-level' and in another '180·9 ft. above sea-level', the assumption being that all objects and structures at the same level below (or above) datum line were in the same 'stratum', i.e. contemporary with one another! I have described this system as 'incredible' and I repeat the description. So incredible is it, and yet so widespread, that the excavator's own proud account of it may be repeated. He says:

In order that our deep digging might be satisfactorily carried out, an extensive system of levelling was necessary. The levels of every building and of every wall were therefore taken, especial attention being paid to door-sills and pavements as being for purposes of stratification the most important parts of a building. In addition, both the locus and level of every object found, whether it was regarded at the time as important or not, were noted in order not only to correlate each object with the building in which it was found, but also to facilitate the study of the development of art and technique. As some thousands of objects were unearthed in the sections that we excavated, it may be thought that this procedure was unnecessarily laborious. This, however, was not the case. The levelling instruments were set up early in the morning and remained in position all day; and it was quite a simple matter to take the level of each object directly it appeared.

It was, however, admitted that this method was not wholly free from complexity; that there were

limitations to the deductions to be drawn from the levels at which objects are found. For instance, if a jar or a seal lies either below or at some distance above a pavement or door-sill, it is difficult to decide to what period it belongs. We, therefore adopted the rule that all objects found in or near the foundations of a building be assigned to the period of that building rather than to the previous phase, unless they actually rested on the remains of a pavement of earlier date; for it is more than probable that they were dropped or left behind when the foundations were being made.

The chapters on the pottery and other finds in the excavator's subsequent report include page after page of elaborate but insignificant tables based on this procedure.

In other words, be it repeated, the so-called 'stratification' of the Indus valley civilization, one of the major civilizations of the ancient world, was dominated, not by local observation, but by the level of the sea nearly 300 miles away! This mechanical classification can only be categorized as the very parody of scientific method. It bears little more relationship to scientific archaeology than astrology bears to astronomy.

To appreciate its utter absurdity, we need only recall that, except perhaps at the earliest level of a site (hardly ever adequately explored), an ancient city in the East is never level. Very rarely is a city completely destroyed and completely rebuilt at one moment and at one horizon. Normally, a house is reconstructed or replaced as it decays, or at the whim of its owner. The town as a whole is constantly in a state of differential destruction and construction. Individual building-sites rise above their neighbours; the town-site itself rises and assumes the contour of a hill; buildings on its slopes are contemporary with buildings on its summit. A doorway or a potsherd may be found at one spot 10 feet below a doorway or a potsherd of precisely the same date at another spot. Such differences, of vital importance to the scientific interpretation of the site, are ironed out and obliterated by the bench-level. If it be necessary to illustrate further the grievous fallacy of this method, two diagrams (Fig. 11) may serve. They are self-explanatory.

Yet, for all the obvious absurdity of the datum-line system just described, the substitution of so-called 'levels' – whether abstract building levels or purely arbitrary depth-lines – for factual stratification dies hard. It recurs, for example, in a revised edition (1950) of *A Manual of Archaeological Field Methods* prepared by a leading American university. There, as sturdily as ever, thrives the old outworn system, with its mechanical 'unit-levels', governed not by changes of soil but by 'the length of the shovel-blade (6 to 12 inches)'.[1] True the word 'stratification' is not unknown to the authors. It represents a phenomenon, they admit, which 'may be visible in the walls of the excavation'; but, we are assured, 'any stratigraphy of artifact types and

1. It may be noted in passing that mechanical 'foot-levels' were used as long ago as 1865 by W. Pengelly, F.R.S., in the excavation of Kent's Cavern at Torquay. See his interesting MS. Journal in the possession of the Royal Society. But it is sad to find the same outworn method advocated by a distinguished university in 1950.

animal bones will appear after a study has been made and need not bother the excavator in the field' [*sic*]. The notion of peeling off the successive strata in conformity with their proper bed-lines, and thus ensuring the accurate isolation of structural phases and relevant artifacts, is not even considered.

Enough of criticism; let us turn to a more positive aspect of the matter. The preparation for the record of the section begins with the first spadeful dug. From the outset, the strata are carefully observed, distinguished, and *labelled* as the work proceeds. It is, of

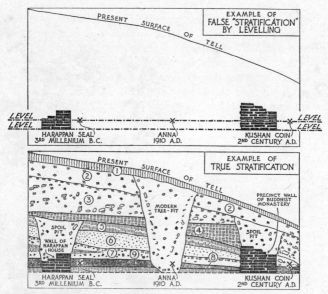

Fig. 11. Diagrams illustrating the stratification of a city-mound (below) and the fallacy of recording by mechanical levels (above)

course, as the work proceeds that 'finds' are isolated and recorded, and their record is necessarily integral with that of the strata from which they are derived. The supervisor must therefore make up his mind clearly from moment to moment as to the limits and nomenclature of his strata; and his decisions, whether ultimately approved or modified, must be susceptible to accurate delineation, if only for the subsequent correlation of his 'finds'. In other words, both he and the spectator or the future reader must know exactly what he thinks he is doing.

I have found in practice that there is only one foolproof method of ensuring this. The successive layers must be defined and clearly labelled as they come to light. By labelling I meant the actual pinning of a label by a nail or peg into the side of the trench in (preferably on the top edge of) each layer. The label bears the number of the layer within a circle (I reserve encircled numbers for this purpose, to avoid all risk of confusion with numbers having other connotations), supplemented by a name: for example 'lower brown', 'red clay', 'porridge' – it matters not what, so long as a distinctive word or phrase is used to emphasize and cross-check the differentiation. Numbers may on occasion be erroneously duplicated, but the addition of a name avoids risk of confusion. And incidentally the use of a name tends to give individuality to a layer and helps the mind in a pictorial reconstruction of the section.

Accordingly, I like to see my sections plastered from head to foot with orderly arrays of labels (Pl. 3), which serve three main purposes: they demand clear and decisive thought on the part of the supervisor who invents them, they show on the ground and on the drawing precisely what his small-find labels mean, and they make it possible for the director or a substitute-supervisor to understand at once the diagnosis up to date. Incidentally, they enable that diagnosis to be checked – always with the proviso that any material alteration in it will probably mean either a relabelling of the relevant 'finds' or at least a recording of the original as well as the corrected diagnosis. As a general guide to the young, it is wiser to insist upon the overstratification than the under-stratification of a section in the first instance: it is easy subsequently to group layers and their contents but it will never be safe to subdivide them.

Now a word as to systems of numbering. Layers or strata it is obviously necessary to number downwards from the top of a cutting, so that the numbers are mostly in the reverse order of accumulation, the latest (topmost) layer being layer 1. This somewhat illogical procedure is unavoidable since it is necessary to give layer-numbers to small-finds as they come to light, without waiting for the completion of the section. The same disability does not apply to *cultures,* which emerge as recognizable entities at a later stage of the work and are not used for labelling purposes. Here the logical system can, and certainly should, be followed: namely, to number the earliest culture or phase as number I, with II, III, etc., in sequence above them. Unfortunately, usage in this matter is chaotic. A number of Mesopotamian and Iranian sites (Arpachiyah, Uruk, Uquair, Gawra, Giyan) have been numbered from top to bottom, so that, for example, Giyan V and Gawra XX are early, and Giyan I and Gawra I are late. On the other hand, Sialk VI is late, and so with Nineveh, Hissar, Susa (new classification) and other rationally classified sites. It should unquestionably be laid down as standard that cultures or cultural phases are numbered (with Roman numerals) from the earliest to the latest (Fig. 9). The only circumstances which may present difficulty to this method is failure to reach the bottom of a site. Where this happens, the earliest phase uncovered may not in fact be the earliest on the site, and therefore not truly its number I. Chanhu-daro in Sind is an instance of this kind, where the excavator might justify the top-downwards numeration, which he in fact adopted, on the plea that the water-table stopped him from reaching and diagnosing the lower levels. Interim reports on unfinished excavations may provide another excuse for this procedure. But in general, the answer to the difficulty is clear: no site should be dug unless it is sectioned and diagnosed to the lowest level and a complete culture-sequence recovered. Water should not normally be accepted as a bar; at Arikamedu in 1945 we had to dig 11 feet below sea-level, and this depth we achieved, with some difficulty it is true, but without elaborate equipment, whilst at Mohenjo-daro in 1950 we penetrated with the help of pumps to a depth of 10 feet below the water-level under peculiarly difficult conditions, and with more time could certainly have dug lower still.

The purist may complain that two contrary systems have here been recommended: the numbering of layers from top to bottom, and of cultural phases from bottom to top. In fact, there is no conflict whatsoever between the two. They are both logical and practical for their several purposes. A nominal inconsistency is their only demerit, and it is of a kind that only a pedant could carp at. 'Do I contradict myself?' cries Walt Whitman; 'Very well, then, I contradict myself!' Or recall the words of a less blustering fellow-countryman of Whitman's: 'A foolish consistency is the hobgoblin of little minds'; and when the magisterial Ralph Waldo Emerson opes his mouth let no dog bark.

Our section, then, has been dug, diagnosed, and labelled. The task remains to record it on paper accurately and expressively. The mechanism is simple enough. Categorically, the materials required are: squared paper, a light drawing-board (three-ply wood is useful for this), drawing-pins, a good HB pencil, an india-rubber, a scale-rule, good thin string for the datum-line, surveying-pins ('arrows') or 6-inch nails, a measuring-tape, clips for fixing the tape, a 5-foot rod, and a plumb-bob.

At a convenient point, generally at the top, the string is stretched firmly across the section and levelled either by means of a bubble-level or by a surveyor's level laid on the terminal points. As usual, details are important. String of the best quality should be used; inferior string breaks or, worse still, stretches and sags. In any case, the string should be supported on carefully levelled pegs at horizontal intervals of ten feet. Moreover, to avoid errors from stretching or other causes, the level of the string should be checked once or twice during the day.

This string should be marked off in feet or metres or, better still, a measuring-tape should be stretched (not too tightly) alongside it. Then, at every foot or at other selected points, vertical measurements are taken with a weighted measuring-tape above or below the datum and are transferred by the draftsman, on the spot, to suitably squared paper.

As to *scale*, the smallest scale at which the detail of an average section can be adequately recorded is $\frac{1}{2}$ inch = 1 foot (alternatively, 5 cm. = 1 m.), and this may be regarded as standard for large sections. Whenever possible, however, the larger scale of 1 inch = 1 foot (alternatively, 10 cm. = 1 m.) is preferable; it is more accurate, and better lends itself to annotation.

In the process of drawing the section, there is a common tendency on the part of the inexperienced draftsman to exaggerate inequalities in the surface of a stratum, so as to obscure its general contour and character. He should be reminded that, on the normal scale of $\frac{1}{2}$ inch = 1 foot, the picture will be one-twenty-fourth of the size of the original. An inequality, therefore, rising actually 2 inches above the average level of a stratum will, in a normal scale-drawing, vary by

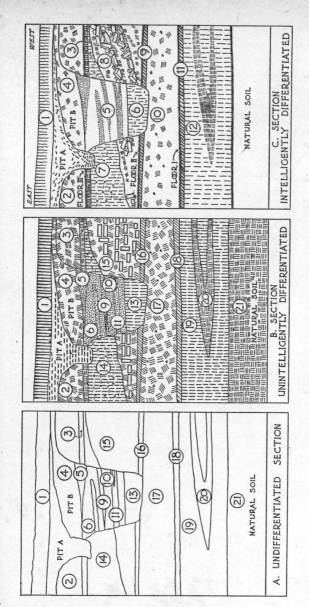

Fig. 12. Technique of section-drawing

only one-twelfth of an inch above the level, and so will form a nearly negligible break in the surface. Almost invariably the draftsman, seeing the trees rather than the wood, will over-emphasize the obstacle, albeit that the feature is exceptional and misrepresents the general meaning of the layer.

Furthermore, there is the question, not merely of the over-emphasis of accidental features, but of the over-emphasis or under-emphasis of whole layers; resulting, in fact, in a permanent misinterpretation of the section. I can best demonstrate this by three diagrams (Fig. 12). In diagram A, the draftsman is assumed to have delineated the individual strata correctly and fairly, with reference to his horizontal datum-line. But this delineation, although indicating the presence of strata, does little or nothing to indicate their varying character and significance. It is an almost meaningless collection of lines – a procession of letters not yet divided into words. A more ambitious draftsman may attempt to indicate something of the individuality and diversity of the strata, and diagram B illustrates such an attempt. This fails in two main respects. First, the general evenness of tone throughout the section produces the unmeaning monotony of a sentence spoken without inflection, and so fails largely to convey the intended impression. The draftsman has not realized the varying significance of the facts which he is recording; he has again failed to see the wood for the trees. Secondly, he has not realized that his rendering is not, or should not be, merely a transcription of accurately measured or even accurately emphasized lines: it is, or should be, also an accurate *picture* of what he sees. Not only should lines of demarcation be transcribed from measurement, but also the size, shape, and position of brick-bats, bones, sherds or other materials which, by their character and quantity and by their 'angle of rest' in the soil, combine to indicate the nature of a stratum and the method of its accumulation. An intelligently drawn section is far more than a diagram; it is, as I say, a picture, representing not merely the skeleton but also something of the vital flesh and blood of its subject. Diagram C is diagram B corrected in this sense.

It must be confessed that a well-drawn, i.e. intelligently recorded, section is relatively a rarity. But it is nevertheless a basic necessity of modern field-work. The published sections are the readiest index of the value of an excavation-report.

In these diagrams, and elsewhere, I have used certain symbols for the easy conventional representation of different types of soil or deposit. They have no special merit but are reasonably expressive. Some measure of standardization in the choice of symbols would be useful but has not yet been attempted in Britain. (See, however, Fig. 13.)

SYMBOLS
FOR SECTIONS

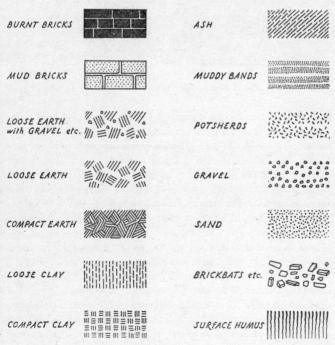

BURNT BRICKS

MUD BRICKS

LOOSE EARTH with GRAVEL etc.

LOOSE EARTH

COMPACT EARTH

LOOSE CLAY

COMPACT CLAY

ASH

MUDDY BANDS

POTSHERDS

GRAVEL

SAND

BRICKBATS etc.

SURFACE HUMUS

Fig. 13. Chart of symbols adopted by the Archaeological Survey of India

Before leaving the delineation of sections, reference must be made to an alternative method which was occasionally (though not normally) used long ago by Pitt Rivers, and has from time to time found favour with others, amongst whom Dr Gerhard Bersu is notable (Fig. 14). This may be called the 'pictorial' method in a sense somewhat different from that in which I have used 'picture' in preceding paragraphs. The strata are not outlined (as in Fig. 12) but are, to a greater or less extent, differentiated from one another by what may

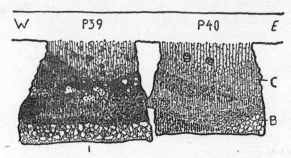

Fig. 14. 'Pictorial' method of section-drawing. After G. Bersu

be called a sort of chromatic shading. The result is an *impression* of the section, more akin to a photograph than to a diagram. The different 'tones' are not consistently framed or demarcated, nor are they numbered.

Granted that, in the hands of an artist, this impressionistic technique has merits, it is equally plain that in the hands of one who is a mere delineator rather than an artist chaos will prevail. A technique which is beyond the reach of most excavators is, on that ground alone, ruled out where a workable alternative exists. The impressionistic technique cannot be defended on the grounds that it is 'less conventional'; in its own fashion, it is no less conventional than the linear technique, only, it is a different convention. And it has this crowning disadvantage: it lends itself to nebulousness, to a blurring of detail and a lack of precision in diagnosis. Even some of Dr Bersu's skilful drawings show this, and a less skilful performer is liable to be utterly lost. This is a grave defect. If I have tried to emphasize one thing more than another it is the need for considered precision in our work. Any medium or convention which is likely to encourage woolly thinking is to be deprecated: and, save at its rare best, the impressionistic technique is woolly. I do not commend it to the average worker.

One more detail. It is useful, in the drawing of a large section, to include a human figure as well as a linear scale. The figure provides an effortless indication of approximate size, and the saving of effort on the part of the reader is worth a little extra effort on the part of the draftsman.

CHAPTER 5

The Layout of an Excavation

AN ill-considered excavation is liable to develop into a chaos of pits and trenches, difficult to supervise and record, and often embarrassed by intrusive spoil-tips that eventually either control the work or are in a constant and costly process of secondary removal. On approaching an excavation, the trained observer can at a glance evaluate its efficiency. It is an axiom that an untidy excavation is a bad one, whether the untidiness reside in the general layout or in detailed execution. The guiding principles are not difficult: they are 'Have a plan', a carefully thought-out scheme, and execute it in orderly fashion.

Two contrasted examples will illustrate this. The first (Pl. 4a) is an official photograph of a well-known excavation in the East, conducted by an archaeologist of considerable repute and long field-experience. Nevertheless, a mere novice might guess, and guess correctly, that chaos reigns. Look at the crowded workmen, picking and shovelling tumultuously in all directions; the absence of a supervisor or indeed of any possibility of supervision; the absence also of 'small-find' or pottery receptacles; and of course a complete lack of any systematic identification of strata. Needless to say, the subsequent report faithfully reflected this concentrated confusion.

The second illustration (Pl. 4b), from the same subcontinent, un-blushingly represents an excavation of my own, on the principle that the professor may properly be expected to practise. It shows a site neatly parcelled out in readily controllable areas; small groups of workmen are directed by supervisors (distinguishable in the photograph by their sun-helmets); the basket-carriers are working in orderly procession along clear pathways; and in the middle distance on the right, the survey-party is conveniently at work at a table shaded by an essential umbrella. The subsequent analysis and detailed publication of this excavation was a relatively easy task. For it is not the least of the merits of orderly field-work that it is *easy*. Every man knows what he is doing, and records are almost inevitably clear and sensible, the considered product of several pairs of critical eyes.

Plan your work, then, and methodically pursue your plan. True, there must always be an element of chance and of opportunism in an excavation, however carefully planned. But scientific digging is not on that account a gamble. The experienced excavator, who thinks before he digs, succeeds in reaching his objective in a majority of cases.

The nature of the plan necessarily depends upon the character and needs of the site. For purposes of discussion, we may here classify our problem under three categories: trial-trenching or *sondages*, area-excavation, and what I shall call substantive trenching. The excavation of burials will be considered separately (p. 113), and caves, in view of the slightness of my experience in their exploration, I propose to omit altogether; they require a monograph by one who knows.

(i) TRIAL-TRENCHING OR 'SONDAGES'

The old practice of cutting trial-trenches, of making *sondages*, as a preliminary to, or even in lieu of, area-excavation was frequently a substitute for intelligent thinking and clear aiming. It was to a large extent 'shooting into the brown' on the off-chance of bringing down a bird. Trial-trenches rarely prove anything, save of the most general kind. I have in mind a long and wide trial-trench cut by an eminent archaeologist across a famous town-site without apparent result; whilst subsequent systematic excavation, initiated on an altogether different basis, proved that the trench had in fact passed through and utterly failed to reveal a building of unique character. The answer on a site of that kind is, not a trial-trench, but a methodical area-excavation, which can always be discontinued if unproductive but at least reveals coherently within the area selected.

Trenches in general, save of the somewhat special 'substantive' kind described below (p. 86), are bad for more than one reason. They 'mess up' a site. Unless very wide (when they are, in effect, cumbersome area-excavations) they are liable at any considerable depth to become excessively confined and difficult to work in, their stratification cannot be viewed comprehensively and at adequate range, and, above all, lateral enlargement complicates the record to an extent which endangers its accuracy. At Maiden Castle in Dorset I dug the northern portal of the eastern entrance in 1935 by trenching, and can still recall the appalling complexity of my record as the work proceeded and my trenches widened. In the following year I dug the southern portal as an area by the 'square' method, to be described below, and both excavation and record developed easily side by side, without risk of error and without headache.

On the other hand, prejudice against trenching cannot be extended to sites where the preliminary problem is solely and simply to search for a superficially invisible structure. If a line of ancient entrenchments, for example, is thought to have passed somewhere through a certain field, a trial-trench across the field is the obvious method of proving or disproving the theory, and it would be pedantry to protest. The example of Napoleon III's Colonel Stoffel in this respect has already been cited (p. 23). The principle here advocated is that trenching should be employed, not as a normal method, but only when very special circumstances demand it. Too often does it form the basis of an excavation to which other methods are more suitable.

(ii) AREA-EXCAVATION

If a site is *known* to have been occupied, an area-excavation, not a trial-trench, is usually the effective answer. But let us first consider the pre-requisites.

An area-excavation must be:

(a) conveniently and clearly subdivisible for record and control;

(b) capable of easy, progressive expansion in any direction without breaking down or impairing the preliminary datum-lines;

(c) capable of preserving for constant reference at a maximum number of points complete vertical sections until the last phase of the excavation;

(d) capable, ultimately, of easy integration into a continuously exposed regional excavation;

(e) readily accessible to all points for the removal of soil, without hindrance from intervening cuttings or traffic across excavated surfaces; and

(f) sufficiently open to the sky to ensure the easy inspection of well-lighted sections at all required depths.

Only one type of layout normally supplies all these needs: namely, a layout based upon a *square* (Pl. 5). A series of squares, a grid, dug so that a balk is left between each pair of adjacent squares until the extreme end of the work, supplies all the six pre-requisites. The individual square is a clearly defined sub-unit for record and supervision; supplementary squares can be added in any direction in accordance with developing needs, without affecting any previous datum; the supervisor retains in each square (until the end of the work) a complete section on all four sides of him, together with such additional sections or part-sections as he may care to add within the compass of the square; the stratification of adjacent squares, and therefore accumulatively of the whole site, can easily be correlated and recorded along a number of arterial lines, so that ultimately the barriers between the squares can be removed without loss of vertical evidence and the whole plan laid bare, level by level; the barriers or balks provide ready paths of access to the various squares, and from them to the spoil-dumps; and the squares, unlike most trenches, are sufficiently spacious to let in ample light and to provide elbow-room for interpretation and record.

Experience shows that in soils of average stability the horizontal dimensions of a square should approximately equal its anticipated maximum depth. Thus, if it is intended to dig to a depth approaching 20 feet, the square should be laid out with 20-foot sides. This ratio allows for the necessary stairs and balks. Similarly, a 30-foot square can be dug to a depth of 30 feet, whilst a depth of 10 feet or less (the normal range in Great Britain) demands only a 10-foot square. The smaller the superficial area of the square in relation to its depth the better, provided always that there is ample light and working-room. With a due regard to these factors, a 10-foot square may be regarded as the minimum sub-unit.

These measurements include provision for the balks between squares. In most soils a balk 3 feet wide will carry any amount of traffic, and that width may therefore be regarded as standard on all but the shallowest sites. (For 10-foot squares a 2-foot balk is usually adequate.) The 3-foot balk implies that the string marking the top edge of the actual cutting is $1\frac{1}{2}$ feet within the perimeter of each square as pegged out; for example, the actual cutting of a 20-foot square will be 17 feet square, and of a 30-foot square it will be 27 feet.

Similarly a 10-foot square with 2-foot balks will be cut with 8-foot sides.

The pegged squares will form the basis of record and survey, and the supervisor must ensure their initial exactitude; otherwise, all sorts of complications and errors will arise. At each corner of the square a strong peg, not less than $1\frac{1}{2}$ inches square in scantling and 1 foot 3 inches long, with one end pointed, is firmly driven into the ground, its faces set diagonally to the proposed square; but the exact corner-point is marked by a 2-inch nail driven vertically into the top of the peg and left projecting about an inch for the occasional affixture of string or measuring-tape in connexion with survey. On one occasion, where the surface-soil was too soft to hold the corner pegs with complete security, I found it worth while to have them set in concrete, so important are they to the accuracy of the work.

From these fixed points, the marking out of the actual cutting with string as a guide to the diggers, allowing for the necessary balk (see above), is a simple secondary operation.

The squares thus pegged out are conveniently named by means of letters in one direction (say, east to west) and by numbers in the other direction (say, north to south). They will thus be known individually as A1, A2, A3, etc.; B1, B2, etc. The appropriate designation must be painted clearly on the nearest face of each of the four corner-pegs, which for this purpose have been set diagonally in the ground. Thus a peg set at the junction of four squares will have a different designation on each face; e.g. A1, A2, B1, B2. The need for clear and abundant labelling cannot be over-emphasized if error is to be eliminated from the records, particularly on a large excavation.

In the actual digging of a square, a principle of universal application in archaeological excavation may be stressed: namely, the use of the *control-pit*. This is the supervisor's own special charge, and upon it the accuracy of the general digging in large measure depends. It is a small cutting, about $2\frac{1}{2}$ feet square, cut by the supervisor himself or by a trained man under his eye, to a depth of $1\frac{1}{2}$–2 feet lower than the average level of the work. Its purpose is to enable the supervisor, with a minimum disturbance of the strata, to anticipate the nature and probable vertical extent of the layers which are being cleared by his main gang. It is a glimpse into the future of his stratigraphical work. Without it, neither the supervisor nor his diggers, working blindly from the top, can avoid the confusion of the lower part of one stratum with the upper part of the next below it. In other words, stratification must, by its nature, always be controlled from the *side*, i.e. from the side of the control pit, since it obviously cannot be controlled prophetically from the top: *vertical digging first, horizontal digging afterwards*, must be the rule. Control-pits must be sufficiently numerous to minimize risks arising from the unevenness or interruption of strata, and sufficiently small in area to restrict the confusion of evidence which is inherent in their exploratory nature. The control-pit is indeed a means of concentrating errors which would otherwise be spread over the whole area. Its evidence in detail must be used with proportionate circumspection.

And, above all, constant reference must be made to the stratification revealed by the sides of the square as the digging proceeds. The four sides must be constantly correlated with one another. Any marked discrepancy between them, or between the equivalent sections in adjacent squares, must be considered and an explanation sought. During the search for an explanation, the supervisor may find it desirable to suspend or restrict the actual digging.

This raises a further point, again of universal application. In view of the occasional necessity for a temporary suspension of digging in one square or another, the director of an excavation must always have in readiness a sufficiency of 'reserve-jobs' to meet contingencies of this kind. Such reserve-jobs may include the removal of unimportant top-soil from a new square, or the reinforcement of a gang engaged elsewhere upon the digging of a deep stratum. Remember that, when a gang stops digging, from two to six workpeople – pick-man, shovel-man and, in the East, probably four basket-carriers – are thrown out of action. And idleness is both costly and infectious.

In the last three paragraphs matters have been dealt with which are not peculiar to the 'square', although they are liable to present themselves on a busy area-dig in an acute form. I turn now to the actual recording of the square.

Be it repeated that a great merit of the 'square' method is that it localizes both control and record. The supervisor's responsibilities are clearly defined, and the area covered by his field note-book is precise. The basis of his record is the careful identification, embodied in an accurate measured drawing, of the stratigraphy of each of the four sides of his square and of such supplementary sections as may be required. As in all excavations, the layers are demarcated and labelled with a serial number whilst the excavation proceeds (see p. 72). Each side of the square is also labelled with its compass-point, which is added to the index-number of the square: e.g. B3N indicates the northern side of square B3. And each side is carefully measured and drawn to a minimum scale of $\frac{1}{2}$ inch to 1 foot, or to a maximum scale of 1 inch to 1 foot, or the metric equivalents (see p. 74). A sketch (or even measured) section should also be included in the notebook; and reference should be made to relevant sections not so included.

In the process of excavation, it may be found convenient sometimes to work diagonally across the square; for instance, if diagonal walls are found, since sections at right angles to the line of a wall are necessary to avoid a distortion of the relevant strata. An example is illustrated in Pl. 4b, where diagonal balks can be seen within the grid-squares. In such cases, the diagonal section must of course be correlated with the side-sections and, if necessary, drawn separately.

All 'finds' will be recorded by strata with reference to the nearest recorded section, normally with the nearest side of the square. Structures, pits, or important objects, together with the position of all measured sections, will be planned carefully in the supervisor's notebook in relation to the four surveyed corner-pegs of the square. 'Finds' will be classified in the notebook by serial numbers, section-label, stratum, and sketch (see below).

(iii) SUBSTANTIVE TRENCHES

The epithet 'substantive' is here applied to trenches which are not merely tentative cuttings made in search of some ill-defined objective but are in themselves a definite objective. In the category is included the cross-trenching of a line of fortifications, to establish their structural sequence and to link it up with the sequence of occupations within the enclosure. Examples are illustrated in Pls. 6 and 7a, one of them a revealing section which, in 1944–5, related the stone defences of the third city of Taxila (Sirkap) in the Punjab with a dated 'palace' in the vicinity and so threw a new light on the chronology of this important site.[1] A further use of the substantive trench is shown in

1. *Ancient India*, no. 4 (New Delhi, 1948), pp. 41 ff.

Pl. 7b, where the method was employed to establish the stratigraphical relationship of two cemeteries, representing different cultures, on the famous prehistoric site at Harappā, in the Punjab. In 1946 the two cemeteries were linked by a carefully cut and surveyed trench nearly 450 feet long, and the resultant section (which has been published) was conclusive. In the photograph, one of the cemeteries is beside the figures in the foreground, the other lies amongst the trees in the background, and the lines of datum-pegs, together with a regular series of cross-balks designed to equate the sections on the two sides of the trench, are seen.

In all these examples, the principle is the same. The lateral extent of the trench is defined at the outset, and the flanking datum-lines are accordingly fixed once and for all. There is no risk of their obliteration by any lateral, crab-like movement of the cutting, and the recorder's task is predictable from start to finish.

The established method of recording objects found in a trench which it is not intended to enlarge laterally is represented by the following extracts from a recorder's notebook:

No.	Measurements	Layer	Object	Remarks
①	IV 6″ × 3′–5′ 6″	③ Brown sand	Iron knife blade 5″ long	(Sketch)
②	III 1′ 4″ × 2′ 5″– 6′ 2″	4 Loose reddish earth with occasional patches of ash	Spherical agate bead	In a local patch of wood-ash

The figure in the *first column* is the serial number of the find. I make the practice of enclosing it in a triangle to avoid any possibility of confusion with layer-numbers, etc. It is immediately written on the envelope containing the object and /or on the label attached to the object, and subsequently on the object itself; also on an index-card in duplicate (one for the site-index and one for the index of objects classified by categories), which will include likewise all the other particulars of the record.

The figures in the *second column* are the essence of the record, and are derived as follows. Before the digging of the trench is begun, two parallel lines of pegs are laid out, each at a distance of 1 foot from one of the intended edges of the trench. Thus, if the trench is (for example) to be 10 feet wide, the two lines of pegs will be 12 feet apart. The pegs themselves are not less than 1½ inches square in scantling and 1 foot 3 inches long, with one end pointed. They are driven firmly into the ground – firmly enough to avoid any risk of accidental dislodgement – and are set *diagonally* with reference to the proposed trench, i.e. with one angle facing the latter. In each line they are placed with these edges 3 feet apart, measured *horizontally*, not along the actual contour of the ground (unless that be level); and an imaginary cross-line joining opposite pairs of pegs in the two main lines must be at right angles with the latter. See Fig. 15.

Every peg is then numbered clearly on each of the two faces nearest to the proposed trench with a serial-number in black paint. With the addition of the Arabic zero, Roman numerals (I, II, III, etc.) are used

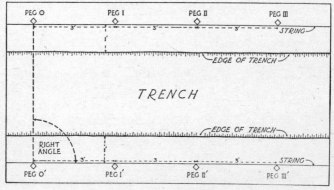

Fig. 15. Layout of a trench for three-dimensional recording

for the double reason: (*a*) that they are easier to paint than Arabic numerals, and (*b*) that there is no risk of confusing them with the actual measurements of the record. The figures on one of the lines of pegs are distinguished by a dash (O′, I′, II′, III′, etc.). If subsequently it is desired to extend the trench backwards from zero (e.g. down the reverse slope of a rampart), capital letters (A, B, C, etc.) are used for the successive pegs of the extension, the letters on one of the lines being similarly distinguished by a dash (A', B', C', etc.).

Along the front edges of each line of pegs a string is then tightly stretched, and is pegged down where this is necessitated by the contour of the ground. These strings are the base-lines from which measurements are subsequently taken.

So much for the preliminary layout of the trench. The supervisor must now be provided with an angle-measure, made lightly but strongly of two 3-foot or preferably 4-foot arms graduated in feet and inches and fixed firmly to each other at right angles (Pl. 18, 11). On each arm is fixed a bubble-level. The other normal measuring-instruments – tape, 5-foot rule, and plumb-bob – complete the equipment.

When the digging of the trench is in progress, the position of every significant find is measured in the following sequence:

(A) *Longitudinal measurement.* The point at which a line at right-angles from the main datum-string to the object cuts the former is measured along that line from the last preceding peg. The point in question is obtained by means of the angle-measure, with such extension of the outward arm as may be required and with the assistance of a plumb-bob. Thus if the point be at 10 feet 4 inches from the zero peg, it will actually be measured from peg III (9 feet) and will be recorded as III 1' 4".

(B) *Outward measurement.* The distance outwards, at right-angles to the datum-string, to a point vertically (by plumb-bob) above the object is measured with the angle-measure, levelled by its bubble-level and extended by means of the 5-foot rule if necessary. Note that the measurement is recorded from the datum-string, *not* from the actual side of the trench. Thus, if the measurement is 2 feet 5 inches, the distance of the object from the side of the trench will be about 1 foot 5 inches. The recorded measurement is affixed to the longitudinal measurement with a multiplication sign: thus in the present example the measurements so far will be III 1' 4" × 1' 5".

(C) *Downward measurement.* This represents the vertical depth of the object below the level of the datum-string at the intersection established under (A) above. It is obtained by tape (or rule) and plumb-bob from the levelled arm of the angle-measure, and it is added to the record with a minus sign. If the depth is 6 feet 2 inches, the total record will now read III 1' 4" × 1' 5" – 6' 2".

In the *third column* is noted the number allotted to the layer – a number best shown in a circle, a symbol which is in practice useful for distinguishing layer-numbers from other figures – and the descriptive word or phrase by which the layer is named. These facts are of importance, since the *material* in which an object is found is usually certain and provides a check upon the measurements, which may sometimes mislead in irregular strata or near the junction of two strata.

The *fourth column* is self-explanatory. The *fifth column* is useful for additional information and, above all, for a sketch of the object. Even a bad sketch is better than none at all.

It is scarcely necessary to add that the utility of such a record – or indeed of any stratigraphical record - is proportionate to the accuracy of the measured section or sections with which the record is subsequently to be equated. The two sides of a trench are rarely identical, and it will nearly always be desirable to prepare an accurate drawing of both, together with occasional cross-sections. Moreover, during the actual digging it is sometimes useful to project certain categories of objects (from the three-dimensional record) on to the actual sides of the trench by means of labelled or coloured pegs. I have known occasions upon which such a visual representation of a distribution in the actual trench has been illuminating and convincing.

CHAPTER 6

The Excavation of a Structure

FROM the more general questions of technique we turn to specific problems. How would you excavate the buried remains of an ancient building? 'Find a wall and follow it' might be the obvious answer. But the previous chapters have been written in vain if the novice who has read thus far is prepared to accept the answer without protest. He will by now appreciate that to follow a wall in all literalness would be to destroy the related evidence upon which its interest in large measure depends. Let us consider in some detail the nature of that related evidence.

Unless a structure is dated by a contemporary inscription or by unimpeachable documentary evidence or (exceptionally) by its intrinsic character, our knowledge of its date or cultural context must be derived from the stratigraphical association of objects of recognizable types. Furthermore, the specific character of the strata themselves – whether resulting from construction, destruction, decay, or other causes – will throw light upon the vicissitudes through which the building has passed. Only the most careful excavation and observation can recover such evidence with sufficient exactitude for use. The dating or cultural setting of a building is based ideally on three categories of objects: (i) those supplied by strata which accumulated before the building was constructed; (ii) those supplied by strata contemporary with the construction; and (iii) those supplied by strata subsequent to the construction. Categories (i) and (iii) bracket the structure chronologically or culturally, whilst category (ii) defines the point within the brackets.

To understand the full meaning of a building in decay, it is necessary to understand how it was originally constructed. I have accordingly urged elsewhere (p. 157), for this and other reasons, that a knowledge of building-construction be included amongst the qualifications of an excavator. In its simplest form, a masonry wall is built normally as follows. A trench, known as the 'foundation-trench', is cut along the line of the proposed wall in order that the foundations of the latter may rest upon the solid sub-soil rather than upon the relatively unstable soil that is commonly found on the surface – whether natural *humus* or disturbed 'occupation-earth'. Rarely, when the surface-soil is itself solid, or when the building is a slight one, or when the building is jerry-built (an abnormal crime in ancient times), the foundation-trench may be absent; on the other hand, a foundation-trench may actually be cut even into the live rock, in order to give a level seating for the wall. The preliminary assumption in all instances must be that a foundation-trench is present.

This feature is of great importance, and all care must be taken in its identification. Obviously, layers into which it is cut antedate it, and must be distinguished beyond all doubt from layers which accumulated *against* the structure and therefore post-date or are contemporary with it. In loose sandy soil, the foundation-trench will be V-shaped, with an appreciable space between its sides and those of the initial wall built in it. But in a stiff clay sub-soil the sides of the trench may be vertical and may have been completely filled with the foundations of the wall. Much may depend then upon the character of the wall-facing when cleared of the soil; a trench-built wall will necessarily have an untrimmed, relatively rough face, whilst a wall built 'free', and therefore accessible to the mason, will generally show a more careful coursing and trimming. Needless to say, a wall with any sort of plaster 'rendering' or facing, or with 'struck' or neatly finished mortar jointing must have been built free, cannot have been laid in a foundation-trench. A wide experience of different materials is necessary for the identification of a foundation-trench, and the result of the investigation must always be noted carefully, with diagrams, in the notebook.

After the building of the wall to a suitable height, the sides of the foundation-trench (if V-shaped) will be packed and the adjacent surface levelled, if necessary, to carry the floor. Subsequently, the utilization of the floor will result in wear-and-tear, possibly patching or renewal, and probably the accumulation upon it of an 'occupation-layer', consisting of extraneous material – hearth-ash, mud, food-debris, broken pottery, lost ornaments or coinage – which may help to date the period or periods of usage. Later again, disaster or decay may cover the occupation-layer with building-debris (indicating, incidentally, something of the character of the superstructure), and eventually the whole site may be carpeted with vegetable-mould.

Let us take an example. Fig. 16a illustrates the accumulation of strata under, around, and over the wall of an ancient structure. On the right-hand side of the wall-section, over the natural soil, two layers (9 and 10) represent village-occupation of Culture A, with post-holes indicating wooden huts and associated with potsherds, spindle-whorls, etc. Into these layers is cut a shallow foundation-trench to take the footings of Wall Y, and the flanks of this trench are filled with layer 8, which is also spread (on the right) as a basis of Floor 1. Layer 8 contains only relics of Culture A, but one or two relics of Culture B are imbedded in Floor 1 ; and the superimposed layer 7, resulting from the occupation of the building, represents Culture B exclusively. Over this occupation-layer, a new rammed floor (Floor 2) is laid, and on it is a further occupation-layer (6) of lesser extent, still containing objects of Culture B but in a somewhat evolved form. On this occupation-layer, a cascade of bricks mixed with burnt timber and clay (layer 5) indicates the destruction of the building by fire. Thereafter the stump of the wall is used as the foundation for a mud-brick wall (X) of lighter construction, associated with an earthen floor (layer 3) containing relics mostly of Culture C. This new structure represents an intrusive culture of inferior quality, immediately preceded by the violent destruction of Culture B, and may (if the evidence is found to be typical) be interpreted perhaps as a semi-barbarian supersession of Culture B in an evolved phase of the latter.

On the left-hand side of the wall-section, the same two pre-wall strata (9 and 10) are continued, but are superseded at the wall-level by a well-metalled street (Road 1). This metalling is renewed at intervals (Roads 2 and 3), the upper metalling being inferior to the lower and suggesting a decline in municipal standards. Finally, in association with the mud-brick wall (X) of Culture C, metalling ceases, and traffic gradually wears the street into a hollow, removing earlier strata in the process. This process of road-deepening may be seen in many Eastern villages of the present day, and serves to remind us that the passing of time may be represented stratigraphically by denudation no less than by aggradation.

Fig. 16b shows the unhappy consequence of the wholesale clearance

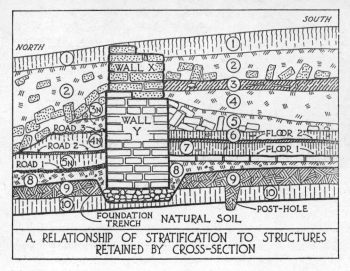

A. RELATIONSHIP OF STRATIFICATION TO STRUCTURES
RETAINED BY CROSS-SECTION

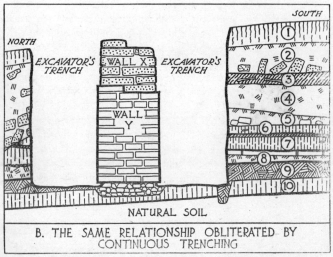

B. THE SAME RELATIONSHIP OBLITERATED BY
CONTINUOUS TRENCHING

Fig. 16. Sections illustrating the relationship of strata to a wall, and their
removal by summary excavation

of the wall along its two faces. The relationship of the wall with the adjacent strata has been lost beyond recall, and the sequence indicated above is irrecoverable. Excavation has devolved into irreparable destruction.

So important is this matter of section-interpretation, that I will give another example, dug out of an old report on the excavation of the Roman amphitheatre at Caerleon in Monmouthshire. In the early stages of this excavation, conclusive evidence as to the date of construction was hard to find, for the good reason that an amphitheatre, being a place merely of visitation, was largely devoid of the sort of material which may be expected to produce dated 'finds'. As the work proceeded, this deficiency was gradually compensated for in a variety of ways, and Fig. 17 illustrates one of them.

In this illustration, the wall in section on the left is the external wall of the amphitheatre. It is built on deep footings, the upper part of which is mortared whilst the lower part is dry-built. The footings occupy a foundation-trench, partly vertical and party V-shaped, cut through three dark occupation-layers which therefore antedate the construction. We then come to the faced walling, the base of which is in contact with a road-surface that had clearly been laid down in connexion with it. The section goes on to show that this road was subsequently renewed on at least four occasions. Now logically, the date of the construction of the amphitheatre plus the earliest road should have been bracketed by the dates of the material from the three pre-road occupation-layers and from the subsequent road-repairs. The pre-road occupation-layers fulfilled their function admirably by producing material of c. A.D. 75, indicating that the amphitheatre was not earlier than that date; but the road-repairs were unproductive, and the later end of the bracket therefore remained open. The section did not on that account fail us; it will be observed that to the right of the amphitheatre-wall is a culvert (in section) built in a trench which has been cut through the same three strata as the wall-trench and has been covered by the same make-up and road surface that covers the wall-trench and equates with the wall. It is therefore exactly contemporary with the amphitheatre. But further exploration in the vicinity showed that the culvert was structurally connected with a neighbouring bath-building dating from the last two decades of the first century A.D. To that date therefore belongs the construction

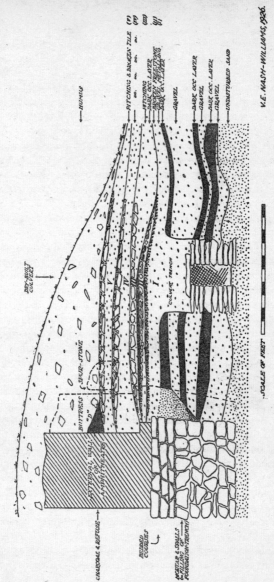

HUMUS

PITCHING & BROKEN TILE (V)
PITCHING (IV)
DARK OCC. LAYER (III)
GRAVEL PERCOLATING (III)
GRAVEL & OCC. LAYER (II)
GRAVEL (II)
DARK OCC. LAYER (I)
GRAVEL
DARK OCC. LAYER
GRAVEL
UNDISTURBED SAND

DRY-BUILT CULVERT

SPUR-STONE

BUTTRESS 2"

CULVERT TRENCH

EXTERNAL WALL OF AMPHITHEATRE

CHARCOAL & REFUSE

BEDDED COBBLES

MORTAR & SPALLS IN FILLING OF FOUNDATION-TRENCH

SCALE OF FEET

V. E. NASH-WILLIAMS, 1926.

Fig. 17. Stratification in relation to the external wall of the Roman amphitheatre at Caerleon, Monmouthshire, 1926

of the amphitheatre – an inference subsequently confirmed from other sources, but in itself sufficiently well founded.

The moral of all this is clear: the identification and interpretation of the stratigraphical evidence associated with a building are of cardinal importance, and are rendered possible only by the preservation of extensive cross-sections in the process of excavation. In other words, the preliminary excavation of a wall consists, not in clearing it continuously, but in cross-sectioning it at frequent intervals, each cross-section being closely examined and correlated with its neighbours. Only when an agreed interpretation of these cross-sections is achieved and recorded can they properly be removed, stratum by stratum. Even so, it is wise to keep a typical cross-section in position for reference until the close of the excavation.

If we turn from general principles to their practical application, there is less room for dogma. In all cases the 'square' method which I have recommended for area-excavations (p. 83) is suitable, and on sites where buildings of varying plans are piled one on top of the other, as on many Eastern sites, no other method lends itself so readily to clear systematic record. But on a shallow site, where the excavator is confronted with an essentially unitary structure, as on some Romano-British sites, it may be found convenient to take the individual rooms of a building as the basis of record. Even so, it is safer to begin on the grid plan until the dimensions of the problem are apparent; and having begun on the grid I should myself hesitate to change horses.

Two or three other points may be dealt with briefly.

'GHOST' WALLS

The excavator may have the misfortune to light upon a site where the walls have been completely destroyed by stone- or brick-robbers in ancient or modern times. A notable example of this is provided by the Romano-British site of Verulamium where Matthew Paris records that, amongst others, an eleventh-century abbot 'turned over the soil to a considerable depth that he might find masonry structures' which he 'reserved for the fabric of his church'. The excavator of the site found, in fact, evidence everywhere of systematic brick-robbing, and learned to recover the plans of buildings by carefully following the robbers' trenches (leaving intermittent cross-sections as described above). For the most part, the robbing had been so skilful and economical that the trench was scarcely wider than the wall that it had contained; so that when, after the removal of the wall, the unwanted debris was thrown back and the site levelled for cultivation, the mixed filling provided a perfect negative of the plan (Pl. 8a). By cutting across the debris-filled trench at frequent intervals, it was often possible to recover the lines of the former building with accuracy, and even, in favourable instances, to equate some of the stratification with them. Perhaps the most remarkable example of the recovery of a plan from 'ghost' walls of this kind was afforded by the north-west gateway of Verulamium where, in 1931, Miss Kathleen Kenyon found that a great part of the structure had been almost completely removed but was able, by the careful clearing of the debris from the former wall trenches, to reveal the whole layout in negative whilst preserving the stratified floors intact (Pl. 8b).

STRAIGHT JOINTS

The junction of two walls is often a key-point in the interpretation of a plan. If the walls are well and truly bonded together, with identical masonry and coursing, they are obviously of the same build and date. There is, however, a 'catch' for which it behoves the excavator to keep a vigilant watch. By the removal of some of the facing-stones of an older wall it is possible to 'tooth-in' a younger branch-wall with some semblance of bonding; but the difference in structural period is usually betrayed by differences in material or coursing, or by the incompleteness of the bonding.

On the other hand, the absence of bonding – a 'straight joint' – does not necessarily imply a difference of date. The medieval builder, it is true, was usually concerned to see that all his walls were properly bonded; the close integration of a Gothic building, the interplay of stresses and strains, demanded this. Accordingly, in a medieval structure a straight joint is normally significant chronologically. But in the more static architecture of earlier periods a straight joint may be a matter of indifference or even of choice. Where two adjacent walls carry very different vertical loads, it may not be inadvisable to leave them to some extent free of one another. Or, in the days when the plan of a building consisted, not of a blue-print, but of the actual foundations planted on the ground under the direction of the architect or master-mason, the main lines may have been laid down first and subsidiary features added as the work proceeded. One or other of these explanations may be sought for the fact that the towers of the Roman fortress known as Burgh Castle in Suffolk show a straight joint with the fortress-wall up to a certain height, above which they are bonded in; or, similarly, that the towers of Verulamium are built free up to a height of 6 feet and are thereafter of one build with the town-wall. In both instances, towers and wall are essentially parts of the same design. A more remarkable instance is the systematic use of the straight joint in Nebuchadnezzar's great Ishtar Gate at Babylon (sixth century B.C.). The foundations of the structure are of a varying depth, and to quote Koldewey:

It is conceivable that those parts of the wall where the foundations are specially deep do not sink so much in the course of time as those of shallower foundations, and settlement is unavoidable even with these, standing as they do upon earth and mud. Thus where the foundations are dissimilar there must be cleavages in the walls, which would seriously endanger the stability of the building. The Babylonians foresaw this and guarded against it. They devised the expansion joint, which we also make use of under similar circumstances. By this means walls that adjoin each other but which are on foundations of different depths are not built in one piece. A narrow vertical space is left from top to bottom of the wall, leaving the two parts standing independent of each other. In order to prevent any possibility of their leaning either backwards or forwards, in Babylon a vertical fillet was frequently built on to the less deeply rooted wall, which slid in a groove in the main wall. The two blocks run in a guide, as an engineer would call it.[1]

TIMBERWORK

In airtight peat or clay or alluvium, or on the other hand in a very dry climate, timber will retain its form and something of its substance for thousands of years. On the other hand, a solid timber such as a railway-sleeper begins to deteriorate in the British climate after about ten

1. R. Koldewey, *The Excavations at Babylon*, trans. by A. S. Johns (London, 1914), pp. 36–8.

years. Ancient woodwork found in Egypt or in the deserts of Central Asia is dated in millennia, and the rough timbering which Dr Grahame Clark uncovered with great skill in the peat at Seamer in East Yorkshire in 1949–51 may be as much as 9,000 years old. Dr van Giffen, a master of timber-excavation in the sympathetic soils of the Low Countries, found remarkable vestiges of wooden buildings – posts and wattle walls – of structures of the first century A.D. in the Roman forts at Valkenburg near Leiden (south Holland).[1] But for the most part, the excavator of ancient timber structures must content himself with less tangible results. When carbonized, their vestiges may last indefinitely; otherwise they are generally a mere stain or a more or less loosely filled hollow in the earth, and have to be treated substantially like the 'ghost' walls of which I have spoken above. On the whole, they are not an easy problem. The stains and hollows may sometimes be missed even by the expert eye, and a timber-structure should never be explored by the novice without the closest supervision.

We may set aside carbonized timber as a relatively straightforward matter. An example of the more subtle kind is provided by the first-century sheds uncovered within the Roman fortress at Richborough about 1930 by Mr J. P. Bushe-Fox. The sheds had been built on sleeper-beams, some of which had been laid on uprights, and Mr Bushe-Fox first recognized them in the faintly discoloured lines and pits which began to show up in the light-coloured sand of the site when the ground was cleared under suitable weather conditions. The coloured lines were formed by the earth which had occupied the matrices of the vanished timbering, and vertical hollows, similarly filled, showed the former presence of the posts (Pl. 9a). By carefully scraping and sectioning the site, the excavator was eventually able to uncover a series of these buildings and to reconstruct them (on paper) with a substantial measure of certainty.

The same method, with variations, must normally be followed in work of this kind. Certain soils, notably gravel, are more reluctant than others to yield their evidence. A sandy sub-soil is usually the most responsive, and at Harappā in the Punjab, in a cemetery dating from $\pm$ 2000 B.C., not only was the outline of a coffin visible as a brown outline, but Dr K. A. Choudury, of the Indian Forest Research

1. *25–28 Jaarverslag van de Vereeniging voor Terpenonderzoek* (Groningen, 1948), with English summary.

Institute, was able to photograph and identify with complete certainty the *impressions* of a specific timber (deodar) in the matrix of sand. The coffin (Pl. 9b) was found first as a dark stain in section and was then carefully cleared from above, the final clearance being effected by gentle scraping and lightly brushing with a small, soft brush. The somewhat similar outline of a coffin was traceable round a late Roman burial at Verulamium,[1] and other examples are recorded from Britain.

It would, however, be difficult to find more brilliant expositions of timber-excavation than those afforded by the work of Mr C. W. Phillips at the Skendleby long-barrow in Lincolnshire and the famous Sutton Hoo ship-burial in Suffolk. The general method adopted in the excavation of the long-barrow will be cited in a later chapter (p. 122). Here we are concerned only with the hurdle-work which was incorporated in the mound and was revealed in a trench dug close to and parallel with its longitudinal axis. In the excavator's words,

the trench was 5 ft. in width, and an examination of its sides soon showed a series of what were called for the sake of convenience 'verticalities' at irregular intervals. These vague vertical breaks in the substance of the barrow could only be interpreted as the traces of decayed barriers of some kind, presumably of wood. A heavy rain fell on the night after these were noted, and brought away a thickness of between 6 in. and 1 ft. of material from the side of the trench towards the upper side of the barrow. This fall had taken place along a definite division in the material of the barrow along its middle line, and it was at once apparent, from the impressions of upright posts and pieces of wood fixed between them, that some sort of a fence had been set up here before the barrow had been built, and then had been buried in it. . . . The reason for the 'verticalities' became clear at once, for they were traces of similar fences setting off at about right-angles from the central fence in the direction of the lower side of the barrow (Pl. 10).[2]

All this evidence was of course in 'negative'; the soil was totally un-favourable to the preservation of the actual woodwork.

Accident helped in this discovery but in no way detracts from the astuteness of the excavator's observation. The feature thus revealed was substantially an addition to knowledge and will doubtless fit, in

---

1. Wheeler, *Verulamium Report* (London, 1936), pl. cxv A.
2. *Archaeologia*, lxxxv (London, 1936), 60.

due course, into a new structural and ritual pattern of the neolithic age. But at Sutton Hoo accident can claim no share of the credit. The general circumstances of this astonishing discovery are well known: about the middle of the seventh century A.D. a man of high rank had been interred with 'the richest treasure ever dug from British soil' in a ship some 80 feet long, which had been buried under a mound in a great trench cut into the sand.

Since the whole ship and its contents had been involved in sand for some 1,300 years, it is not surprising that there were virtually no remains of wood except for small fragments which were found here and there preserving their form if not their character through contact with rusted iron. . . . Traces of the existence of wood could frequently be seen in the form of thin layers of discoloured sand, associated with bands of more or less the same material leached white by the action of the acids liberated in the decay of the wood. The normal colour of the sand on the site was yellow, except where it was the product of the decay of turf or had been under decaying wood. . . . No difficulty was found in distinguishing the filling of the trench from the undisturbed sand even where the colour was the same in each case. The filling dropped away easily from the sides of the trench and following it was merely mechanical.[1]

In these circumstances, the excavation of the hull was a particularly delicate operation, and extracts from Mr Phillips's account of it may be quoted. The work which had been done before he took over direction

showed that none of the wood of the ship remained, though all the numerous clench-nails which had held its planking together were exactly in place, the ship having been completely filled up with as much of the sand excavated from the trench as could be got in again. These conditions were ideal for the preservation of its form, and it was clear that the only way to carry out the work was to cut a very wide trench right through the mound which would give ample walks on each side of the burial-trench. The faces of the cutting were stepped backwards in terraces and their faces timbered up, and the boat was carefully emptied of all content, beginning with the burial chamber. . . .

Since all but the burial chamber area had been filled in directly with sand while the ship was still whole, none of the clench-nails which held

1. *Antiquity*, xiv (1940), 10.

the ship together could move from their place even when the wood which they secured had disappeared. By careful work from the inside it was possible to remove all the content of the boat without displacing any of the nails, which remained in their places on the sides of the excavations. This process was aided by a change in the consistency of the sand which was to be found where the boat's timbers had once been. A dusty blackish layer, accompanied by some leached sand, could be felt for carefully by slowly shaving down the sand, and warning was given of its approach by the appearance of the bright red patches signalling the near presence of clench-nails. In this way all the boat which survived was emptied so that the face of the excavation everywhere was the sand which had pressed against the timbers of the boat from the outside, and which sometimes still bore in recognizable form the imprint of the grain of wood. . . . [Pl. 15.]

The ship had twenty-six ribs. . . . The preservation of the ribs was bad. All that remained ... was a dirty line of sand running across the ship from gunwale to gunwale keeping close to the hull, and frequently still retaining a marked rectangular cross-section. In some cases the sand had formed a rough cast of the decayed wood so that, if this was breached, discoloured sand tended to pour out of the hole leaving a rectangular-sectioned cavity. In excavating the ship these rib traces were left enclosed in strips of sand.[1]

These examples of timber-excavation must suffice. The tools most generally useful are a broad-bladed knife, a small spike of some sort, and a soft paint-brush. In the clearance of the Sutton Hoo burial-chamber, a stout shovel mounted on the end of a long ash handle was used for shaving down and removing the sand on a horizontal plane in a search for the significant changes of colour.

MUD-BRICK

In the dry climate of parts of Africa and Asia, bricks of unbaked mud, often integrated by an admixture of straw, have long been used for building, and may present some difficulty to the excavator, though

1. *Ant. Journ.* xx (1940), 158, 183, 188, etc. See also the account of the excavation of the burial chamber, ibid., p. 158. A simpler but nonetheless instructive set of problems attended the excavation of the Oseberg ship in Sweden. The student is referred to the account of these (in English) in A. W. Brøgger, Hj. Falk, and Haakon Schetelig, *Osebergfundet*, i (Kristiania, 1917), 369 ff.

generally of a less formidable nature than that presented by vanished timberwork. A writer on archaeological technique has written:

> The principal difficulty faced by an archaeologist in dealing with mud-bricks lies in the fact that the material used in their construction is not unlike that of the earth in which they have been buried for centuries. As a result there have been a number of cases where long narrow rooms turned out to be heavy walls; in other words, the excavators recognized a slight change in colour or consistency of the ground during the digging but removed the walls and left the rooms unexcavated!

I need hardly add that this unhappy experience was derived mainly from that land of archaeological sin, Palestine, and reopens a vista of incompetence which is by now sufficiently familiar to us.

The problem once more is that of intelligent supervision; though the trained workman is here an asset of almost equal worth. The texture of the earth, the feel of it, the sound of it as the pick or shovel strikes it, are all factors which, almost equally with direct visual evidence, tell the experienced digger when he is or is not on a mud-brick wall. The instructed peasant learns to think through the point of his pick or the blade of his knife. Decayed mud-brickwork may fill the interior of a room and present on plan an undifferentiated surface where it and a mud-brick wall-top abut upon each other. But tapping carefully and obliquely with a small pick will often produce a distinguishable hard note when the point, penetrating the filling, strikes the face of the actual wall. Scraping the surface carefully with a knife, sometimes aided by damping, may reveal a slight but significant line where filling and wall meet, or between individual bricks. The composition of the mud wall will sometimes indicate whether it represents brick or filling; flecks of charcoal and scraps of pottery rarely occur in bricks but are not infrequent in filling, and I have sometimes found them in the coarser mud which may be used as the equivalent of mortar. Their presence, therefore, is a useful guide, though their absence proves nothing. Petrie adds that 'in the last resource the stuff should be searched with a magnifier to see the hollows left by decomposed straw: in kneaded brick these hollows lie in every direction; in blown dust and wash they lie nearly all horizontal'.

The initial tracing of a mud-brick wall may thus be a fairly lengthy process, involving careful inspection and digging in different lights and different degrees of dampness or dryness of soil. When the wall-face has been definitely located, further care must be taken to ascertain whether it was anciently 'rendered' with a mud or plaster facing. If not, it can be gently brushed horizontally or scraped with a knife. When thus newly cleaned, the individual bricks will frequently show up clearly, and they must then be completely recorded (size, bond, quality, jointing); for the chances are that, as the wall dries out and bleaches in the sun, much of the detail will be lost. In order to retain the general picture, it is sometimes possible to reduce the mud-joints slightly by gentle brushing or scraping, and so to leave the separate bricks in shallow relief. On the other hand, if the joints are of harder, coarser material, as they sometimes are, it may be preferable to scrape the smoother surface of the bricks, thus leaving the joints in relief (Pl. 11). In either case, this work should normally be done *after* record not before.

In all other respects, a mud-brick wall should be dug exactly as a masonry wall, with a similar system of cross-sections through the attendant strata.

CHAPTER 7

On Digging Town-sites

THE natural sequel to a chapter on structures is the consideration of the structural complex of a town-site. (The problems of a military site are technically similar.)

The site of an ancient town may to-day be a tolerably level tract of countryside, or it may have piled itself in the course of ages into the form of an artificial mound or *tell* up to 100 feet or more in height. Something has been said of the latter process elsewhere (p. 57). Here the question is one of tactical approach to the problem of excavation.

Let us consider what information we want. Our primary need is to ascertain the chronology and cultural setting of the site. Without these two basic facts, its structural layout will mean little. But they in turn will mean little without a knowledge of the plan of the town, of its domestic economy from period to period, and the social and political condition of its inhabitants. These problems are necessarily interlocked, but they can to some extent be separated for the purpose of preliminary investigation.

On a level site, the technical approach is relatively straightforward. There the cultural and chronological sequence can be recovered in introductory fashion by one method only: by a restricted area-excavation in the interior of the town, preferably somewhere near its centre. Although the rule is by no means invariable, cities commonly grow in a reasonably symmetrical fashion; the original civic centre is likely to remain the focus and to represent therefore the maximum depth of accumulated occupation. This accumulated occupation must be probed carefully to the bottom, preferably by means of one or more squares – a group of four adjacent squares is often a useful unit – in accordance with the method described on p. 83. *But* on no account should this procedure be repeated at random. Petrie cannot be gainsaid when he protests against the multiplication of trial-pits. Such pits, 'if they hit anything of importance,' he remarks, 'are likely to injure it, and certain to destroy its connexion with other things. French explorers have a love for *faire quelques sondages*, a proceeding which often ruins a site for systematic work, and which never shows the meaning of the positions or the nature of the plan'. On the other hand, a restricted probe, carried out by methods more subtle and thorough than Petrie's, is a necessary preliminary stage on a 'flat' site of unknown potentiality.

A secondary if not simultaneous stage is the investigation of the system of fortifications which normally characterizes an ancient town. The moments at which a town built or rebuilt its defences were manifestly of special importance in its life-history. The construction of a fortification may indicate the newcomer in a strange land, as in the mottes of Norman England; or it may mark the achievement of full city status, and may reflect a period of peaceful consolidation rather than of military duress, as in the walled towns of Augustan Gaul or late second-century Britain. Or it may reflect the advent or threat of a formidable rival or of political anarchy; as when anxious edicts of Honorius urged cities to build or repair their walls and authorized them to use statues, altars, and temples for the purpose. It may have been designed to defend the populace, or to control it; as, perhaps, in the almost feudal citadels which dominated the Indus cities of Harappā and Mohenjo-daro in the third millennium B.C., or certainly in William the Conqueror's Tower of London. Fortifications thus not merely outline the town-plan (or some part of it) but may focus and express the city's vicissitudes and something of its sociology. Further, the character of their brickwork or masonry is a fair reflection of the economic condition of the city at the time of construction, of wealthy and leisurely civic pride or of more slovenly necessity. And to what extent were the defences maintained? – were there long periods of immunity during which maintenance was allowed to lapse? Finally, were they riven by an attacker, as were the mined and counter-mined walls of Dura-Europos on the Euphrates? – or did they crumble into decay as a counterpart to economic decline? All these and other questions are of the first importance to the inquiring antiquary or historian. It is along the lines of the defences rather than in the buried relics of the bazaar that the excavator may expect first to recognize the major moments, the framework, of the story of the site.

Let him therefore, early in his work, cut across the line of the fortifications at selected points where it seems likely that the evidence will be most comprehensive. And let his cross-trenches be both wide and deep, no mere otter's bites – wide enough to escape accidental features and to provide ample room and light for observation; deep enough to reach down into the natural soil and so to ensure that the story is complete. Furthermore, let the trenches be carried far enough into the town to relate the defensive system in its various phases with the successive occupations of the town itself.

The accepted three-dimensional method of recording such a trench is described on pp. 87–90.

To the sectioning of the defences should be added the careful excavation of a gateway, where successive road-levels and guard-room floors may be expected to amplify the architectural evidence and to lend it precision.

The completion of these works – the examination of the defences and the central area-excavation – may be assumed to have given us a reasonable conspectus of the site. The next stage is less predictable in detail, although its general purpose is clear enough: namely, to recover a representative part of the town-plan at various periods or, at any rate, at the topmost period, and to ascertain the character and economy of its various types of building. The best course will probably be to extend the original area-dig at the level of some specific stratum, to link it up with the excavated gateway, and to recover the intervening layout of buildings and streets at the selected level or levels. Thereby an orderly, coherent development of the work is ensured, and future excavators will know readily where they stand in relation to it. This was approximately the method adopted by Sir John Marshall at Taxila (Sirkap) in the Punjab, with the most revealing results (Pl. 12). The extent to which such work can or should be carried subsequently downwards depends on the funds available and the current state of knowledge. Although I would not accept Marshall's methods of excavation and record, my view is that he was perfectly right in uncovering, and preserving uncovered, only the two uppermost strata of Sirkap in the area tackled by him. He was dealing with an entirely unknown culture and polity. On the other hand, in a Romano-British town I should to-day normally advocate the *complete* clearance of the available area in depth, even at the expense of extensive destruction. As so often, no general rule can be postulated; each instance must be considered on its merits.

If we turn from a 'flat' site to a *tell*, say, 50 feet high (Pl. 13), complications confront us. Probing from top to bottom in a mound of this depth becomes a major engineering feat and involves a disproportionately large opening at the top. Moreover, there is not infrequently the risk that such a probe will over-emphasize the latest and possibly best-known phases at the expense of the earlier and less-known. Let me give two examples.

Some 18 miles north-east of Peshawar in the North-west Frontier Province of Pakistan, near the village of Chārsada, is a famous group of mounds which represents the ancient capital city of Puṣkalāvatī, set athwart one of the great trade-routes of ancient Asia. Its strength was such that even the veteran army of Alexander the Great took 30 days to capture it in 326 B.C., and such was its prestige that Alexander went out of his way to receive its surrender in person. In the seventh century A.D., when the Chinese pilgrim Hiuen Tsang visited it, it was yet 'well peopled'. To-day the vast site is derelict, bitten into and divided by the streams of the Swat river, but its largest mound, the Bālā Ḥiṣār or High Fort, still stands to a maximum height of about 100 feet. Here in 1902–3 the then recently reconstituted Archaeological Survey of India carried out its first excavation. The summit of the highest mound was selected for the work, and trenches were dug into it to a depth of 20 feet. The result was the discovery of scraps of medieval and later buildings of familiar Sikh and Islamic types and a few possible fragments of somewhat earlier historic dates. Nothing that was not predictable was brought to light, and the real problems of (potentially) one of the most important sites of Asia were not touched. The young director, fresh from Athens, his mind doubtless obsessed with the prestige of a towering acropolis, had carried out the excavation in the one spot where a maximum accumulation of relatively modern material could have been foreseen.

Similarly at another site, far away on the steppe of Afghan Turkestan, there lie the great mounds which represent the ancient Bactra, 'Mother of Cities', carfax of trans-Asian trade-routes and outpost of Hellenism *in partibus*. Bactra was already a city in the fourth century B.C., and it suffered from the savagery of Chingiz Khan in the thirteenth century A.D. To-day only the tiny village of Balkh lies within the immense circuit of its derelict walls, and several square miles of the buried history of Asia, indeed of the world, lie accessible to the adventurous explorer. Accordingly, in 1924–5, Monsieur A. Foucher, to whose memory all honour is due as a student of Buddhist art, was deputed to carry out a series of excavations on behalf of the French Archaeological Mission to Afghanistan. The results were, as he freely and naïvely admits, disappointing to a degree. Why? He chose for his operation the highest point of the towering *tell* which represents the citadel of this vast city, and dug down metre after metre into the ruins of – a relatively modern mosque and a 'Turkish' bath! True, in a city with a walled circuit of 7 miles there was room enough for error: Foucher himself exclaims, 'We compared ourselves, my wife and I, to two ants sent into the depths of the jungle to carry out an autopsy on the corpse of an elephant.' But why, from so wide a possible choice, did he choose of all things the ultimate summit of the citadel? In a letter to his Paris correspondent, he tells us: '*Because*', he writes, '*one cannot escape the magic power of names*, and you yourself, if I could have consulted you from afar and had asked, as in Hernani: "Where should I begin?", would incontestably have replied: "On the Acropolis."'[1] The inescapable magic of names! What a superbly Gallic reason for plunging into the one spot in the whole of Bactra that a less charmingly sentimental investigator would unhesitatingly have shunned: the one dominant spot which could have been prophesied to bear upon its heights the latest and most familiar of medieval buildings.

No, a little cold-blooded deliberation at these two sites would easily have pointed the proper way. I happen to know them both, and am prepared without undue rashness to prescribe. The premisses are that both sites stretch back into a remote but undefined antiquity; that both have also been wholly or partially occupied in Islamic times; but that, since our extensive knowledge of Muslim architecture is unlikely to be enhanced appreciably by the costly excavation of the buried fragments of a medieval citadel, this phase may profitably be by-passed. The outstanding importance alike of Chārsada and Balkh lies in their earlier phases, when they were metropolitan centres of Asiatic trade and meeting-places of oriental and occidental cultures. To reach these earlier strata the approach is not in fact difficult. At Chārsada the attacks of man, weather, and water have, over a large

1. A. Foucher, *La Vieille Route de l'Inde de Bactra à Taxila* (Mém. de la Délég. Arch. Française en Afghanistan, Paris, 1942), p. 98.

part of the principal mound, removed the higher strata to a depth of some 40 feet. In other words, Sikh and Muslim may safely be presumed to have vanished here, leaving the pre-medieval strata exposed to immediate attack. There, at the eastern foot of the High Fort, is the obvious spot for an area-excavation designed to reach the ancient Puṣkalāvatī and to achieve – who knows? – another Mohenjo-daro at its base? At Balkh also it is not difficult, by an examination of the sides of gullies and other cuttings, to find a number of places where the familiar top-stuff is absent, and where penetration to the earlier levels can be reasonably assured. But at Balkh there is one obvious and immediate goal. Nearly half of the defensive system shows only Islamic workmanship and may for our purpose be ruled out, at any rate in the initial stages (later, it too should be fully recorded); but a part of the remainder is of composite character and obviously incorporates earlier work. In particular, along the southern side the Islamic wall is carried by a huge rampart which is itself, to judge from slight indications, a complex structure. Here is a major problem for settlement. Until the excavator of Balkh has dug a great trench, recorded in three dimensions, through these southern fortifications and linked their successive phases to occupation-levels in the adjacent interior, he has not got to grips with his problem.

To turn from these two examples to the general run of *tells* is to turn to variable phenomena, susceptible to no fixed rule. Much depends upon the height of the mound and the extent of its erosion. As a general practice, however, it is desirable to bite boldly into the periphery at some carefully selected point, penetrate the inevitable scree, and establish the successive cultures with, if possible, the successive systems of fortification. This desideratum is commonly realized by *tell*-excavators, but there is an unhappy habit of nibbling sporadically at the flanks of the mound instead of contemplating a methodical, coherent cutting which will, with ordinary luck, link up and sort out many important factors once and for all. An established method of cutting such a section is to step it from top to bottom, so that the gangs have convenient working-platforms at intervals and, above all, so that the lower stages of the cutting are not unconscionably deep. Nevertheless, there are few published *tells* where a section of this kind has been completed. Pl. 11 shows a complete section through the margin of the highest *tell* of the chalcolithic Indus city at

Harappā in the Punjab. Its total depth is 50 feet but, owing to the compactness of its material, I was able to cut it vertically, without stepping. Incidentally, the recorder and draftsman completed their work in detail, foot by foot, as the working-platform was gradually lowered, so that, when natural soil was eventually reached, the digging and the recording ended almost simultaneously. As usual, the log-book record was three-dimensional (cf. p. 87).

Apart from the marginal bite, as on a 'flat' site, the clearance of a gateway is highly desirable, combined with an area-dig in the adjacent interior on a sufficiently large scale to establish firmly the cultural context of successive gateways and fortifications. Further in the interior, an elevation may indicate the position of a citadel or temple and may also be subjected to an area-excavation, which should subsequently be linked up systematically with that adjoining the gateway, and thereafter continued to the designed limits of the enterprise.

The ultimate goals of a *tell*-excavation should be (*a*) to establish its cultural or chronological range by the marginal sections indicated above, and (*b*) to uncover *completely* a specific phase or phases of its occupation. I emphasize this point after seeing many incredibly messy *tell*-excavations where everything has been attempted at once, with cuttings and soundings at varying depths and the whole site permanently wrecked or obscured by tip-heaps. Let the rule be to *finish* a clear-cut scheme which can be transmitted lucidly, on paper and on the ground, to future generations of investigators. Leave your *tell* for others as you would wish to find it. Too many excavated *tells* of Asia are, to adapt Petrie's phrase, 'ghastly charnel houses of murdered evidence'. Fortunately, there are still some thousands of intact oues awaiting a more human and legitimate execution.

CHAPTER 8

Burials

'Where necessary, the dolmens were blasted, the circles of stones were removed and the cistvaens constructed with large flat slabs were made available for study.' *Mysore State Archaeological Department, Annual Report for 1942.*

FROM the living we turn to the dead. The varieties of burial-ritual devised by man in his care alike for the departed and for their survivors are legion. The body may be buried intact or after cremation; it may be left awhile to the weather, the kites, and the jackals, whereafter a few representative bones may be collected and piously interred. Burials may be communal or individual. The dead may be thrust with no durable equipment into the earth; they may be accompanied by the treasury of Sutton Hoo, or by a sumptuous army of attendants as at Ur; they may go naked to St Peter or with a harem to Paradise; they may be enclosed in a humble pot or in relays of costly sarcophagi; their grave may be marked by no lasting monument or by 'a mound on the hill, high and broad, by wave-farers wide to be seen'; or their ashes may be tipped into a river which will bear them happily from our ken. Fear, habit, a little affection, and much affectation go to the making of these things. It is fortunate for the prying archaeologist that his technical problem is often a relatively simple one. His difficulty begins when he comes to reconstruct the ritual represented by the particles of evidence uncovered by his skill (for an example, see above, p. 18); and if he steps beyond ritual to its fancied significance, he will scarcely find the answer in the cartload of books which, says the Chinese proverb, contains all wisdom.

Here is no place for the anthropology of this vast subject. From the technical point of view only, I will deal in turn with certain broad categories such as are known to me as an excavator or observer.

ROUND BARROWS AND CAIRNS

Round barrows (of earth) or cairns (of rubble), ranging in Britain from the end of the Stone Age to the Viking period and abundant at various periods in many other parts of the world, provide a useful starting-point. They may be a few feet or more than 50 feet in diameter, and their present altitude shows an equivalent variation. But, whatever their size, their excavation can, in a majority of instances, follow one of two alternative procedures. The best introduction to them is to emphasize how *not* to proceed.

The day is not long past when barrow-digging, or rather barrow-hogging was a polite amusement on a summer's day. Something has been said about this in Chapter II (see also Pl. 1): and it will suffice to recall how in 1849 Dean Merewether 'opened' thirty-one barrows in twenty-six days in the Avebury district. This is probably a world record, but there are several runners-up whom it would be waste of time to catalogue. The method was to plunge downward into the centre of the mound in the hope (often, alas, fulfilled) of finding a primary or secondary burial, or both. The crime lay, not merely in the neglect of all the structural and ritual *minutiae* which are a large part of the interest of a barrow, but that, working downwards in a central cavity upon the strata of successive structures or burials no investigator, however experienced, could correlate them owing to the simple fact that they were largely removed in the process. Not, of course, that Merewether and his kin had any notion of stratification. Nevertheless, even after stratification had begun to be dimly understood, the practice of driving a narrow trench through the middle of a barrow long continued. I remember seeing an excavation of this kind which in fact revealed the primary burial but – so narrow and dark and dirty was the trench – failed to discover a surrounding ritual ditch 6 feet wide, although the trench passed over it at two points.

The central pit and trench are therefore alike ruled out of court as methods of excavation. Nothing in archaeological excavation can be more definite than that.

Now for the more positive side of the matter. The underlying principle is that the whole barrow shall be removed and, whenever possible, subsequently replaced. This principle was laid down by Pitt Rivers and cannot be gainsaid. At any point in or about the mound, structural features or secondary burials are liable to occur, and nothing short of a complete record can nowadays justify the excavation of a type of monument which has in the past suffered so grievously from piecemeal work.

A satisfactory method to this end, adopted, for example, by Sir Cyril Fox at Ysceifiog in Flintshire[1] and by myself on Dunstable Downs in Bedfordshire[2] was as follows (I quote Fox):

Two parallel rows of numbered pegs were driven in 1 ft. apart on either side of the barrow, at right angles to the face on which it was proposed to work. As the removal of the barrow advanced foot by foot, the face was maintained in a straight line between pegs similarly numbered, and on the discovery of a deposit its position was fixed – firstly, by measuring its distance from the appropriate right-hand peg along a line stretched to the equivalent peg, and secondly by measuring its vertical position above or below the original ground-level. In practice it was found that positions could in this manner be fixed very easily. The centre of the deposit marked CII on plan [Fig. 18], 1 ft. 6 in. above the floor of the barrow, was thus quickly recorded as 25′: 18′ + 1′ 6″. The scale of feet on this plan indicates the position of one row of pegs. . . . As the work proceeded the floor was tested at frequent intervals and holes dug when any indication of disturbance presented itself.

In this clear description it is of course implied that a carefully measured cross-section of the barrow is drawn along every face which revealed any feature of interest. Fox in fact published seven sections of the Ysceifiog barrow (Fig. 19).

At the risk of repetition, I would add the following details. First, the datum-pegs must be substantial and firmly driven in. They must also be broad enough to bear a clear, painted numeral (I prefer Roman numerals, both as distinctive and as easier to paint). Thirdly, a two-inch nail must be driven into the top of the peg at the exact point of measurement. Incidentally, this nail is useful for holding the loop of a measuring tape, and the transverse string for each successive cutting. Fourthly, a continuous string along each datum-line from nail to nail is useful for intermediate measurements. Fifthly, it is convenient to record in the fashion already recommended for three-dimensional recording (above, pp. 87–90), with ruled columns arranged across two pages of the notebook.

The great merit of this system of excavation is that the excavator is working throughout in the fullest possible light and comfort, and the recording is rendered exceedingly easy. Its demerit is that, unless

1. *Arch. Cambrensis*, 1926, pp. 48 ff.   2. *Arch. Journ.* lxxxviii (1931), 193 ff.

special and rather cumbersome arrangements are made, the records are exclusively parallel with one axis of the mound, and the other axis is not adequately recorded. In a majority of instances, this partiality does not matter, but it *might*.

The alternative method in general use meets this objection. It

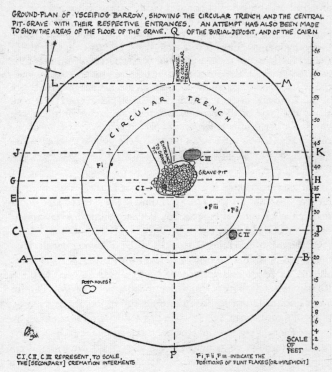

GROUND-PLAN OF YSCEIFIOG BARROW, SHOWING THE CIRCULAR TRENCH AND THE CENTRAL PIT-GRAVE WITH THEIR RESPECTIVE ENTRANCES. AN ATTEMPT HAS ALSO BEEN MADE TO SHOW THE AREAS OF THE FLOOR OF THE GRAVE, Q, OF THE BURIAL-DEPOSIT, AND OF THE CAIRN

CI, CII, CIII REPRESENT, TO SCALE, THE [SECONDARY] CREMATION INTERMENTS

Fi, Fii, Fiii INDICATE THE POSITIONS OF FLINT FLAKES [OR IMPLEMENT]

Fig. 18. The Ysceifiog barrow, Flintshire, showing the layout for excavation. After Cyril Fox

is known as *quartering* or the *quadrant method*. The mound is marked out into four quarters by two strings, laid preferably to the cardinal points of the compass, and over the approximate centre. Opposite quarters are then excavated in turn, a balk 1½–3 feet wide being left

SECTIONS Nos 1 to 6 ARE PARALLEL ; No 7 IS AT RIGHT ANGLES TO THESE

1. SECTION AT 20 FEET A–B ON PLAN

2. SECTION AT 26 FEET C–D ON PLAN

CREMATION II — CREMATION II IS PROJECTED INTO THIS PLANE

3. SECTION AT 33 FEET E–F ON PLAN

FLINT FLAKE — FLINT FLAKE Fii IS PROJECTED INTO THIS PLANE

LIMESTONE-BOULDER AND DARK-SOIL (EDGE OF CAIRN)

4. SECTION AT 37 FEET G–H ON PLAN

CREMATION I — CAIRN OF LIMESTONE BOULDERS AND PEBBLES — IMPLEMENT Fi IS PROJECTED INTO THIS PLANE

TRENCH CUT IN GRAVEL — BEAKED IMPLEMENT OF FLINT — PIT SUNK THROUGH GRAVEL TO SAND — PRIMARY BURIAL — TRENCH CUT IN GRAVEL AND SAND

7. SECTION FROM SOUTH TO NORTH P–Q ON PLAN

CAIRN OF LIMESTONE — THE ENTRANCE TO THE BURIAL PIT IS PROJECTED INTO THIS PLANE

TRENCH CUT IN GRAVEL — PIT SUNK THROUGH GRAVEL TO SAND — ENTRANCE TO PIT — PRIMARY BURIAL [GRAVEL FILLING OMITTED] — TRENCH CUT IN GRAVEL — ENTRANCE TO TRENCH [GRAVEL FILLING OMITTED]

0 5 10 15 20 25 30 35 40 45 50 55 60 65
SCALE OF FEET

SYMBOLS USED:

ABOVE GROUND LEVEL { HUMUS — YELLOW CLAYEY SAND WITH FEW STONES — GRAVEL — ORANGE-BANDED GREY SANDY CLAY }

UNDISTURBED SUBSOIL { CLAYEY SAND — GRAVEL — FINE WHITE SAND } SHOWN IN SECTIONS FOUR AND SEVEN ONLY

NOTE
THE FILLING OF THE TRENCH CONSISTS OF A VARIETY OF MATERIAL. IT IS MOSTLY GRAVEL; BANDS OF CLAYEY SAND OR SANDY CLAY WITH OR WITHOUT STONES ALSO OCCUR. THE FILLING OF THE BURIAL PIT IS STIFF CLAYEY SAND ON WEST SIDE, GRAVEL WITH CLAY BANDS ON EAST SIDE

Fig. 19. Selected sections across the Ysceifiog barrow (nos. 5 and 6 omitted).
After Cyril Fox

between each quadrant in such a fashion as to give a complete transverse section across the mound in both directions. The example here illustrated (Pl. 14) is, for convenience, taken from a level site (a burial-pit at Brahmagiri, Mysore State), on which the system shows up clearly. It will be observed that the balks are staggered so that the two halves of each transverse section are in the same plane, although one half of each is necessarily in reverse in relation to its fellow – a detail easily adjusted in the final drawing.

Recording by this method is rather less-simple than by the other. Each quadrant is numbered or lettered or named by compass-point, and it is desirable to fix a line of pegs at 1-foot intervals along one of the cardinal lines of the layout. From these pegs, the usual three-dimensional measurements are taken in each quadrant until, in the ultimate phase of the work, the balks are themselves cut away. In the example illustrated, it was easy on the level site to lay out a measuring-tape in lieu of pegs.

Apart from these two standard methods of excavation, other methods have been improvised in recent years in emergency-work carried out under a time-limit on doomed mounds. With skilful handling, some of these improvisations have produced important results, but they are not on that account justified save in emergency. In particular, there has been some reversion to the axial trench, subsequently expanded about the centre of the mound. With a builder's bulldozer in the offing, anything saved is better than everything lost; but, though this obsolete method be then as inevitable as quarter-day, it is just about as desirable. The two standard methods are the best to date.

Whilst no attempt can be made here to catalogue the varieties of structural or stratigraphical problem which a burial-mound may present, a few of the more common features may be noted as a guide to the beginner. The primary burial is usually central under the mound as originally formed but not necessarily as later enlarged. It may be a hole in the ground, with or without a small mound or heap of stones immediately covering it; it may be in a wooden (dug-out) coffin or in a stone cist, which may be 'large' (3 feet or more in length) or 'small' (under 3 feet) and buried beneath or standing upon the natural surface. The stones should be examined for intentional markings. Secondary burials may be inserted into the original mound, or placed upon it and covered by added material, or even inserted into the added material; the shape and extent of the cuttings containing secondary burials are therefore vital pieces of evidence, to be looked for and recorded with the utmost care. The area containing the original burial may lie within a circular ditch, which may either be covered by the original mound or lie alongside it, and may either be continuous or interrupted or, significantly, approached by a ramp. The shape and character of the ditch – whether flat-bottomed, and whether beaten and hardened as by ritual traffic – must be considered and discussed. And the bottom of the ditch must be searched for material which, on analysis, may show whether the ditch was exposed for any appreciable time, or whether it was covered immediately after the funeral (cf. p. 63). Alternatively, a 'processional way' round the primary interment may be built up above the natural surface, as, apparently, in the Pond Cairn at Coity, Glamorgan, brilliantly recorded by Sir Cyril Fox.[1] Here, the burial and, as it seems, an initial infant-sacrifice, were covered by a cylindrical stack of turves, and around the stack a circular space about 5 feet wide was enclosed by a surrounding stone wall 15–20 feet wide and perhaps 5 feet high (a south-western feature in Britain). This interspace appears to have been used for elaborate ritual, and the excavator's discussion of the phenomena should be studied by all barrow-diggers in whatever part of the world they be.

The edge of a barrow or cairn may be retained by a stone kerb, or revetment or ring-wall, up to 18 inches high,[2] or may be anchored by earthfast buttress-stones.[3] How far, or in what manner, timber may have been used alternatively round British barrows we cannot say until many more of them have been completely excavated under modern conditions. The practice is known from Holland, where Dr van Giffen has excavated examples;[4] and in Holland also timber circles were sometimes set up within the mound. Three barrows in Britain (on the Yorkshire Wolds, in Lancashire, and in Montgomeryshire) have produced analogous evidence,[5] but whether, as one

1. *Archaeologia*, lxxxvii (1937), 142 ff.

2. Ibid. lxxxix (1943), 108, 110 (Llandow tumulus, Glamorgan, excavated by Fox); and *Proc. Prehist. Soc.* 1938, p. 112 (Breach Farm, Glamorgan, excavated by W. F. Grimes).

3. Ibid. lxxxvii (1937), 134 (Simondstown cairn, excavated by Fox).

4. A. E. van Giffen, *Die Bauart der Einzelgräber*.

5. Grahame Clark in *Proc. Prehist. Soc.* 1936, pp. 30 ff.

excavator thought, they represent the dead man's hut is mere speculation. The whole matter deserves further investigation in the field, and timbering should be very carefully looked for, not merely at ground-level, but also in the stuff of the mound itself, in all future barrow excavation. The timber inside certain Indian Buddhist stupas, which have been compared with round barrows, is an analogous problem.

LONG BARROWS AND CAIRNS

Long barrows in Europe represent a group of burial-customs prevalent in certain regions approximately between 2500 and 1500 B.C., i.e. at the end of the Stone Age and the overlap with the early Bronze Age. Like round barrows they vary widely in form, size, structure, and usage, but in general they were intended for multiple burial, normally by inhumation though occasionally by cremation. As their name implies, they are distinguished by the fact that one axis is longer than the other, but the difference may range from only a few feet to a third of a mile.[1] It follows that no uniform procedure can be commended to the excavator.

The first long barrow scientifically excavated – and one of the few –

1. Thus a long barrow on Thickthorne Down, Dorset, was 90 feet wide and only 110 feet long. On the other hand, the monstrous 'bank barrow' in Maiden Castle, Dorset, was 60 feet wide and no less than 1,790 feet long. True, a writer in *Arch. Journ.* civ, 11, has disputed the identification of the latter as a barrow and prefers to call it (as indeed the excavators nicknamed it) a neolithic racecourse or *cursus*. But (a) more than 500 feet of it are still a mound and cannot have been used as a *cursus*; (b) seemingly comparable long mounds in Dorset (e.g. in Long Bredy and Broadmayne parishes) are still mounds from end to end and were never 'racecourses'; (c) the flattened portion of the Maiden Castle structure coincides exactly with the extension of the Iron Age Camp and is susceptible to explanation by that fact; and (d) the Pentridge *cursus*, which has been cited as an analogy on the ground that a small long barrow is incorporated in one of its margins, bears no resemblance to the Maiden Castle plan. The Pentridge *cursus* is over four times as broad, and to say that 'if the Pentridge *cursus* was reduced in scale and the offset long barrow placed between its ditches centrally, the two structures would not differ materially one from the other' is to exceed the limits of legitimate hypothesis. To assume at Maiden Castle a racecourse completely blocked for at least a third of its length is like assuming a bottle of which one-third is cork! And in fact since this note was written further excavation has shown beyond doubt that the work was originally a mound from end to end. – *Proc. Dorset Nat. Hist. and Arch. Soc.*, lxxiv (1953), 36.

was the famous Wor Barrow on Handley Down, Dorset, excavated by Pitt Rivers in 1893. The published photograph of the finished work, in which 'the figure standing at attention in the middle distance marks the site of the central interment', is itself a monument of the General's scientific discipline. Save for four pyramids of chalk and turf left to indicate the original height of the mound, the barrow and the filling of its peripheral ditches have been completely removed. The pyramids represented the axis of a broad trench, 45 feet wide, which was cut at the outset centrally along the length of the mound, leaving the flanks for subsequent clearance. Objects found in the ditch-filling were recorded three-dimensionally, and in the report were projected diagrammatically on to two schematic sections of the ditch (Fig. 2, pp. 26–27).

It is no detraction from the outstanding merit of this classic excavation to suggest improvements of method. In the first place, it is a primary desideratum to record a complete longitudinal section of a structure of this kind; i.e. along the original axis of approach into the chamber (here of wood). This is particularly necessary in chambered barrows, where the record of successive entries can best be shown by a section from the entrance or forecourt inwards. (Supplementary cross-sections are of course also necessary.) Secondly, under the greatest height of the mound, i.e. along its longitudinal axis, internal structures (as at Skendleby, p. 101) are most likely to be best preserved, again demanding a central longitudinal section. Thirdly, it is likely that the two longitudinal halves of the mound will be approximately symmetrical in structure, and hints or evidences in the first half dug can be followed up and verified in the second half if the halves are dug in succession, not as at Wor Barrow simultaneously. Fourthly, in an extremely irregular neolithic barrow-ditch a series of carefully drawn cross-sections is needed. Pitt Rivers's projection of all the finds, some drawn twice the scale of the ditch and others only one-third the scale (Fig. 2), on to a purely diagrammatic section is useful but is no substitute for an accurate picture.

There is indeed no reason why a mound such as Wor Barrow should not be dug by the quadrant-method already commended for round barrows. Only when the length of the barrow greatly exceeds its width does that method tend to become cumbersome. Whatever the method, however, the first step is to mark out, and preferably peg out, the barrow longitudinally into equal halves, and then to tackle one half only at a time.

As an example of the excavation of a longer barrow of this kind, I may again refer to the very successful work carried out in 1933–4 by Mr C. W. Phillips on the Giants' Hills mound at Skendleby in Lincolnshire. Mr Phillips describes his method as follows:

The first step taken was to lay out a rectangle 180 by 80 ft. round the barrow and drive in a strong post at each of the corners. A line of levels was run from the nearest Ordnance bench mark, and a local bench mark was cut on one of the posts. A contour survey of the barrow was then made.

In the case of barrows with large ditches there are two main lines of investigation which may be pursued. First, there is the actual barrow with its primary interments and any original structural features it may have. This gives information about its builders, its value depending on the degree of preservation of the contents and the absence of disturbance. Secondly, there is the evidence of the part which the monument has played in the life of the district since it was completed. Some of this may be recovered in the form of stratified traces of casual human settlement in the ditch before the shelter afforded by it was destroyed by silting. In the case of a long barrow ditch of normal size this may usually be relied upon to give evidence down to the close of prehistoric times. There is the further possibility of intrusive secondary burials in the boby of the barrow or in the ditch.

The season of 1933 was devoted to establishing the second of these two points by digging a large section of the ditch on the upper side of the barrow. In 1934 the barrow proper was excavated, and as much more of the ditch as was necessary to prove its character all round the barrow.

In opening the barrow a central spine was left intact right down the middle to show the original height, and this was carried across the ditch at the east end. At the same time 5-ft.-wide balks at right-angles to the central spine were left at stated intervals.

It was originally expected that the east end would contain the burials, but, when a complete excavation of the eastern third of the barrow had shown that this was not the case, a 5-ft.-wide trench was driven along the central spine right through to the west end. In this way the burial area was approached from the side, and, when found, fully opened out. Also the remarkable hurdling in the western part of the barrow [see above, p. 101] was revealed and studied, further cross-cuts over the whole of the barrow being made at various points to establish the section and find out about the hurdling offsetting from the central 'fence'. Another investigation was the careful clearance of the revetment-trench found across the eastern end on the old ground-surface. Trenches had also to be run along the sides of the barrow to follow up the post-holes which were found to flank it along the greater part of its length on both sides. The whole of the extreme west end was also excavated to find out as much as possible about the eight posts which were found to have stood here.[1]

In all this admirable work, the excavator would probably himself be the first to admit an element of opportunism, due to the novelty of the evidence revealed, the immensity of the task, and the consequent necessity for selection as the excavation developed. But the whole project was well and truly based upon the elements essential to a long-barrow excavation, namely: (a) the provision of firmly fixed datum-lines; (b) the preparation of a contoured survey before excavation; (c) the maintenance of a longitudinal section or spine during excavation; (d) the thorough exploration of the ditches; and (e) the careful removal of the (greater part of the) mound. The structural hurdles, first identified at Skendleby, and the marginal posts will now be looked for in all long-barrow excavations, and the search for them can therefore be legislated for in the primary layout.

A further word in regard to the contoured survey of an unexcavated long barrow. The contours may not adequately indicate the actual extent of the mound, particularly on a slope. It may therefore be necessary to add a basal form-line, differentiated from the contour-lines, to indicate the approximate line of junction between the structure and the natural surface of the ground.

The two long barrows which I have chosen as examples are both devoid of the stone structures – chambers, passages, peristaliths, entrance-complexes – which characterize many of the kind. To these the general principles apply: above all, the restriction of excavation to *one half of a feature at a time*, and, wherever possible, to work upon the longitudinal axis or 'approach axis' as the base. Thus, in the excavation of megalithic 'port-hole' cists in India – i.e. large cists with a small circular entrance through an end-stone – half the cist was excavated first, in such a fashion that the section bisected the port-

1. *Archaeologia*, lxxxv (1936), 42–4.

hole. By this means it was possible to ascertain exactly what portion of the filling had been inserted through the port-hole, and so to reconstruct a feature of the ceremonial usage of the tomb. The procedure need not be further elaborated; nor need the method of digging and recording the sections through the ditch, where a simple adaptation of the three-dimensional method described elsewhere (p. 87) is applicable.

'FLAT' CEMETERIES

Where burials, for example in urn-fields, are not marked on the surface of the ground, their investigation becomes an ordinary area-excavation of the kind already described (p. 83). Within the squares of the grid it will obviously be necessary to leave additional 'keys' or cross-sections to interrelate certain of the burial-groups vertically. Otherwise, the main problem will be that of isolating the individual graves and planning their outlines by very careful horizontal digging, often with a knife or trowel. In dealing with inhumations, the excavator may advisedly look particularly for discolorations or impresses which may indicate the former presence of coffins or shrouds. See Sir Leonard Woolley's account of the cemetery at Ur,[1] or the reference above to a coffin-burial of the Indus Civilization at Harappā (p. 100), all or mostly dating from the third millennium B.C. It is manifestly important to determine whether burials overlap (and so indicate perhaps a culture-sequence) or have otherwise been disturbed anciently. Care must also be taken to discriminate between authentic grave-goods and objects which may happen to have reached the grave with the infilling. No rule can be laid down for this; much must depend upon the precise position of the objects in question, and upon the general character of the infilling. Where any shadow of doubt exists, it must be stated in the report.

1. *Ur Excavations II: the Royal Cemetery* (London and Philadelphia, 1934), pp. 137, 165, 184, &c., and pl. 14.

CHAPTER 9

Watch-makers' Jobs

'THAT be a watch-maker's job', remarked the ancient, after long and meditative observation of an archaeologist on all fours, plying a pen-knife and a water-colour brush upon the reluctant soil. And watch-makers' jobs are not the least amongst the employments of the director and his supervisors. 'The archaeologist, who the moment before may have been writing notes in a different part of the field, has to take his turn with the pick, or more probably with a knife, and may spend the next few hours crouched in the same hole, in the same uncomfortable attitude, engrossed in the cleaning, recording and safe removal of some one particularly fragile object.'[1] I do not altogether applaud the dispersal of effort and the shortage of skilled assistance implied in that quotation; save in the direst emergency, the general does not have to lay his guns or repair a breech-block. But the principle is right enough; the extraction of delicate objects from the earth demands the highest skill, patience, and knowledge available, and is not lightly delegated.

First, however, a word or two of warning may be uttered. Avoid any semblance of excitement when an object of some special distinction first begins to emerge. I have seen a director of excavations leap excitedly into a trench on such an occasion, communicating a false and emotional atmosphere to the incident and interfering therefore with cool, objective workmanship. It is essential to check any sort of excitement instantly, and to insist firmly on quiet routine.[2] In particular, let the adjacent gang get on with its allotted task without intermission. Nothing unusual has happened. Discipline is now more

1. Sir Leonard Woolley, *Digging up the Past* (Pelican Books, 1940), p. 40.

2. More charmingly expressed by a French writer on excavation: '*Il faut laisser les vestiges en place aussi longtemps que possible*, ne jamais se presser et conserver son calme. Le moment le plus dangereux est celui d'une vraie grande découverte; l'exaltation risque de devenir telle que le fouilleur oublie la moitié des consignes, pousse des exclamations admiratives et s'aperçoit trop tard que sa documentation est incomplète. Il est vraiment grand s'il a le courage de s'asseoir et d'allumer une cigarette pour réfléchir.' A. Leroi-Gourhan, *Les Fouilles préhistoriques (technique et méthodes)* (Paris, 1950), p. 7.

than ever necessary if proper values are to be maintained. And secondly, the removal of some special object is very rarely an adequate justification for an ugly untidy piece of excavation. The rules of stratification must be adhered to; if possible, a part of the object should first be uncovered in such fashion that the remainder is still embedded in, and projects from, a clean-cut local section. Apart from the importance of its relationship with environment, this section may reveal unexpected information, such as the stain of a vanished casing which on plan had evaded recognition. In other words, ordinary rules may not be jettisoned without very exceptional cause. The warning may seem unnecessary, but experience shows otherwise.

Having said that, I turn from precept to example. And first I propose to turn to the ship-burial of Sutton Hoo (p. 102), where Mr W. F. Grimes has described the 'exciting and exacting task' of removing the treasure from the burial-chamber.[1] The following extensive extracts are reproduced by permission.

The bronze bowls . . . were standing one inside the other, with a number of iron objects in association. Three angons [long iron javelins] were actually pushed through the drop handle of the larger bowl, with spearheads and other implements and weapons near at hand. . . . Corrosion was so far advanced that it was unlikely that any free metal could survive in any of them. . . . The weapons were corroded not only to one another but also to the side of the bronze bowl with which they were now in contact. . . . It was abundantly clear that they could not be mechanically separated on the spot. . . . They were therefore cleaned up with care and freed from sand – a task which took some time because of the large amount of undercutting and the generally restricted conditions – and the whole complex of bowls and iron objects was lifted intact. . . .

Beneath [a silver dish] was an assortment of articles, most of them in a fragile and parlous state, the recording, removal and packing of which took the undivided attention of all working on the site. The most urgent were the organic materials – especially a number of small cups which were thought at one hasty glance to be made of wood. But there were also leather and other materials, all of which owed their preservation to their having been more or less encased in fabrics and a flock-like substance which had kept them in a state of perpetual dampness whilst shutting out air. Delay here would have been fatal. The cups already

1. *Antiquity*, xiv (1940), 69 ff.

showed signs of distortion and were damaged in other ways. And a hot drying sun poured into the bottom of the ship. If they were to be preserved for future treatment it was obvious that quick measures were called for; equally obvious that the best hope for their preservation would lie in a reconstruction of the conditions which had already preserved them for so many hundreds of years. The cups were therefore closely packed in damp moss in boxes with well-fitting lids to exclude as much air as possible, and stored in a cool place away from the sun. The leather and fabrics were put temporarily in bowls of water.

There is little to be said about the removal of the remaining objects from beneath the dish. The small silver bowl was taken up with its contents untouched but protected with a thick layer of moss. . . . The fine leather bag in which the small dish lay was our despair. It had become ragged with decay, was cracked and fissured, with all its native toughness gone. The remnants were cleaned and photographed *in situ*; after that interest concentrated on the size of the largest piece that could be detached unbroken from the underlying wood of the trough in which all these objects had been deposited. . . . The trough and the objects surrounding it were left until later; the wood was protected from the drying action of sun and air by a thick covering of damp cloths.

In the western end of the burial-chamber, was revealed

an iron object which proved to be of quite unexpected size and character. As with cleaning its various features became clear we called it a lamp-stand. It was much corroded but appeared to be fairly strong, and in spite of its size was lifted quite easily. The surrounding sand was completely removed and the weight of the stand evenly supported by three people. It was placed on a wide plank of a suitable length on which its unsupported parts were propped with packing covered with cotton wool.

Near the lamp-stand was an iron-bound wooden bucket in an advanced state of decay. The iron binding was badly corroded; the wood had become friable. The vessel had therefore collapsed upon itself and become a more or less shapeless mass. Even so it seemed possible that careful removal might enable some sort of reconstruction to be attempted later – and there was the further possibility that the bucket might contain other material of interest.

Surplus sand having been removed, the bucket was bound firmly round with webbing, particular care being taken with the lower part, upon which the greatest strain was to be placed. A piece of thin iron plate of slightly larger area than the bucket was then obtained and gradually introduced beneath its base, the sand being cleared away in front of the forward edge of the plate with a trowel. With the plate completely inserted the bucket was ready for lifting. But the iron was too thin to sustain the quite considerable weight of the bucket without buckling – which would of course have disturbed the already broken pieces. A flat spade was therefore inserted beneath the plate, which prevented any lateral pressure being inflicted on the bucket while providing a large surface for its support. Bucket and plate were then lifted together on the spade and placed on strong boards so that the spade could be withdrawn. In this way no part of the bucket was seriously disturbed.

Mr Grimes remarks parenthetically that he has 'used an almost similar method in removing very fragile Bronze Age pottery. The consolidation of two Bronze Age urns from Coity, Glamorgan, was only possible because they were lifted intact in this way and the crumbling pottery hardened and treated in the workshop before its contents (which helped to reinforce it) were removed.' I may add that in similar circumstances, in the removal of a considerable prehistoric clay oven, I have likewise used the iron-plate method with success. The preliminary binding of the fragile object – preferably with an ordinary surgical bandage – is an important stage, and may sometimes have to be supplemented by a surface-coating of plaster or melted paraffin-wax to give additional solidity. The particularly fragile clay oven was coated with a considerable jacket of wax, and survived the operation of removal perfectly. It is now in the Dorchester (Dorset) Museum.

Enough has been quoted from the Sutton Hoo account to indicate the general methods used. Mr Grimes observes that the account

is not a story of new and elaborate technical methods, but rather of the way in which simple readily available means were employed to deal with an unexpected range of materials, each . . . with its own set of problems. In some cases one could visualize an instrument or method by which the solutions would have been the more easily obtained. I longed several times for a broad-bladed implement, a kind of fish-slice, which (in various sizes) would have been ideal for lifting such things as the horn mounts, the silver bowels, and even the wooden bucket. But only a specially made tool could have combined all the necessary qualities: strength to sustain weight and pressure, thinness and a sharp edge of a suitable outline for easy insertion beneath the object to be removed.

Excavation of a barrow, 1844 (*Gentleman's Magazine*, 1852) (See p. 21)

(*a*) An Early Iron Age pit at Scarborough, Yorkshire, cut to show three interrupted phases of the filling (See p. 45)

(*b*) Section showing sixteen successive layers of plastering on the wall of the temple of the moon-god Sin at Khafajah, Iraq (See p. 46)

Stratification at Brahmagiri, Mysore State, India (See p. 65)

(*a*) Chaos: excavation in the East, 1935

(*b*) Discipline: excavation at Arikamedu, South India, 1945 (See p. 80)

Layout of an area-excavation (Taxila-Bhir Mound, 1944) (See p. 83)

Section pegged for three-dimensional recording (Maiden Castle, 1935)
(See p. 86)

(*a*) Section pegged for three-dimensional recording (Taxila-Sirkap, 1945)
(See p. 86)

(*b*) Similar section linking two cemetery-areas (Harappā, Punjab, 1946)
(See p. 87)

(a) 'Ghost' wall at Verulamium, Hertfordshire, 1931 (See p. 98)

(b) Verulamium, north-west gate: part of the plan recovered by clearing trenches made by wall-robbers (See p. 98)

(a) Roman timber-building at Richborough, Kent, traced by coloration of the soil (See p. 100)

(b) Burial of about 2000 B.C. at Harappā, Punjab, showing outline of wooden coffin (See p. 101)

Traces of hurdle-construction in the neolithic long-barrow at Skendleby, Lincolnshire (See p. 101)

Section through the mud-brick defences of the Harappā citadel, Punjab, built before 2000 B.C. (See p. 105)

Air-photograph of part of the Parthian city of Taxila, Punjab, first century A.D. (See p. 108)

A typical *tell* (Tepe Sialk, central Iran). (*Scale, indicated by the small figure on the right shoulder of the mound*) (See p. 109)

Excavation of a burial-pit (first or second century B.C.) at Brahnagiri, Mysore State, India, showing the 'quadrant' method (See p. 118)

Traces of the Sutton Hoo ship, Suffolk (See p. 103)

(a) Silver coin of Tiberius, dated A.D. 26–37, from Chandravalli, Mysore State (See p. 147)

(b) Arikamedu : fragments of Roman amphorae (See p. 142)

16

Rouletted ware of the first century A.D. from Arikamedu, South India
(See p. 144)

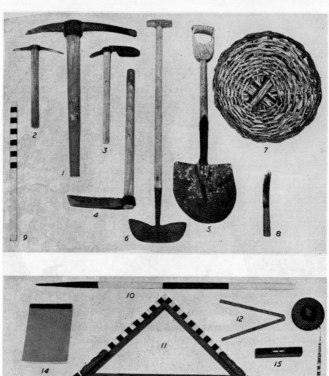

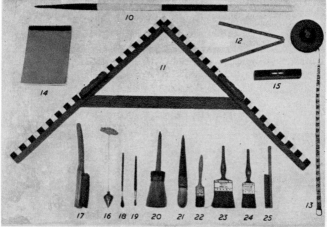

Selection of tools from an Eastern excavation (See p. 181)

Part of section through the 'Fosse' earthwork at Verulamium, showing turf wall embedded in earth and gravel but emphasized by careful lighting

(See p. 201)

Pottery-grid, for use in dry climates (See p. 193)

Tower for high-angle photography (See p. 205)

21

MOSAIC (4 or 5) WALL (2) CONCRETE FLOOR (3)

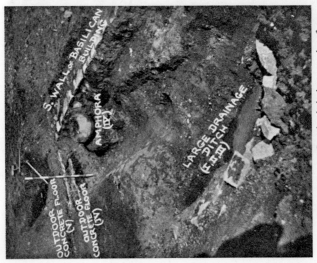

S. WALL of BASILICAN BUILDING AMPHORA (IV) OUTDOOR CONCRETE FLOOR (V) OUTDOOR CONCRETE FLOOR (IV) LARGE DRAINAGE DITCH (I-II-III)

Overloaded photographs of unprepared subjects (See pp. 201 and 218)

22

Reconstruction of an Early Iron Age homestead at Little Woodbury, Wiltshire (See p. 243)

Ministry of Information

(*a*) 'Sir Flinders Petrie in the court-
yard of the School in Jerusalem'

(*b*) 'Copper Jar no. 277'

How *not* to illustrate! Two examples, with captions, from well-known
publications (See pp. 202 and 217)

24

The absence of some luxuries had to be countered by patience and perseverance. Our tools were of the simplest kind. Here we were fortunate in our soil: the sand yielded readily to treatment, and especially, when dry, to brushing for the more delicate objects. For these the usual procedure was a sequence of alternate phases of brushing and drying, the surface sand being removed to expose a new damp sand which in its turn was allowed to dry. Paint brushes were most useful for this purpose. In actually carving sand away from heavy objects calling for no special treatment of the surface – and also for much of the finer work – I was very grateful for a curved bodkin or packer's needle, especially as long as its point remained sharp. The curve of the needle was particularly useful for negotiating hollows, angles, and undercutting; it provided a sensitive 'feeler' for unexpected shapes; and since it was not mounted in a handle it could be used in a restricted space.

Of the general practice of cleaning it remains to be said that each specimen, whatever its material and character, was freed as completely as possible from its matrix: the importance of the first step cannot be too strongly emphasized. (Even sand when damp is strongly prehensile, and the extra strain imposed by its adhesion even to a small area might well result in damage to a fragile specimen.) Care in coaxing the sand away without damaging the surface and in lifting the object so that all the weight was equally distributed, with no strain on any one part, completed the process. Such precautions may appear to be obvious, but were especially important on a site where all except the most precious metal was badly decayed and corroded.

In the circumstances, dealing as we were with a wide range of objects and materials all calling for laboratory treatment, and not knowing what else we might have to face, it was sound policy to remove even the most unpromising of finds with as little interference as possible. Chemical and other methods have now replaced more direct mechanical treatment of antiquities; here mechanical treatment was reduced to the minimum necessary to remove the object from the ground. In addition, even with much broken and apparently worthless objects, much time and trouble were expended in attempts to maintain the various parts and fragments in their relative positions, as a very valuable first step in reconstructing the original or obtaining maximum information from it by more leisured laboratory examination at a later stage. This was not always successful and sometimes was impossible, even from the beginning. But every attempt was made to see that no scrap of evidence from Sutton Hoo was lost by lack of care and patience in the field.

By way of comment on this account of a difficult and successful piece of work, I would reinforce Mr Grimes's plea for a 'broad-bladed implement'. Independent experience has shown me the constant necessity for a selection of implements of this kind. They can be bought or made without undue difficulty and should be a routine item in the excavator's equipment, beginning with the broad-bladed kitchen knife which every supervisor should carry (p. 179) and including fish-slices and the unnamed flat instrument ('turner'?) with which fried eggs are removed from the adhesive surface of the frying-pan.

From Sutton Hoo we may travel to Ur of the Chaldees, where Sir Leonard Woolley had much experience of the 'watch-maker's job' and has something to tell of it. One of his masterpieces was the recovery of the harp from Shub-ad's tomb, and he shall tell the story in his own words.[1]

The first thing to come to light was the gold cap of the upright, which seemed to be loose in the soil and gave us no hint as to what lay below. As the work went on there were found two or three gold-headed nails and, searching for their possible connexion, we found a hole running down into the earth across which could be seen the shafts of more nails obviously in position, i.e. the hole represented some wooden object which had decayed away altogether but the nails once fixed in it were being kept in place by the soil against their heads. A stick was therefore inserted into the hole for so far as it would go and plaster of paris was poured in round it; when that had had time to set the digging continued and there was found the lower part of the upright modelled in plaster with the gold-headed nails in it; measurement of the soil and the calculation of the distance apart of the dislodged nails gave the full length of the upright and enabled us to refix the gold cap at the original height. Below, the plaster had expanded into the 'shoe' of the instrument and its flow had then been stopped by the not altogether decayed bitumen which had held the shoe to the base; this, with the line of shell and lapis inlay which emphasized its curve, was at once hardened with paraffin wax. This brought us to the sounding-box which, being of wood, had completely perished, but the broad band of mosaic along its edges was for the most part in position, though rather distorted, and could be cleared little by little and secured as it appeared by waxed muslin. The wood had apparently been painted black with a line of red paint running

1. C. L. Woolley, *Ur Excavations*, II (London and Philadelphia, 1934), pp. 74 f.; and *Digging up the Past* (Pelican Books, 1940), pp. 85 ff.

parallel to the edge a little inside the inlay border. The top edge was first treated and then the side could be laid bare and the form of it ascertained; the rectangle of the near side was complete (it was indeed lifted in one piece) and the back of the inlay of the far side could also be cleaned and secured. The gold and lapis-lazuli calf's head which decorated the front of the instrument seemed to be in rather bad condition, for the whole of the top of the head, consisting of lapis tesserae representing hair, had fallen down into the hollow left by the decay of the wooden core, and the metal was a good deal bent, but nothing was missing; in the end it was restored without much difficulty.

Thus the available evidence, some of it positive, some negative, was preserved, and an acceptable reconstruction of the whole instrument rendered possible. The whole success of the operation depended on the recognition at the outset of the potential significance of a hole running down into the earth. Similarly,

one of our richest graves at Ur, that which contained the famous golden helmet, was located by the discovery of a copper spear-head sticking point upwards in the earth. The soil was cleared from round it, and there came to light a length of thin gold tube which adorned the top of the shaft; below this there was a hole in the ground left by the wooden shaft itself when it turned to dust. We followed the hole downwards, and it led us to the grave, against the corner of which it had been leaning when the earth was thrown back into the pit; with this forewarning we were able to trace the entire outline of the grave before we started to lay bare its contents, and so could record in order all the offerings heaped and crowded round the coffin.

Where the actual woodwork is preserved, other methods must be adopted in accordance with circumstances. Thus in 1951 a La Tène sword in its bronze-bound wooden scabbard was found in the water-logged clay at the bottom of an ancient ditch at Stanwick in Yorkshire. It was carefully cleared to a rough outline with trowel and pen-knife, and sufficient mud was then washed from it with a small soft brush to enable a photograph and an approximate life-size drawing to be made of it on the spot. Meanwhile a local carpenter was preparing a box to receive it, with an ample allowance for packing material. When the drawing was completed, a stiff 3-ply board was carefully inserted beneath the object, which was then immediately placed without further cleaning in the box in a thick matrix of wet newspaper. The package was then taken by the next train to the British Museum laboratory, care being taken to maintain the dampness of the packing. The subsequent treatment, applied with great skill by Dr H. J. Plenderleith, lies outside the scope of the field-worker.

Lastly, it is fair to include amongst 'watch-makers' jobs' the removal of a Roman mosaic pavement, the condition of which usually demands the utmost delicacy of handling. The surface of the mosaic may have sunk into hollows: many of the tesserae, even though in position, may be fractured; and the fine mortar in which the tesserae were originally embedded may largely have lost its grip. The conventional procedure has been described in categorical form by the late Mrs T. V. Wheeler, F.S.A., who herself applied it successfully.[1] Her account is here reproduced.

1. Dig a trench 1 foot wide and 18 inches deep round the area of the pavement to be lifted some days before the work of removal is started. A considerable amount of moisture is thereby drained away.

2. Build a shed or shelter of sufficient size to cover the pavement and the drainage-trenches.

3. Remove all dirt scrupulously from the pavement and from the joints between the tesserae. The condition of the pavement will dictate the means to be employed. These may vary from scrubbing with brush and soapy water and/or gently scraping with a blunt knife, to the delicate use of an orange-stick or bellows.

4. Place coke-buckets on bricks *on* the pavement and keep fires burning day and night until the mosaic, its bedding and the earth beneath are absolutely dry. The heat not only drives off any remaining moisture but also disintegrates the Roman mortar. This drying-out is the most important part of the whole process and may take from two to five days according to local conditions of dampness.

5. Before or during the drying of the pavement, prepare a flat board, a few inches larger in each direction than the fragment or section under treatment. A platform of ⅜-inch board, reinforced with cross-battens, is adequate.

6. Remove the fires and clean the mosaic finally.

7. Brush a coat of ordinary glue, prepared in a dixie nearby and sufficiently thin to run into and fill up all interstices, over the surface and leave it to set.

1. *The Museums Journal*, xxx (London, 1933), 104 ff.

8. Brush a second coat of thick glue heavily over this hardened surface.

9. Press down into this hot coat a piece of stout canvas newly wrung in boiling water. The canvas should be squeezed down with the fingers until it is certain that all air-bubbles are eliminated. A final coat of glue on top of the canvas will ensure adhesion to every tessera.

10. Replace the fires in the drainage-trenches for an hour to drive off moisture.

11. Remove fires and allow the glue to harden. The time that this will take will again depend on local conditions, but upwards of eight hours should be allowed. Again, it is essential to make sure that the glue is set before attempting the work of removal.

12. The mosaic can now safely be released from its bedding. Cut into the mortar of the bedding with trowels, slate-rippers or, if available, bar-chisels, leaving a good clearance of 2–3 inches below the lower surface of the tesserae.

13. Slip in planks underneath as the bedding is removed. These should project beyond the edges of the pavement, for use in reversing it.

14. Lay the prepared board on to the surface of the pavement.

15. Using the lower planks as levers, turn the pavement, now sandwiched between wood, on to the prepared board, which now becomes the working-platform. The pavement, or section of pavement, can now be removed to a work-shed on this platform.

16. Remove all Roman mortar. If the heat from the fires has penetrated properly the greater part will come away if gently tapped with a wooden mallet. Care must be taken to scrape away any obstinate mortar from the side and back of each tessera, and bellows used to blow fine dust from between them. The tesserae are now in position facedownwards on the glued canvas and are clean.

17. A slight sprinkling of water applied here will soften the glue sufficiently, without releasing its grip, to press the now convex surfaces of the former hollows into their original horizontal position.

18. Nail a two-inch frame round the working platform.

19. With soap or thick grease fill up all breaks in the pattern, so that the modern cement will be kept back from the ultimate level of the face of the finished pavement.

20. Mix a sufficient quantity of modern cement with broken Roman material, imitative of the mortar used in the original pavement, to pour into the joints between the now-isolated tesserae.

21. Tap the frame on every side, to ensure that the mixture is filling all joints and that all air-bubbles are eliminated.

22. Lay a reinforcement of wire-netting and steel rods within the frame and fill up with cement. If the section is of considerable size (and it is possible to handle a section 6 feet by 3 feet by this method) a second layer of reinforcement may possibly be needed. The cement should be brought to a smooth surface within the frame and left for two days or more to set. Where large pavements are to be removed, sections of a workable size should be determined upon, and marked with tell-tales on the canvas, which, initially, may cover the whole surface. The canvas may then be cut along the lines laid out and each section lifted separately.

23. The frame can now be knocked away and the pavement reversed, canvas-side up.

24. Flood boiling water on to the canvas until the glue is sufficiently dissolved to allow the canvas to be lifted, not pulled, away. Any remaining glue should be removed with boiling water and a nail-brush. If, in this process, any tessera is found to be loose, it should at once be reset.

25. The breaks in the pavement may be treated in accordance with the policy desired. If restoration is envisaged, the newly-cut tesserae will declare themselves as modern and so prevent deception. If restoration is not desired, the breaks should be brought to a smooth surface at the general level of the mortar-bedding.

The pavement should now be strong enough to withstand any reasonable handling and ready for exhibition.

CHAPTER 10

Tactics and Strategy

THE main subject of this chapter is the overall planning of field-research, a phrase disguised above under the somewhat inflated term 'strategy'. In retrospect every archaeologist is constantly arranging his facts into a pattern, his laboriously collected words into a coherent sentence. Less frequently does he place his inquiries in advance with an equivalent regard for sequence. There is some excuse in the fact that at the present time field-archaeology is still dominated in Britain by special conditions arising out of a hard war and a harder peace. It is conditioned, too often, by the incidence of a bomb-hole or a housing scheme or an aerodrome, or by sheer economic duress, rather than by long-term planning. Yet even between wars, strategic planning, though sometimes talked about, was rarely carried into effect. Other factors – personal or international competition, sheer lack of imagination – obstructed it. Sites were dug because they 'looked good' or because they *might* produce information, rather like carrying out a surgical operation at random on a patient in the hope of finding somewhere the cause of an undiagnosed disease. It was thus that the neolithic surgeon used to cut a hole in a man's skull in the hope of letting out a headache; but not thus, I need hardly say, is the orderly way of science. As archaeologists we are excessively prone to opportunism: we do not sufficiently plan or create our opportunities. Admittedly a happy chance has from time to time added unexpectedly and even dramatically to knowledge; for instance the finding of that famous seventh-century boat-burial in the mound at Sutton Hoo. Nevertheless, the progress of science depends less on these hazards than on the methodical, logical use of the disciplined imagination in the evaluation of cause and effect. It depends in no small measure upon careful strategic planning.

The nearest approach to planning during the past half-century or more is probably to be recognized in the discovery and enlargement of the Minoan civilization of Crete. The vivid quality of the civilization itself, the imaginative genius of its prime discoverer, and its central geographical position have combined to give a certain unity to the multifarious but more or less related work which has been carried out by several nations in the adjacent lands. But even there co-ordination has been notoriously inadequate and the results proportionately scrappy and unsatisfying. A great opportunity has been missed. In the circumstances, as illustrations of what I mean on the one hand by tactical and on the other by strategic planning, I may be forgiven the presumption of taking two examples from work in which I happen myself to have been concerned, where it is at least possible to speak at first hand of the conscious and careful sequence which was present continuously from the outset in the mind of the director. The first of these two examples is an example of *tactical* planning in the development of a local problem. That problem was the unravelling of the history of Verulamium in Hertfordshire as a Roman and pre-Roman city, with its potential bearing upon the Caesarian campaign which culminated hereabouts in 54 B.C.

I may recall that Verulamium, in the valley below the medieval and modern town of St Albans, is a site of some exceptional interest in the protohistory of these islands. There or thereabouts in pre-Roman times reigned, as his coins tell us, King Tasciovanus, the father of Cunobelin; and since Cassivellaunus was a predecessor on the same tribal throne, it was assumed that there also Julius Caesar had found and stormed the headquarters of his great opponent in 54 B.C. Later events included the martyrdom of Albanus, a Christian citizen of Verulamium and our most authentic Romano-British martyr, and a visitation by St Germanus of Auxerre who thus provided one of the few unquestioned fifth-century contacts between Britain and the Roman world. Altogether, the site was fraught with archaeological possibilities of an alluringly miscellaneous kind. The historical and geographical sequence of human occupation in the St Albans region through the five centuries presented a challenging problem.

The visual starting-point was the large walled and embanked area, some 200 acres in extent, which manifestly represented the developed Roman municipality. The conventional theory before excavation was that this area represented also the pre-Roman capital and one of the first functions of the excavators was to check this view. Accordingly, deep pits were sunk to the natural surface within the walled area, and at the same time sections were cut through the defences.

The former failed to reveal any pre-Roman occupation; the latter showed that the defences were not earlier than the second century A.D.

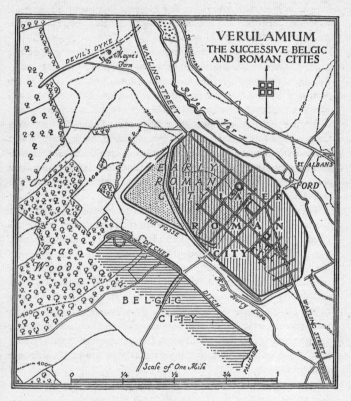

Fig. 20. Successive sites of pre-Roman and Roman Verulamium. (Based on the Ordnance Survey 6-inch map, Herts. XXIV, by permission of the Controller of H.M. Stationery Office)

That may be regarded as Stage I of the investigation. Stage II was directed inevitably to the examination of the next most evident structural relic in the vicinity; an unexplained earth-work known as 'The Fosse', which projected on the hill-side from under a part of the

137

circuit of the second-century defences. Here, in and under the rampart, was found a considerable quantity of native pottery, presumably indicating the proximity of the pre-Roman site; but an admixture of early Roman material indicated a post-conquest date. Stage II, then, had identified the site of an earlier Roman town, but left the pre-Roman settlement still in the air.

The early pottery recovered from 'The Fosse' served at least as a pointer. The earth-work lay just below the brow of the plateau flanking the valley which carried the main Roman site, and the obvious next step, Stage III, was to pursue the inquiry on to the plateau itself. Here, in the depths of a tangled game-preserve, lies a complex group of unmapped and unimpressive earth-works. Some of these were disused field- or woodland-boundaries, but amongst them was a nucleus which was proved by excavation to be a portion of the pre-Roman city. A part of our question was thus answered; the associated remains, however, were of post-Caesarian date, and evidence was still lacking for the Caesarian episode. (Fig. 20).

There was still an unexplained feature which appeared to relate to the pre-Roman site. A mile to the north of it were traces of a cross-country dyke or barrier facing away from Verulamium. Excavation, which may be classified as Stage IV, showed that (a) this dyke was likewise of pre-Roman date, and (b) it had originally barred an open gap of chalk-land between the hill-top woodland on the one hand and the marshy valley on the other. It was presumably a boundary of the pre-Roman civic territory at a point where natural obstacles were missing. Its major office in our task of exploration was, however, as a pointer to draw fresh attention to a seemingly related but mysterious cross-country dyke of far more formidable size on the opposite side of the valley.

This further dyke, known to fame as Beech Bottom, is a remarkable construction. It is 100 feet wide and upwards of 30 feet deep, with a bank on both lips. It is sited along the bottom of an east-west valley, and there is only the greater size of the more southerly marginal bank to show that the work faced north. It was clearly a major traffic-barrier rather than a military work in the narrower sense. About a mile of the dyke is still visible, but a further half-mile has been traced by excavation or safe inference. Its examination had already been begun as Stage V when a happy chance supplied more definite evidence than unaided science could have expected. Workmen digging a sewer at measured depths through the dyke, at a point where it had been filled up, found a coin-hoard of the second century A.D. deep in the filling but still a dozen feet above the bottom of the ditch. The coins – a shovelful of them, it was said – were immediately scattered amidst the ready hands and pockets of the cosmopolitan gang of workmen concerned. But a strenuous search that night in a multitude of local places of refreshment and entertainment produced about forty of them, enough to indicate the general character and date of the hoard. It was clear that the ditch in which they had been found was of some considerable age by the second century A.D., and that solid fact, combined with its entirely un-Roman character and siting, placed it fairly and squarely in our pre-Roman period.

But this was not all. If the dyke had served any logical purpose at all, it must have barred a fairly open stretch of country between two river valleys and fords: that of the Ver, beside which Verulamium stands to the south-west, and that of the Lea to the north-east (Fig. 21). Along this line the eye is carried to a height above the ford across the Lea, where are the remains of the greatest *oppidum* in this part of England, that which adjoins the little country town of Wheathampstead. The present fame of this *oppidum* may be measured by its appearance in an historical novel; but it was not in fact until Stage VI of our planned advance that the significance of the mighty earth-work became tolerably clear; it had previously attracted little or no attention. The profile of its defences is of the same kind as that of Beech Bottom, only more so. The enclosure is some 90 acres in extent, on a platform above the Lea, just as pre-Roman Verulamium stands on a plateau above the Ver. A significant difference between the two sites began to emerge, however, as excavation proceeded. Whereas the Verulamium site began in post-Caesarian times, when, in the age of Tasciovanus, Roman things and forms were already beginning to penetrate the backwoods of yet unconquered Britain, there was no hint of Romanization in the equipment of the Wheathampstead *oppidum*. In other words, this *oppidum* preceded the last two decades of the first century B.C.; and, that being so, it was an easy further step to ascribe its great defences to a phase of inter-tribal or even international rivalry such as marked the age of Caesar's British campaigns.

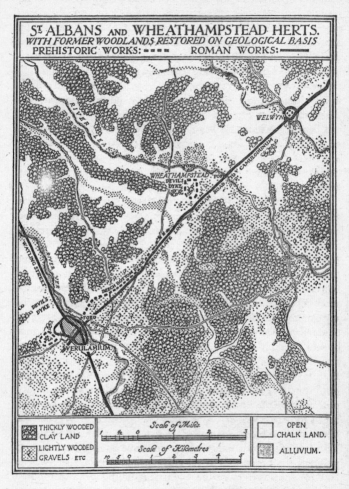

Fig. 21. Map of the earthworks of Wheathampstead and Verulamium, with
intervening dykes. (See p. 138)

Here, if anywhere, may we locate the headquarters of such a one as Cassivellaunus. At least we are approaching closely to his time and environment, and no rival site is known. The name of Wheat-hampstead has now, with no great questioning, entered the books as the scene of Caesar's culminating British victory.

Thus in six progressive stages, developing gradually and logically from known to unknown, the vista of a formative phase of proto-historic Britain began to unroll itself. In reverse, the picture is that of the initial overlordship of a powerful Belgic king, competitively exploiting a countryside which had previously, it seems, been but thinly inhabited. Thereafter, during the Augustan Peace on the Continent and the centralization of native rule in south-eastern Britain, the emphasis changes: fortifications, hereabouts at any rate,[1] are now of trivial size, and continental trade percolates with increas-ing freedom. The phase culminates in the formal extension of the *Pax Romana* to lowland Britain in A.D. 43; thereafter fortification was discounted by over-confidence, which was in turn countered by the Boudiccan revolt and by the consequent construction of new defences of no mean order ('The Fosse'); and finally, in the spacious days of the second century, the town took shape on evolved, conventional continental lines. We are not here concerned with the details, only with the sequence of thought and action – an elementary illustration of archaeological tactic on half a dozen miles of landscape.

From the Hertfordshire parish-pump, I turn to the wide horizons of Asia, to planning on a large scale to which the term 'strategy' may properly be applied. Again, the example is from my own experience, on the renewed plea that first-hand witness has an actuality which may sufficiently counterbalance defects. As Director-General of Archaeology in India from 1944 to 1948, I had, in spite of war and acute political difficulties, an opportunity such as few archaeologists have had of strategic planning within the far-flung boundaries of a whole sub-continent. The northern and southern parts of that sub-continent differ alike in the character of their respective problems and in the amount of work previously done upon them. Central and south India, with which I am here concerned, had scarcely been worked at all. In the whole of that great southern region, some half a million square miles in extent, there was in 1944 no firm archaeological

1. At Colchester their size was sustained by dynastic wealth and ambition.

datum-line prior to the Middle Ages. In the north of India, contacts with prehistoric Mesopotamia and, later, with Persia and the lands of the classical West had provided reasonably fixed pegs upon which to hang some part of the prehistory of the frontier-lands. In the south, most of these pegs were absent. Sporadic exploration of an unmethodical kind had there revealed great quantities of material; urn-fields had been gathered up like rice-crops, megalithic tombs had been ransacked (sometimes, as recently as 1942, with the aid of dynamite – p. 113), town-sites had on occasion been broken into and miscellaneous debris recovered from them; but nowhere had this archaeological loot been interrelated systematically with itself or correlated with any external datum. Of the museums of the region it would have been sufficient to quote the words applied by Petrie to nineteenth-century museums in general: 'Our museums are ghastly charnel-houses of murdered evidence; the dry bones of objects are there, bare of all the facts of grouping, locality and dating which would give them historical life and value.'

In this world of chaos there was, however, one potential fixed point. Since 1775, Roman coins, generally in hoards of gold or silver, have turned up from time to time, mostly in south India where they represent the Imperial luxury trade abundantly vouched for in classical and Indian literature. Here was a chance of securing the required datum. Could we but find a significant association of Roman coinage or other datable Roman imports with a native Indian culture, we should have at once a firm base from which to advance upon the general problem of the ancient chronology of the Indian peninsula.

Accordingly it was one of my first acts as Director-General in 1944 to draw up a list of sites known to have produced Roman coinage and to send two members of my staff on a 3,000-mile tour of the listed sites with a view to selecting one of them for investigation. My envoys worked steadily down the west coast of India and round Cape Comorin without encountering any very hopeful sign. But the solution was in fact imminent from another source.

In July 1944 I visited the Madras Museum and found in a cupboard there a part of a Graeco-Roman amphora of a type familiar in the Mediterranean region about the beginning of the Christian era. It had, I was informed, been dug up recently at a coastal site near Pondicherry, then the capital of French India, 80 miles south of Madras.

I shall not lightly forget the (to me) dramatic moment when chance put into my hand here on a hot afternoon of a south Indian summer an answer which I could almost believe that fate had sent me 6,000 miles from my little Roman Britain to discover: an answer which I had indeed sought but had scarcely dared to expect. By arrangement with the French authorities, I lost no time in visiting Pondicherry, and saw in the public library there a collection of objects which had been recovered during the previous two or three years by French antiquaries at a site known locally as Arikamedu, 2 miles south of the town. The collection comprised a considerable quantity of Indian pottery, beads and other objects, together with a remarkable assemblage of material of Mediterranean origin, including many sherds of amphorae, fragments of glassware, part of a lamp, and an untrimmed crystal intaglio representing Cupid with an eagle. To these may be added another gem bearing allegedly a head of Augustus but no longer available. More important than all these, however, were several sherds of red-glazed ware of the kind made at Arretium and other Italian centres prior to *c.* A.D. 45. The meaning of these things had not been suspected by their finders, but to an eye trained in the West it was instantly and easily apparent. Dated pottery, by virtue of its relatively limited durability, was better evidence even than dated coins, with their less computable survival-value. It remained to ascertain, by careful digging, the precise relationship between this Arretine ware and the Indian culture or cultures found on the same site.

Our subsequent (1945) excavations have been fully recorded. It will suffice to note here that the relationship was readily established, and that the site will therefore go down in the history of south Indian archaeology as that from which the classification of ancient south Indian cultures effectively began. With the aid of the dated imports referred to, it defined for the first time the chronological position of an extensive complex of south Indian pottery and other equipment dating from the first two centuries A.D.; and it was not long after the conclusion of the work that the importance of Arikamedu was found to extend far beyond the vicinity of the site itself. This extension was the result of carefully planned, progressive research, proceeding steadily from known to part-known to unknown, and its main stages may be recounted in the present context.

The first step was to discover the distribution of the more distinctive of the Indian wares thus newly dated. A tour of south Indian museums met with immediate success. Amongst the distinctive products of Arikamedu was a type of dish (Pl. 17) decorated on the internal base with concentric rings of a rouletted pattern otherwise foreign to Indian ceramic but familiar on certain classical wares including Arretine ware itself. Some of these rouletted dishes were doubtless imports from the Mediterranean, others were local Indian imitations. A search of museums showed that dishes of this kind had been found in southern India at a number of places separated by some hundreds of miles from one another (Fig. 22). The famous Amarāvatī, for example, which supplied the Buddhist sculptures displayed in the entrance-hall of the British Museum, had produced sherds of them, now in the Madras Museum. At other places, such as Maski and Kondapur in Hyderabad State and Chandravalli and Brahmagiri in the northern end of Mysore State, this distinctive decoration, type, and fabric had been found in ill-published and ill-conducted excavations. Maski, Kondapur, and Chandravalli had been, in part at least, towns of the central Indian Āndhra Empire which flourished at the end of B.C. and the beginning of A.D., and at Chandravalli stray denarii of Augustus and Tiberius had also been found. The historical and archaeological environment was therefore consistent with the Arikamedu dating. At all these sites the newly dated rouletted ware introduced at once an element of chronological precision; and on all of them it was manifestly associated with an elaborate and distinctive ceramic industry which differed largely from that at Arikamedu but could now, presumably, be regarded as contemporary. Already the fixed-point of Arikamedu had indicated the possibility of dating, by means of a little careful excavation, a widespread and important Indian culture more than 300 miles away.

A visit to one of these sites, Brahmagiri, in 1945 indicated other and wider possibilities. Trial excavations of a somewhat unorthodox kind, assisted on occasion by high explosive, had here been carried out by the State Archaeological Department and had revealed remains of an extensive ancient township. But the outstandingly interesting feature of the area was this: that adjoining the town-site was a large cemetery of megalithic tombs of a kind widespread in peninsular India but never hitherto adequately dated. Further, the Brahmagiri cists were marked by the circular entrance-opening or 'port-hole' which is present on many other Indian examples and on comparable tombs in

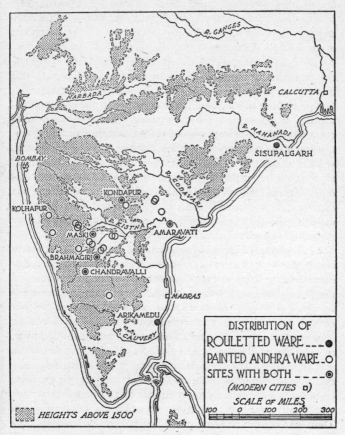

Fig. 22. Map of India showing sites which have produced 'rouletted ware' of the first century A.D.

western Asia, northern Africa, and Europe (including Britain) and *may* be a significant common factor. Indeed, these Indian tombs greet the eye of the visiting European prehistorian with a friendly familiarity

145

and at the same time with a challenge: their date and origin at once become matters of more than local importance. Their general character has indeed been familiar since the work (referred to on p. 23) by Meadows Taylor in Hyderabad State in the middle of the nineteenth century, and James Fergusson drew renewed attention to them in his *Rude Stone Monuments* in 1872. The curiosity of others, too, has not been lacking, and in the aggregate some hundreds of these cists in central or southern India must have been despoiled at one time or another for the benefit of public or private museums, from Oxford to Madras. The result has been merely to pile up the mountain of our ignorance. Until the undated contents of these tombs could be related to a fixed chronological point, their further spoliation was waste and worse than waste. But here at last, at Brahmagiri, was a clear opportunity for the establishment of such a relationship; for the equation of the culture represented by the tombs with evidence from an adjacent town-site containing a known factor – the dated rouletted ware of which sherds had already been unearthed there. It remained to ascertain the precise nature of this equation by the normal methods of scientific excavation.

Accordingly, as has already been recalled in Chapter 4, in 1947 a simultaneous exploration was carried out on the Brahmagiri town-site and in the adjacent megalithic cemetery. The former revealed three successive and distinctive cultures, of which the uppermost was associated from the outset with our rouletted ware of the first century A.D. This topmost culture is now identified as that of the Āndhra phase to which reference has already been made. Below it, and partially overlapping it, was a culture identical with that which was being revealed at the same time in the neighbouring megalithic cists. The overlap between the two, assessed in the manner described on p. 65, was amply sufficient to indicate that the megalithic culture with its elaborate iron equipment, lasted into the first century A.D. Thus, for the first time a fixed chronological point was obtained for a group of megalithic tombs of characteristic south Indian type.

But this was not all. A reasonable computation of the time-value of the megalithic strata – a computation which need not be reviewed here – suggested a backward duration of some two to two-and-a-half centuries from the terminal date in the first century A.D.; that is, the culture had arrived somewhere about 200 B.C. Below that was an

8-foot accumulation of occupation material representing an altogether different and more primitive culture. Whereas the Āndhra pottery had been turned on the fast wheel and the megalithic pottery (it seems) on the slow wheel, the crude wares of the lowest culture had been hand-made, without any sort of wheel. Again, whereas the overlying cultures were both in an advanced stage of the Iron Age, the lowest was essentially in the Stone Age (polished stone axes, rough microliths), although bronze was not altogether unknown – the first evidence, incidentally, for anything approaching a Bronze Age in south India. Yet, in spite of the disparity of the two cultures, there was clear evidence that this crude chalcolithic community had outlasted the arrival of the megalithic intruders: in other words, that the chalcolithic culture, elements of which had long been recognized, without context, in many parts of south India, had lasted into the second century B.C., and extended backwards from that date through 8 feet of deposit.

It would be irrelevant here to consider the details and implications of this happy concurrence of evidence, although in fact it was to the wider interpretation of the culture-movements represented by it that our work was directed. Suffice it to observe that we had recovered a picture of a rudimentary stone-using society overrun suddenly (during the Time of Troubles following the break-up of the great Aśokan Empire) by an elaborately equipped invasion of iron-users and megalith-builders, followed in turn by the sophisticated civilization of the surgent Āndhra empire: three hitherto unclassified but widespread cultures now for the first time arranged in clear sequence with a chronological datum-line at one end of the sequence and in consequence a new significance in subcontinental protohistory. So important was it to establish this datum-line beyond all shadow of doubt that a small parallel excavation was in fact carried out simultaneously on another Āndhra town-site some 45 miles away. This site (Chandravalli) yielded parallel evidence in the association of our rouletted ware with local Āndhra coins, overlying 'megalithic' fabrics, and incidentally produced from one of the Āndhra layers a denarius of Tiberius dated A.D. 26–37 (Pl. 16). It would be difficult to imagine a more satisfactory conclusion to our campaign: at one end of our story, our key-evidence associated with Roman ware of the first half of the first century A.D., and at the other end of our story identically similar evidence associated with a Roman coin of the same period.

This story of the 'opening up' of central and southern Indian chronology by gradual pervasion from our starting-point at Arika-medu may here be carried one further stage. In front of us loomed the great problem of linking up the newly found chronology with that of the northern Indian plains, where lay the great cities of Indian epic and protohistory. The problem threatened difficulty of a special kind. The cultures of these north Indian cities have been fairly exten-sively 'sampled' in a very rough-and-ready fashion, and are found to differ in every respect from those of the south. Correlation was there-fore only feasible on a site where south and north had actually met and had existed for some time side by side.

Search revealed exactly such a site, potentially, at a point where the northern plains bend southwards along the broad coastal strip between the Bay of Bengal and the Eastern Ghats or inland hill-barrier. In Orissa, adjoining the old temple-city of Bhubaneśwar and not far from the sacred east-coast town of Puri, home of the notorious Juggernath, lay the embanked site of an ancient city, now known as Siśupalgarh, which fulfilled the necessary geographical conditions. Excavation in 1948 and 1949 showed that it also fulfilled the archae-ological requisites which we had postulated: for in stratified relation-ship with a distinctive and widespread northern ceramic lay sherds of our now-famous rouletted ware, identical with that which only three years previously we had found nearly 700 miles to the south-west in association with first-century Arretine. North and south were now for the first time firmly interlocked.

I need not pursue this matter further. Enough has been said to illustrate how three seasons of carefully planned, progressive work were able to draw a clear archaeological datum-line across many hundreds of miles of a sub-continent, and to open up spacious new vistas of cultural relationship. Generations of fumbling from site to opportunist site might easily have failed to approach this result – have indeed in the past failed to do so. The two necessary factors were present: Opportunity and Planning. To these might be added the factor of Luck, but I do not much believe in Luck. Hard thinking and steady execution are at least its honest and dependable substitutes. *Have a plan*, and *make* the opportunity, remembering with hope and at the same time with humility the dictum of Gibbon that 'the winds and the waves are always on the side of the ablest navigator'.

*

Lastly, a problem in which strategy merges closely into tactics may suitably be considered in this chapter since in fact matters of major policy are involved. From time to time the question arises: shall stress be laid (in some particular programme of work) upon horizontal or upon vertical excavation? By 'horizontal excavation' is meant the uncovering of the whole or a large part of a specific phase in the occupation of an ancient site, in order to reveal fully its layout and function (cf. Pl. 12). By 'vertical excavation' is meant the excavation of a restricted area *in depth*, with a view to ascertaining the succession of cultures or of phases and so producing a time-scale or culture-scale for the site. The two procedures are of course complementary, not antagonistic, and the excavator may be expected to attempt, if rarely to achieve, both methods of approach. But in a great majority of instances, a priority has to be determined, having regard to the state of current knowledge and the resources available.

Let us consider the nature of the evidence which the two methods may be expected to supply. Vertical excavation alone, whilst supplying a key to the length of an occupation, to its continuity or intermittency, and to some part of its cultural equipment, cannot be expected to reveal save in the most scrappy fashion the significant environment – economic, religious, administrative – of a human society. In other words, it leaves us in the dark as to those very factors which fit a past culture or civilization into the story of human endeavour and so make its recovery worth while. It is the railway time-table without a train. On the other hand, the extensive horizontal excavations which were in effect the normal practice before stratification was adequately understood generally produced an abstraction – often a very confused and misleading abstraction – unrelated with any sort of precision to the sequence of human development. They were trains without a time-table. The trains sometimes ran vigorously enough, but we knew not when they were running or where they started, or their intermediate stopping-places, or their destination.

At certain stages of research both these incomplete methods may have a substantive value; indeed, they are themselves stages in the progress of research. I am not, for example, of those who scorn the horizontal excavation (in the nineties) of the Roman town of Silchester. True it was dug like potatoes, without a shadow of the scientific nicety of the contemporary excavations in Cranborne Chase; and the resultant plan is the uncritical synthesis of a varying urban development through more than three centuries. But it gave at once, and with a rough accuracy, the general impression of a Romano-British town such as fifty years of subsequent and often more careful work have failed to equal. More exact vertical and horizontal digging on both this and other similar sites has indeed begun to reveal the sociological evolution essential to our historical perspective; but who amongst these later and wiser excavators has not constantly referred back with profit to the crude, primitive assemblage of Silchester?

So also elsewhere. The Glastonbury lake-village, excavated uncritically with results that are often infuriatingly baffling, has nevertheless given us the complete layout of a small Early Iron Age settlement and so enabled us to assess in broad terms the social and economic significance of such a settlement as no exacting and partial probing could have rendered possible. For that, even in moments when the evidence in detail completely fails us, we may be properly thankful. And let us for a moment look further afield. One of the most dramatic and revealing of all excavated cities is prehistoric Mohenjo-daro, beside the Indus in Pakistan. Technically the methods adopted by a succession of excavators there became almost an international scandal, and neither Professor Piggott nor I have been at pains to spare the lash. But the primary marvel of the great Indus city is not that it did (or did not) develop in such-and-such a fashion between, let us say, 2500 and 1500 B.C., *but that it existed at all* in the remarkable form that extensive, if disproportionately summary, excavation has revealed to us. Its house-walls, towering accumulatively above our heads, its long straight streets, its lanes, its elaborate drainage system, its citadel – these and other things in bulk re-create a whole phase of human society even though in detail they fail to analyse it for us. Analysis – by careful vertical digging – should, of course, have accompanied all this summary horizontal clearance; but there can be no question that Mohenjo-daro takes its place as the representative of one of the great civilizations of the ancient world in some measure by virtue of the crimes of its explorers.

And since we have arrived in Pakistan, let us take again one more familiar example from that land. For a thousand years the city of Taxila stood upon successive sites in the northern Punjab, and one of these sites, of the first centuries B.C.–A.D., was extensively cleared by Sir John Marshall so that a considerable portion of a remarkable rect-angular town-plan was ultimately revealed (Pl. 12). The clearance did not conform with modern technical standards, and in fact more than one phase is represented without discrimination in the published plan. Nevertheless, the outstanding interest of Parthian Taxila is the general character of its buildings and their relation to a street-grid without known analogy in this part of Asia. Had the excavator concentrated on vertical digging on this deep site he would have given us valuable information for which we are still waiting; but he could scarcely have given us also the picture which we owe to him of a teeming city with its streets and temples, its palaces and its shops. He would have given us a useful catalogue but not, as in fact he has, a vivid chapter of social history.

The four examples of horizontal digging which I have given – Silchester, Glastonbury, Mohenjo-daro, and Taxila (Sirkap) – are not very happy in that none of them was excavated with adequate skill. Technically, they all belong to the pre-Pitt-Rivers era, though Pitt Rivers had in fact established his methods before any of them began. Needless to say, it must not be inferred that horizontal excava-tion is necessarily summary and unscientific! Ideally, the excavation of a town-site would begin with vertical digging, sufficient to estab-lish the time- or culture-sequence, and would proceed to the careful horizontal digging of successive phases, one at a time. Obviously the process cannot be reversed, and at the three sites mentioned, only the careful vertical excavation of areas not yet touched can partially replace the squandered evidence. A better example of horizontal excavation on a small scale is provided by Little Woodbury near Salisbury, where Dr Gerhard Bersu cleared the greater part of an Iron Age farmstead and was able to reconstruct both its architecture and its economy. The site was a shallow one, and the technical problem was incomparably simpler than on a deeply accumulative town-site;

nevertheless, it is chastening to reflect how little of the real meaning of Little Woodbury could have been recovered merely by vertical samples of it.

With the proviso, then, that all horizontal digging must proceed from clear and comprehensive vertical sections, the question of priority is fundamentally not in doubt. Careful horizontal digging can alone, in the long run, give us the full information that we ideally want. Vertical digging will, by itself, serve a valuable purpose in establishing the geographical distribution of a culture and its time-relationship with other cultures from place to place; but this evidence still derives its ultimate significance from a knowledge of the social environment of the cultures concerned. Wise words are said by the authors of the Council for British Archaeology's *Survey and Policy of Field Research in the Archaeology of Great Britain* (1948) in their statement with reference to the Early Iron Age, that to have at least one site in each main region of the country excavated totally 'will now be of more value than merely to sample a number of sites in the same time instead'. But they are equally wise when, on the following page, they also advise that hill-forts be submitted to 'selective excavations to ascertain the date, character, and sequence (if any) of the defences, and whether or no the fort was permanently inhabited. This method . . . should be continued regionally.' It is all a matter of bias, and bias depends upon our knowledge at the moment of the problem of the moment. There is no essential conflict, but the question of priority is worth careful thought in archaeological planning.

Once more, the moral is that the exercise of tactical skill without a controlling strategy is opportunism run riot. Or, to change the metaphor, the excavator without an intelligent policy may be described as an archaeological food-gatherer, master of a skill, perhaps, but not creative in the wider terms of constructive science.

CHAPTER 11

Staff

THE time has come to consider the staff and machinery with which all the various operations described in the preceding chapters are carried out. First, the personnel.

The staff of an archaeological excavation on any considerable scale includes a director, a deputy director, a supervisor for each area under excavation, a trained foreman, a small-find recorder, a pottery-assistant, a photographer, a surveyor, a chemist, a draftsman, and, according to need, an epigraphist or numismatist. In rare cases, certain of these posts may be combined, but it is preferable, and often necessary, to subdivide them. Where distances are short, as in Great Britain, it may be possible to dispense with the chemist and the draftsman in the field, but it is inadvisable to do so. Only an ignorant critic could protest that the list is excessive. Nevertheless, large and relatively costly expeditions in the past have failed of their duty through false economy or lack of prevision in this all-important matter of staff.

To the official and essential nucleus, a valuable addition is student-labour. I have never undertaken an excavation, whether in Britain or overseas, without the assistance of university students, and I suppose that in England, Wales, France, and India 500 students or more have at one time or another worked with me in this fashion. My debt to them has been immense. They impose a constant need for clear exposition and therefore for clear thinking. They ask simple, awkward questions, which have to be answered convincingly or with a frank and wholesome admission of ignorance. You can't fool them. They are the friendliest and most stimulating of critics, and the best of them rapidly become the most co-operative of colleagues. My habit is to work them in pairs, a senior with a junior, and to give the senior considerable, if controlled, responsibility – indeed my site-supervisors are nearly always senior students. A note on their training will be given below (p. 162). The whole problem is almost exactly that of a commanding officer with a bevy of young subalterns.

I append a few observations on each of the posts which I have named.

It would be easy to be trite in describing the qualities of the director. It goes without saying that he must have the combined virtues of the scholar and the man of action. 'Scholarship is by no means all that is wanted,' affirms Petrie; 'the engineering training of mind and sense . . . will really fit an archaeologist better for excavating than book-work can alone.' I shall say more about this matter of scholarship in a moment or two. Meanwhile, it is scarcely necessary to observe that the director cannot be an expert in every branch of his work, any more than a general is an expert in every tank or gun under his command. But, just as a general must be exactly familiar with the performance – the range, fire-power, mobility, and so forth – of every arm available to him or his enemy, so must the director of an archaeological excavation be acquainted with the exact potentiality of the various techniques appropriate to his craft and the nature of the problems which are likely to oppose him. He may himself, for example, be an indifferent photographer, but he must know accurately the capacity of his cameras, lenses, and filters, and must thoroughly understand the preparation of a photographic subject; at all points he must be able to direct or check his expert. I have been blessed with a series of exceptionally competent photographers, but scarcely ever have I had an archaeological photograph taken without carefully checking the subject through the lens before exposure, for lighting, position of scale, angle, and background. Experience of this procedure (and of the converse) has convinced me of its necessity. The director, and he alone, is responsible for the record of his work; he knows, or should know, better than anyone else exactly what his record should express; and he can achieve the best possible record only through a full knowledge of the capacity of the mechanism which he is using.

So throughout the complex operation of modern field-work. The director sets the standard of achievement and must know enough to impose his standards without question on his experts.

But he is, of course, more than a gauge of technical values. He is a leader, and it is a truism that leadership is based not merely upon knowledge but also upon imagination. It is not enough to confront the situation when it is presented; the leader may be expected in some considerable measure to create and define the situation, to be something of a strategist as well as a tactician. The present book deals mainly with the tactics of archaeology, with technical devices and local problems, but the ultimate quality of the field-archaeologist is the wide comprehension of the inter-relationship of major problems; in other words, a disciplined imagination. An outstanding example of this quality is easy to recognize in the work of Sir Arthur Evans, the discoverer of Belgic Britain and Minoan Crete. It is a quality which exalts field-archaeology from a technical science into an art.

Above all, the director must cultivate a scrupulous accuracy and completeness in the observation and record of his factual evidence. Accuracy is a fundamental quality of scholarship, and there is a scholarship of field-archaeology as there is of other scientific disciplines. Let us pause for a moment and consider this matter of scholarship a little further. Excavation has been described by a superior person as 'dirt archaeology', with the implication that it bears something of the same relation to 'scholarship' as landscape-gardening does to botany. But what is 'scholarship'? It might perhaps be defined in the broadest terms as 'accurate and comprehensive knowledge adequately expressed'. Admittedly, other and narrower definitions have found favour. The *Oxford English Dictionary* declares that it is 'learning, erudition; esp. proficiency in the Greek and Latin languages and their literature'; blandly adding that formerly the scholar was often 'one who had studied at the university, and who, not having obtained any fixed employment, sought to gain a living by literary work'. Even that nice definition fails to reach the precision of J. M. Barrie's Fleet Street professor who, in his examination of budding journalists, included the question: '*Pabulum, Cela va sans dire, Par excellence, Ne plus ultra.* What are these? Are there any more of them?' – the correct answer being, 'They are scholarship, and there are two more, namely *Tour de force* and *Terra firma*'.[1] Presumably the author of the phrase 'dirt archaeology' would equally describe Darwin's study of earthworms as 'dirt biology'. Anyway, we need

1. *When a Man's Single*, chap. ix.

not bother our heads any more either about the superior person or about the *Oxford English Dictionary*. 'Scholarship' as a monopoly of classical erudition has in fact been dead since the 1850s when Neanderthal Man, the Boucher-Prestwich hand-axes, and the Origin of Species almost simultaneously smote it hip and thigh.

In the liberal and only valid interpretation of 'scholarship', field-archaeology and excavation, no less than textual criticism, may be a proper qualification of the scholar. Pitt Rivers was a scholar. But excavation is by itself, of course, no more scholarship than is the ability to construe the *Aeneid*. Pitt Rivers was a scholar not merely because he dug well, but above all because his powerful imagination enabled him to visualize and create new standards of scientific accuracy. His super-accuracy was the cardinal quality of his scholarship. It was not simply that he was methodically and pedantically accurate; added to method was a comprehension of the causative relations of things which gave structure and corporeality to his observations and records – 'comprehensive knowledge adequately expressed', as I have understated it. And that comprehension of causative relations is a vital quality in scholarly field-work. It is a quality which cannot be initiated but can be immensely developed by training. It is in fact a necessary part of a modern archaeological education. The evolutionary development of flint implements, of pottery-types, of script, of pictorial or sculptural renderings, is taught to-day to the young archaeologist as a matter of course. But let the budding director himself take up such a study in detail on an objective basis, let him explore for himself the possibilities and pitfalls in the varying categories of evidence bearing upon some selected group of material – let him discipline his mind for some months in an exact appreciation of evidential values and inter-relationships, and he will acquire a part of the grammar of his subject, without which he can never achieve full literacy. It matters not at all that his subsequent studies may take him to Asia or Africa. A detailed study of Bronze Age wares in Wiltshire will prepare him for a detailed study of the chalcolithic wares of Persia. After all, Pitt Rivers chose fire-arms. The procedure is in all essentials identical, and the switch from the one to the other is merely the redirection of trained eyes.

And while we are discussing some of the component elements of the director, let us not omit an understanding of *structural* relationship, which is another aspect of the causative relationship of which I have been speaking. The properly equipped director is one who has had, amongst much else, some specific architectural training. His understanding of the Palace of Minos or the Ziggurat of Ur will be none the worse if he has learned the sort of things that C. F. Mitchell has long taught in his *Building Construction* (12th edition, 1945). Sooner or later, the excavator of neolithic and later cultures will be confronted by structural evidence in stone, brick, or timber, and this evidence may mean little or nothing unless viewed with an understanding of the significance of structural factors. But, in a wider context, the structural sense is one which is invaluable also in the understanding of the inter-relationship of soil-strata. It is a source of constant astonishment to me to find how lacking is the average mind in the understanding of what is and what is not *structurally possible* in the analysis of a section. On all grounds I have no hesitation in urging a systematic course of architectural training (lasting, say, six months) upon anyone who proposes to devote himself to field-archaeology.

There is indeed no limit to the desiderata with which one might saddle the embarrassed director. But before attempting to impose an impossible burden upon him, we may distinguish fairly clearly between two kinds of qualifications; those which can be delegated and those which cannot. Amongst the former are, as I have already suggested, photography and draftsmanship. One of the best archaeological excavators known to me – unsurpassed as a painstaking and accurate analyst of stratigraphy – is devoid of any sort of skill as a draftsman. The chemical, physical, or botanical analysis of soils is manifestly the task of a separate specialist with laboratory equipment. The extent to which the director should be a linguist is more debatable. Technically, the methods of excavation are identical whether a literate or an illiterate culture be in question. Petrie's view was that 'the ancient language of a country, all important as it is in the study of remains, is yet in its critical aspects not so essential during field-work. But the excavator should at least be able to take the sense of all written material which he finds.' That is a fair enough statement. Nevertheless, every expedition concerned with a literate antiquity should have on its staff or within a few hours' reach a fully qualified epigraphist who can gauge instantly and in some detail the potential value of a tablet or a seal or a coin. The necessary linguistic and epigraphical studies are generally such as monopolize the time and capacity of the specialist, and they can rarely be combined with the wider functions and qualifications of the director. With Petrie's reservation, therefore, linguistic proficiency may be regarded as susceptible to delegation.

But the qualities which *cannot* be delegated are the instant understanding of structural and stratigraphical problems, the quick and accurate correlation of the various groups of evidence as they appear, the reasoned appreciation (sometimes miscalled 'intuition') of the immediate needs of the work as it proceeds from day to day, the capacity for undelayed but well-founded decision, and the ability to ensure even progress in all the various departments and sub-departments of the enterprise. To these qualities must be added a clear anticipation of the needs of the ultimate report, and the capacity to present that report in a clear, concise, and intelligible form. In other words, and in brief, a precise and trained mind and an informed and informing imagination are the qualities of the director of an archaeological expedition. And having said that, I am aware that I have carried the reader scarcely at all along the upward path. There are, however, a few practices which I have found of use in an attempted approximation to those qualities in the field, and I note them for what they may be worth.

First and foremost, the director must be a free agent, free from administrative detail. His primary and constant duty is to circulate from site to site and from workshop to workshop. Every section, in its latest manifestation, must be clearly in his mind's eye, and he must be familiar with every development in the hour-to-hour work of his team. If plans or sections are being made, he must himself ensure their adequacy; if his draftsman is drawing pottery, samples must be tested. His surveyor must be overlooked critically, his photographer utilized and supervised. Above all, he must familiarize himself with the groups of pottery as they lie on the tray beside the work or as they come from the wash, and he must occasionally check the marking of them. The indexes of small finds must be inspected daily. At some moment or moments during the day, he must examine the field notebooks of his supervisors. And he must keep his colleagues and employees constantly, in varying degrees, 'in the picture', and ensure that they are, each of them, aware of the importance of their individual contributions to the progress of the work.

This last point is essential to the maintenance of morale and efficiency. It ensures the fullest and most intelligent co-operation of every member of the team. Once more I turn to soldiering for an analogy. One of the great qualities of a certain celebrated commander was his habit of taking almost every one of his soldiers, from general to private, into his confidence before a battle. Almost every British fighting-man at El 'Alamein was a partner to his general's plan and could collaborate intelligently therefore in victory. As often, military and archaeological field-work march alike in this. Tell your unit, before you start digging, exactly what problem you are out to solve, how you intend to tackle it, and, when possible, the sort of time-table which will probably be required. This last is particularly desirable with a relatively inexperienced staff. I recall, for instance, how at Arikamedu, in south India, where we sought and found for the first time extensive evidence of a Roman culture in significant contact with a hitherto unknown Indian culture, I explained beforehand in detail the nature of our problem and our methods, and ended with the warning that significant results need not be expected for a fortnight. In fact, the excavation opened badly; the site had been much disturbed, and for nine days nothing of importance was found. Then, on the tenth day, one of my Indian students emerged excitedly from the muddy depths of a cutting at sea-level with the stamped base of an Arretine dish in his hand. Thereafter the results were overwhelmingly satisfactory, but in those first days with an untrained staff and students and the mercurial south Indian temperament to contend with, we had been saved from something approaching disaster by the timely warning.

This is not to say that all can be foreseen and that there is no place for opportunism in digging. But the whole framework of the problem must be very carefully constructed before the work begins, and the use of opportunity is limited by that framework, which must itself be comprehensive enough to admit it. Here, however, I am again encroaching upon the general problem of archaeological strategy (Chapter 10).

And all the time that the director is attending unrestingly to those various and vital details, the growing accumulation of evidences and inferences is working upon his mind, creating new ideas, suggesting working theories or probabilities for trial, confirming or bending his plan. He alone can (and must) know *all* the latest evidences as they emerge and can fit them into a logical pattern. Nor should he defer this operation until he reaches the remote sanctuary of his study. Inferences of a general or far-reaching kind will constantly refer back anew to detailed observation in the field, requiring fresh trial and appreciation of the material evidence. The more thinking that the director can do in the actual presence of that evidence, the better, and it goes without saying that the factual interpretation must be absolute and final in that presence. Says Petrie:

At the moment that a fact is before the eye – a fact which may never be seen again, and perhaps never paralleled – it is needful for the observer to make certain of all the details, to verify every point which is of fresh value, and to record all that is new with certainty and exactitude. ... Everything seen should be mentally grasped, and its meaning and bearings comprehended at the moment of discovery, so clearly that a definitive statement can be made, which shall be as certain and as absolute as anything can be which depends on human sense.

There is but little place here for the *esprit d'escalier*, and the director must be sufficiently liberated by his staff from routine cares to keep his wits actively and unceasingly about him. A director who knew this and always carefully chose his staff was more than once accused of taking credit for the work of others. The accusation was, of course, correct; he knew his job and chose a staff capable of doing much of his work for him. Perhaps, after all, the greatest qualification in a director is the capacity to select and train a competent staff. Let us turn now to that staff and consider some of its requisites.

THE DEPUTY DIRECTOR

Whilst the director is the operational leader of the expedition, the deputy director is primarily in charge of the administration. He (or she) deals with the well-being and pay of the various grades of staff, and is personally responsible for the smooth working of the machine. He should also be a trained field-archaeologist, in close touch with the director and able in emergency to represent him, but is not officially responsible for the scientific aspects of the work. If he is a specialist in some relevant branch of archaeology, so much the better.

The following are amongst his duties:

(*a*) *Billeting or housing.* This problem, of course, varies widely with local conditions. It ranges from the strenuous task of securing lodgings in a provincial English town to the relatively easy one of building a village of grass-huts in Bengal. Whatever its precise nature, it must be tackled well before the actual work of the expedition is timed to begin. Special attention must be paid to the administrative office, the drawing-office, the photographic dark-room, and the pottery-shed. In certain expeditions to the Near East between the wars, an unnecessary degree of luxury was sometimes sought at disproportionate cost in the living-quarters of the party. On the other hand, the notoriously Spartan conditions under which the Petries used to run their camps reached the opposite extreme. Unnecessary discomfort amongst any considerable body of people for any considerable time can only lower efficiency and is itself a sufficient symptom of inefficiency.

(*b*) *Equipment.* The director is immediately concerned in the choice of equipment, but its preparedness and maintenance are largely the duty of his deputy. The theodolite or its equivalent must be checked, the surveying-poles must be kept freshly painted (a shabby surveying-pole is sometimes hard to see, and is another emblem of inefficiency), there must be an adequate supply of bubble-levels and well-conditioned measuring tapes, there must be good string, pegs, labels, cloth or strong paper bags, notebooks with water-proofed covers, drawing-boards and paper, and so forth. All these are the proper charge of the deputy director, and are a constant drain on his attention.

(*c*) *Accounts.* The ungrateful task of keeping the running accounts of the expedition falls to the deputy. This is no light matter, but a deputy who cannot carry it is an unjustifiable addition to the personnel. Above all, he must deal accurately and promptly with the weekly wages bill, including the tiresome complication of *baksheesh* for special finds where the hateful bonus-system is in vogue. Any sort of error in the payment of wages and *baksheesh* reacts instantly and unfavourably on the relations between master and men.

(*d*) *Supplies.* The organization of food-supplies is the duty of the deputy, with or without the assistance of a 'housekeeper'.

(e) *Hospital.* The first-aid box and, if necessary, a supply of other simple remedies are maintained by the deputy, and a daily 'hospital hour' is normally necessary in the more remote parts of the world. A knowledge of first aid is thus added to the deputy's qualifications, together with a sympathetic firmness in its application.

SITE-SUPERVISORS

I have generally chosen these from amongst my senior students, that is, students with one or more seasons' training behind them. They are in charge of an area sufficiently compact to enable them to keep in immediate contact with all work done in that area throughout the day. Scarcely a shovelful of earth is removed save under their eyes. They are personally responsible for the small 'control-pits', each normally some 2 or 3 feet square, which are cut ahead of the main work to provide a preview of the strata (p. 84). They write up the area notebook, keep sketch-plans and sections, and record special small-finds. They insure that each stratum has its separate small-find box or basket, with tie-on labels and supplementary loose label (p. 188). Their equipment is contained in a portable 'desk' or box, for which they are individually accountable. So far as possible, they have the same workmen from day to day, get to know them individually, and allot them tasks suitable to their various capacities. They are, in fact, platoon-commanders, and on their efficiency depends ultimately the technical adequacy of the excavation. Wherever feasible, they are each assisted by a junior student whom they help to train.

FOREMAN

The foreman is the sergeant-major. He has proved himself as a digger and should be the best workman on the site. He may assist in the uncovering of especially fragile or important objects. But he must, above all things, be by nature capable of controlling his men with firmness and scrupulous fairness. On arrival in the morning and (in the East) after the midday break he calls the roll, and he marshals the men on pay-day. He should know his workmen individually from a somewhat different angle from that of the site-supervisor, and should show patience and assiduity in their training. At the end of each week, he is responsible for providing the deputy director with all information required for the pay-sheet. The best foremen are also enthusiasts. In England, William Wedlake my foreman and colleague at Maiden Castle and in France, Thomas Hepple, who assisted Mr J. P. Gibson and Mr Gerald Simpson on Hadrian's Wall, and W. E. V. Young, Mr Keiller's foreman at Avebury, are three outstanding examples of the foreman-archaeologist and friend. In India, I had one such, a Punjab peasant, whose mind was constantly on his work whether he was on duty or off, and who used to come and discuss the problems of the site with me in the evening. One or more of Sir Leonard Woolley's Iraqi foremen, I believe, used to travel voluntarily some hundreds of miles every year across the desert in order to rejoin his old chief's staff during subsequent work near Antioch. Such friendships are amongst the highest reward that a director can desire. They bridge the class-room and help to link inferred fact with basic earthy knowledge.

THE SMALL-FIND RECORDER

The recording of a 'find' begins at the moment of discovery. Unless it requires special treatment or attention the object is placed immediately in an adjacent box or tray or basket to which is tied a label bearing the code-name of the site, the number of the square or other sub-unit, and the number of the stratum. The last I always place within a circle, to distinguish it unmistakably from all other numbers. A duplicate label, loose, is placed in the bottom of the receptacle. (See Chapter 13, pp. 185 ff.)

At a suitable moment, at the end of the day's work or earlier, the receptacle is transferred to the small-finds shed, where its contents are cleaned, so far as is suitable at this stage, and marked by the small-finds recorder, either with Indian ink or white paint on the objects themselves or on labels tied firmly to them. Sooner or later, it is useful to cover the mark neatly with shellac as a protection.

The recorder's next act is to card-index all individual objects of any possible significance. I always maintain two card indexes, one by categories, the other by sites. See p. 190.

Such objects as require first-aid are then handed over to the field-laboratory for treatment (p. 195). Most of them, however, can be immediately packed for transportation to base, either in boxes or in bags of paper or cloth (pp. 188-9).

A high responsibility rests upon the shoulders of the recorder. He is personally responsible that every object is clearly and correctly marked on as inconspicuous a surface as possible; no object should be spoilt for subsequent photography or display by an unsightly code-symbol. He is also responsible for storing the boxed or bagged finds in such a fashion that they are quickly accessible if required for reference in the field – a very important desideratum, sometimes overlooked. The finds-shed must, in other words, be in impeccable order. Muddle means inaccuracy, delay, incompetence, and the destruction of evidence laboriously garnered. At a small excavation the problem is proportionately simple, but at a large one the recorder will require a staff, which must be subjected by him to the closest supervision and discipline. Every addition to the staff multiplies manifold the risks of inadequate or even incorrect recording, and the recorder must remember that on his unceasing vigilance depends much of the scientific value of his expedition's work. He is a pillar of the enterprise.

THE POTTERY-ASSISTANT

The duties of the pottery-assistant equate with those of the small-finds recorder, and on a small excavation the two posts may be combined. But at most excavations, particularly in the East, where pottery is liable to occur in embarrassing quantities and is usually of the highest possible evidential value, it is essential to have a trained assistant exclusively in charge of this department. And a very exacting task is his. His preliminary qualifications must include an extensive knowledge of previously recorded discovery, so that he can instantly spot analogies amongst his new material and can bring them at once to the notice of the director. He must also have a sound general knowledge of ceramic techniques, so that, for example, he can protect from the omnivorous pottery-washers such wares (e.g. wares painted after baking) as require special treatment. He must be a strict disciplinarian, and possess a clear and orderly mind. And he must have a simple, effective routine for the marshalling of the fairly considerable working staff which, on any large-scale excavation, must be allotted to him. No hampering economy should ever be imposed upon him; if the expedition cannot afford an adequate pottery-department, it should close down at once. The hackneyed assertion is a true one: pottery is the alphabet of archaeology. Its plasticity lends it a special facility in the imitation of other fabrics such as metal-work, leather, basket-work, or other pottery. For example, Roman *terra sigillata* imitates metal-work or glass-work, some Bronze Age beakers imitate woven grass, some neolithic pottery in Western Europe imitates leather-work, some pottery both in Europe and in India imitates Roman *terra sigillata*; and so on. Pottery is thus liable to preserve the influences of other wares and materials and to represent cultural or industrial interactions of various and often vital kinds which would otherwise be lost to us. Its fragility limits its normal durability and, unlike metal-work, which may last for generations or centuries and is also more liable to be treasured for intrinsic value, the date of its destruction (at any rate in mass) can be approximated to its date of manufacture. That same fragility tends to restrict the diffusion at least of the commoner wares to a measurable vicinity of their kilns; although it is salutary to recall that Graeco-Roman amphorae, owing to the popularity of the wines which they contained, found their way in numbers to the shores of the Bay of Bengal, that Roman glass reached India and China where local glass was almost unknown, that Roman Arretine ware found a sale in south India by reason of its superiority over local products, and that Chinese celadon ware penetrated far and wide over Asia and Africa in the ninth and following centuries A.D. partly because of its quality and partly because of the forceful salesmanship of Chinese merchants. But whether because most pottery is fairly local or because some of it is astonishingly and significantly exotic, it is of the first importance to the archaeologist, and the immediate and faultless record of field-evidence relating to it is a primary care of the director and his administration.

The pottery-assistant is therefore a very important person. His methods will vary with his own ideas and circumstances. In Chapter 13 are discussed procedures suitable on the one hand to a temperate (often intemperate) climate and on the other hand to the more predictable tropical or sub-tropical climates where most of his work can be happily done out of doors.

THE PHOTOGRAPHER

The essential qualifications of the field-photographer are (a) that he shall be technically dependable in all lights and colour-schemes, and (b) that he shall be quick and ingenious in the improvisation of scaffolding for his camera and, in particular, of a readily accessible darkroom; he must at all times be in a position to produce the developed plate or film for inspection by the director within 20 minutes of exposure. To these qualities he must add a thorough understanding of the preparation of a subject, whether in the open air or in the studio, although this is ultimately the personal responsibility of the director. Further notes on these matters will be found in the chapter on photography (p. 200).

An intelligent and experienced photographer is a *sine qua non*. From the beginning of the excavation, it is his spare-time job to make a study of the site at different times of the day, and so to be prepared to advise in regard to lighting and position. Here again, the director is primarily responsible, but a good and observant photographer can help him a great deal. Like a doctor, the photographer must be available and prepared at a moment's notice and at all times. On an excavation of any magnitude his duties cannot be combined with those of any other member of the staff.

THE SURVEYOR

The preparation of a measured drawing of a section is the duty of the supervisor, under the eye of the director. The supervisor and the director know more about the stratification and meaning of the sections than anyone else, and the task cannot be delegated.

On the other hand, the preparation of a contoured survey or the plan of a building, though, like everything else, demanding constant supervision, must on a large excavation be delegated primarily to a professional surveyor. I do not propose to include here a detailed excursus on the craft of surveying: many handbooks are available.[1] But there are one or two observations which may usefully be made

1. e.g. T. Baker and G. M. Leston, *Land and Engineering Surveying* (29th ed., London, 1945); R. Parry and W. R. Jenkins, *Land Surveying* (5th ed., London, 1946); R. J. C. Atkinson, *Field Archaeology* (London, 1946); A. H. Detweiler, *Manual of Archaeological Surveying* (New Haven, 1948).

in regard to the application of professional survey-methods to archaeology.

First let us consider the nature of the tasks which are likely to await the archaeological surveyor. These are: (a) the preparation of a site-plan, generally contoured and often of considerable extent; and (b) the planning of a structure or group of structures on a small scale or in detail. For (a), either a plane-table or a theodolite may be used; (b) is normally carried out by triangulation from a base-line. In both categories, it is important to remember the degree of accuracy required. Here I tread upon delicate ground. Throughout this book I have stressed the vital need for accuracy, and I would countenance no withdrawal from the position. But there is a kind of accuracy which frustrates itself by its disproportion to needs or possibilities, or may even result, paradoxically, in an essential inaccuracy. In my experience, professional surveyors are liable to lose the conformation of the wood in the planning of the trees; to lavish so much care upon the slight irregularities (many of them often secondary and accidental) of an ancient wall as to misrepresent its essential character and original intention. I have already remarked upon a similar 'over-accuracy' on the part of the inexperienced in the rendering of a section (p. 74). In all cases, the degree of 'accuracy' must be commensurate with the scale to which the plan is to be published. A plan drawn to the scale of $\frac{1}{8}$ inch to 1 foot will commonly be published to the scale of $\frac{1}{24}$ inch to 1 foot, and on that scale small excrescences of flint work, or small variations due perhaps to subsidence or other deformation, will cease to signify. Omit them therefore; but do so only after careful consideration. In a measured section it would be utterly useless pedantry to measure every small pebble in a gravel layer, and the same need for proportion and common sense is present in the ground-survey. Do not be more 'accurate' than your scale permits; do not overload your machine. We all know the dangerous pedantry of the ultra-careful motorist who, in season and out, laboriously obeys every rule of the Highway Code. We have seen how aggrieved railwaymen or meat-porters can hold up a community by a deliberate adherence to the rules of their trade. With less deliberation, perhaps, but with equal pedantry, the professional surveyor can not only hold up an excavation but can imperil the real accuracy of its records. Watch your surveyor, and train him in the difficult but necessary art of distinguishing essentials without invalidating the impersonality of his record. It can be done.

For archaeological purposes, therefore, I prefer a somewhat simpler instrument than the regulation theodolite. An artillery 'director', designed for quick but essentially accurate survey, meets much of the need and is a far handier machine, and many instrument-makers have equivalent instruments on the market.

Similarly, the use of innumerable 'checks' and diagonals from a base-line to a wall-system, with an accumulation of small errors, is often better replaced by the careful survey of two terminal points on which the plan is swung from a quick series of local measurements. Thereby, the correct local interrelationship of the walls of a building – in other words, its essential character – is often more accurately and speedily recorded than by more elaborate professional methods.

Having said this, I must end by warning the student against the opposite extreme. A very eminent archaeologist of my acquaintance used to set out on a surveying-expedition with two pea-sticks and a visiting card, the former for 'line', the latter (sighted along the edges) for 'angle'. I saw some of his results, and marvelled that they were not more inaccurate than they actually were. But then he was a genius.

THE FIELD-CHEMIST

A small field-laboratory and an experienced and resourceful chemist are essential save in the rare instances where a static laboratory is within easy reach. The work of conservation in the field is limited as a rule to first-aid, and it is highly important for subsequent treatment that the field-chemist shall keep a careful and detailed record of all action taken by him. This record must accompany each object to the base-laboratory, since subsequent action may be conditioned by it. For example, not long ago a work of sculpture arrived in Brussels, seemingly in perfect condition; but shortly afterwards it burst into pieces – the excavator had imprisoned salts within it by impregnating the surface with celluloid and had omitted to inform the recipients.

It is particularly important that the field-chemist shall be able to treat coins in any metal with a minimum of delay, since their evidence will be required at once by the director. For the rest, the chemist's main functions are (a) to prevent further decay, and (b) to consolidate friable objects sufficiently for removal and transportation. These functions will be amplified in Chapter 14 (p. 195).

THE DRAFTSMAN

The work of the draftsman is various, involving a range of qualities rarely possessed by one and the same individual. In practice I have generally found it necessary to employ three draftsmen, although I have known one or two exceptional men who have covered the whole ground.

Whether one or three, it is essential that the draftsman shall thoroughly understand the technique of line-block reproduction (p. 226), and shall so be able to attune his style to the machine: to employ lines of the right thickness and firmness, having regard to the extent of reduction required in publication, and to avoid too close a proximity of one line to another, such as may lead to a fusion of the thin metal strips that will ultimately represent those lines on the blocks. Clean lines and clean hatching, without an unnecessary coarseness of detail, entail a sureness of hand and eye that, combined with experience, are a primary qualification in all types of scientific draftsmanship.

On that common basis, the work falls roughly into three categories: the tracing and lettering of maps and plans, the drawing of objects and the semi-schematic drawing of pottery. In all these things, the critical eye of the director is a present need. As always, the director must be able to impose his judgement with an acceptable authority upon his draftsman. At the same time, the draftsman's initiative must be encouraged; his advice, comments, criticism are, or should be, always worth listening to, and I have often profited from them. Not only in matters of scientific interpretation, but in the attractive presentation of his material, the draftsman can help the archaeologist to 'get over' to his public – his scientific no less than his non-specialist public. Few scientists are so devoid of humanity that they will not look more eagerly and attentively at an attractive diagram than at unrelieved geometry. The placing of a plan upon the page, its relationship to its lettering, scale, north-point and key, the character and placing of its border, the rendering of a bead or bracelet in clear line from an expressive angle, are all factors worthy of consideration. These aesthetic attributes do not imply any special measure of elaboration;

indeed simplicity of expression is as important in illustration as in text. Occasionally, scientific illustration has been excessively elaborate. Good taste is the yardstick, but good taste is a very positive quality, partly a matter of instinct and partly of deliberation. Let the director and his draftsman deliberate frequently together, profiting from their combined good sense and such instinct as may have been vouchsafed them.

The difference between a well-presented and an ill-considered plan is indeed immense. I have referred to the placing of the border: let it be so placed that no space is unnecessarily wasted, but in such a fashion as to enable the actual plan to be balanced with the lettering and pleasing to the eye. Whether the observer fully realize it or not, waste space is distracting and disturbing. Equally, of course, overcrowding must be avoided, but this is a less frequent crime. Above all, let every word and figure in the plan be easily legible after reduction by the block-maker. Far better let them be too large than too small; nothing can be more frustrating and infuriating than an indifferently legible scale – a common failing. And let the draftsman avoid all unnecessary underlines and frills – a vice to which engineering draftsmen have been particularly prone. How far he should let himself go in the matter of additional and scientifically unnecessary decoration is, be it repeated, a matter of taste. The old map-makers who adorned the seven seas with whales and ships and wrote their titles upon scrolls sustained by cherubs, or Stukeley who added appropriately romantic ruins, produced works of art which often disguised a deficiency of scientific information. In recent times, Mr Heywood Sumner has enriched his plans and maps with a *décor* that is often a pleasure to the eye but is sometimes overdone.[1] Again, the Royal Commission on Historical Monuments (England), in its *Westmorland* and other recent volumes, has made a brave attempt to relieve the monotony of small plans of hut-circles and the like by the addition of large and highly ornate titles, which are well meant but not always relevant. On the other hand, a north-point is fair game for the decorator within moderation, and has a well-established tradition of ornament behind it. Generally, when in doubt simplicity is best.

[1] For example, in his *Descriptive Account of Roman Pottery Sites at Sloden*, etc. (London, 1921), his general map has a heavily over-weighted and unnecessary border, but his other plans and diagrams are, in my judgement, perfect.

The *expression* of an object such as a brooch by the draftsman involves a somewhat more developed artistry. *Per contra*, I have known draftsmen who could achieve this but who were quite unable to rule the clean lines of a plan or to produce clear and attractive lettering. Here we need an artist in the more orthodox and creative sense of the term, and he is often one who scorns the more mechanical technique of the architect's draftsman. The artist, however, is inclined to impose his own personality upon the motifs of another age, and the objective accuracy of his rendering is sometimes questionable. He needs watching. The choice of the expressive angle, the extent to which his picture calls for a diagrammatic element or supplement, are matters for the director's consideration, and the director must, by training and experience, know his part.

Mention may be added of a draftsman's trick which I have on occasion found extremely useful – the tracing of fragile objects on to glass before their removal from the soil. Iron objects in particular are sometimes found in so friable a condition that they have to be waxed or plastered (p. 197) before they can be lifted. When that need arises, an immediate record is essential, and the simplest method is to place a sheet of glass (e.g. an old photographic plate which has been cleaned and sponged with a lump of cotton-wool dipped in alcohol) over the object and to trace the latter in Indian ink on to the glass. Negative contact prints can then be made from the inked glass, and in due course further positive tracings made from them, whilst the glass can be again cleaned and re-used. The method is both speedy and accurate.

Lastly, there is the very important question of pottery-drawing. This is in some aspects the easiest task of the three, but likewise involves careful training. Accuracy is all-important, and can be aided by a variety of devices – notably, graduated horizontal and vertical rules with a graduated arm that can be slid up and down the vertical rule. The pot is placed upon the fixed horizontal rule against the fixed vertical rule; the adjustable vertical rule is moved up to it, and the adjustable horizontal rule is moved down to the top of it. The pot is thus framed in a rectangle graduated on all sides in inches or centimetres, and offsets can be taken from them to the pot at appropriate intervals.

A sherd cannot, of course, be so treated. It must be wedged with plasticine at the correct angle and measured from a vertical scale.

Great care is necessary to ensure the correctness of the angle, by planting the rim (if such it be) firmly upside-down upon the board, or by testing the horizontality of the wheel-marks on a wheel-turned sherd. The diameter of a fragmentary rim is ascertained by matching the rim against a chart of concentric circles prepared for the purpose.

The standard practice now is to render half the pot in section and half in elevation. *All pots should be drawn life-size* unless excessively large; the usage sometimes adopted of drawing them half-size saves paper but increases inaccuracy. Normally, no pot should be illustrated in a published report at less than one-quarter actual size (linear), and a decorated pot (e.g. ornamented *terra sigillata*) should be reproduced half-size. Very large pots, and these only, should be reduced to less than one-quarter by the block-maker.

It is sometimes desirable, especially in hand-made pottery, to indicate the texture of the ware by hatching the 'elevation' side of the drawing. This involves artistry of the kind indicated in our second category of draftsmanship, and must be well done. Above all, both in the outline and in the hatching of the drawing, care must be taken to avoid giving an excessively mechanical aspect to a hand-made pot. Lines such as those of base and rim should generally, in such pottery, be drawn freehand, not ruled.

One more point: make sure that the draftsman appends to each of his drawings of pottery and other 'finds' a transcription of the appropriate label.

LABOURERS

Digging is a skilled craft, and many years ago I began a note on this subject with the words 'Abjure voluntary labour'. To-day, in 1955, voluntary labour is Hobson's choice. The old-fashioned British labourer survives only in a few odd corners of the land; indeed, so rare is he that one is sometimes inclined to class him with the mythical Mrs Harris. A note, therefore, which before the war might have run to some length may now be compressed into a few paragraphs, most of which are applicable to labour in general and are not confined merely to the (former) home-product.

Let me say at once that my experience as an employer in Great Britain is based on England and Wales; as an archaeologist, to my great loss, I have never attempted, like the Roman legion, to 'curb the fierce Scot'. On the Continent, I have employed Bretons and Normans, and in India a great variety of races, ranging from the tall, regal Punjabi Musulman to the tiny, volatile Madrasi. With Arabs I have never worked, although I have often enough watched them with a critical eye upon archaeological excavations. They do not appear to be a very different problem from the north Indian Muslims. In fact, I would hazard a guess that, from Carnarvon to Calcutta, the basic factors of labour-control or, in the quaint terminology of the army, 'Man-management' are very much the same. Impartial dealing, a readiness to share discomfort, provision of such comfort as may be feasible without ostentation, and above all an occasional gleam of elementary humour (*never* sarcasm), summarize the qualities required everywhere of the director by his workmen. Something more will be said about these qualities, but first let us consider the technical accomplishments required of the workmen themselves.

The local tools used by the labourer will differ considerably from place to place, and a separate section will be devoted to them (p. 178). But it stands to reason that the workman shall thoroughly understand their usage, and that his mind and muscle shall be accustomed to them. A drawback to the kind of labour that usually comes to the field-archaeologist to-day in Great Britain is that it is often unacquainted with pick and shovel and has to be taught *ab initio*; it consists of unemployed or unemployable invalids, garage-hands, drapers' assistants, university students and the like, to whom picks and shovels are encumbrances rather than instruments. On the other hand in certain parts of Asia – Palestine, Syria, Iraq, some districts of India – are men whose fathers and grandfathers have worked for British, German, or other archaeological expeditions, and who have inherited a useful understanding of the matter. And indeed, to be just, the university student, if he is of the right sort, can usually be trained without undue delay to a fair measure of technical competence; only, he could usually be better employed in more detailed and specialized work and is largely wasted in the basic task of digging.

Tidy excavation implies a skilled knowledge of this basic task. Without tidiness, all is lost. A trench such as that ingenuously illustrated in Pl. 1 could not safely be interpreted or recorded even by an experienced interpreter. The proposed cutting must be laid out carefully by pegged strings at the outset, and must be clearly and vertically cut – as vertically as the nature of the material will permit. The general tendency is to cut a trench with too much outward slope or 'batter' on the sides, with the double result that the stratification is distorted and the cutting becomes excessively narrow as the digging proceeds downwards. This tendency must be watched constantly by the supervisor and corrected immediately. If the batter be allowed to accumulate, the subsequent cleaning down to a vertical face will almost inevitably result in a mixture of material from different levels and a confusion of evidence. A further tendency is to leave blunt angles at the ends and base of a cutting, thus again obscuring the stratification and inducing muddle. Precision must be the order, and precision and tidiness are synonymous.

Another common error of the unskilled digger is to cut down too much material at one time. Picking is generally easier than shovelling, and the pick-man is liable to show an excessive zeal. The result is that the floor of the cutting is encumbered with loose material which is liable to conceal stratification and to get trodden into alien strata. Usually, the less earth loosened at any one time the better; keep the cutting clear so far as the controlled progress of the work will permit.

A corollary of this is: avoid crowding your workmen. A scene such as that illustrated in Pl. 4a implies every sort of disorder. Material is inevitably mixed on the floor of the trench, there is a constant risk of 'finds' being placed in the wrong box or basket, the supervisor cannot see what is happening, and chatter amongst the men swells to an uproar. Noise on an excavation generally implies inefficiency; always with the proviso that the Oriental is a born chatterer and is unhappy without a considerable measure of noise about him. In the East, therefore, noise, as distinct from concentrated conversation, is merely local colour and may be a symptom of happiness. I have stood upon an Eastern site and marvelled at the miscellaneous noise welling up around me from men, women, and children all busily and effectively engaged upon their tasks. But noise amongst British workmen is a bad sign. Almost every gang of them contains at least one addle-pated gossip, who must be isolated and extinguished at once, or the good men will rapidly deteriorate. On the other hand, during off-hours, perhaps when sheltering from rain, the English workman will chatter merrily with the best of them, and a gang of

Welshmen will sing like an angel-choir, in such fashion as to make a virtue of discomfort.

The word 'discomfort' raises another point. The director who looks after the reasonable comfort of his men, for example by the provision of shelter from rain or sun or by ensuring an efficient water-supply – occasionally by a bucket of hot tea on a wet day – is merely doing his duty. But a word of warning is necessary. An over-solicitous attention to 'welfare' may easily result in dissatisfaction. Such is the perverseness of human nature that excess often begets an unreasoned desire for more; in other words, breeds a new kind of discontent. A horse will always nose as of right a pocket from which it has received sugar. Translated into human nature, this expectancy becomes a form of irritation, which is dry fuel to any petty spark of discontent which may happen to be near. The disconcerting result is that ill will arises out of charity; and indeed perhaps the word 'charity' sums up the weakness at the base of the trouble. Charity has no inevitable limit and is therefore susceptible to exploitation. In other words, the charitably minded director suddenly finds that he is being exploited, and, if remedy be not immediately and tactfully applied, the path to hell has been well and truly paved.

One's workmen, then, must be carefully teamed, to prevent the bad from corrupting the good; the fool and the chatterer must be relegated to jobs where they can meditate in solitude upon their (or their director's) folly; the gangs must be spaced to ensure adequate *Lebensraum*; and a proper care for their well-being must not degenerate into an over-anxious solicitude. To all this must be added an alert readiness on the part of the director or supervisor to share any special hardship, such as working in water or mud, or in excessive heat or cold. Furthermore, if, as on very rare occasions, there is some slight element of risk, that risk must be shared or even wholly undertaken by the senior staff. Such active co-operation is essential and is worth more than an infinitude of charitable petting. And at any moment of difficulty or fatigue, the casual jest may be the anodyne. I have seen, towards the end of the day, the lines of young native basket-carriers, upon whose speed and regularity depends in great measure the general *tempo* of an Eastern excavation, falter and chatter and play truant in spite of the despairing efforts of a strong-minded foreman. Basket-carriers are never the most responsible members of the party, and they are necessarily numerous and elusive. A joke and the organization of a basket-carriers' competition were the immediate solution; the whole gang leapt into life, and the foreman leaned upon his stick. *Solvitur jocando*, and this applies throughout the world.

Finally, there is another form of stimulus which has become habitual in some countries: the allocation of bonuses or *baksheesh* (universal Oriental word!) to workmen distinguished by a special aptitude or good fortune in the recovery of 'finds'. This system has in the past been normal in Great Britain, Egypt, and the Near East, although I understand that an attempt is being made to abolish it in Iraq, and under modern economic conditions it has practically died out in Britain. So far as I know, it has never been used in India. It is an unmitigated curse to the director or, rather, the deputy director; it complicates accounting, it adds materially to cost, and, unless administered with a rare combination of honesty and cunning, does almost as much harm as good. It has been found or thought necessary in countries where dealers and collectors stand menacingly at the workman's elbow, ready to tempt with inflated values. Indeed the problem is not an easy one. There can be no doubt that in the past much has been salved for science in the East by the *baksheesh* system. Even in Great Britain, objects, notably coins, have probably been saved in similar fashion from disposal at the local public house (though amongst Britons it is to the 'national sporting instinct' that the bonus is presumed to appeal). But the real answer to all this is not 'bribed honesty', which is what the *baksheesh* system amounts to, but adequate supervision. After all, the director's best guarantee of the honesty of his workmen is, in the words of the French Prehistoric Society's Excavation Manual, 'de ne pas les quitter une minute'. The *baksheesh* system was in fact adopted in the ill-controlled mass-excavations which have long – far too long – been characteristic of Eastern archaeology, as a substitute for adequate supervision. On a properly supervised excavation, nearly all the diggers are constantly under the eye of the site-supervisor, and theft would in any event be difficult.

But there is a little more in the matter than that. Apart altogether from the question of monetary gain to the workman by the sale of objects of marketable worth, the archaeologist has to remember that the requirements of science involve a complete change of values on the part of the peasant, and the bonus-system, wisely applied, undoubtedly helps to impress the new scale upon his mind. When the workman begins to realize that what is to him a mere fragile crock or a fragment of carved bone and nothing more may, to his supervisor, be an historical 'document' of high importance, deserving of a monetary bonus, he is on the way to a mental readjustment which may ultimately turn him into something more than a mere dirt-shifter. Nevertheless, my Indian experience shows me that, by combined example and occasional commentary, the intelligent supervisor can achieve this end without the embarrassments entailed in *baksheesh*. For example, a workman finds an old horse-shoe; he is told that it was made 2,000 years ago. He in turn remarks upon its general similarity to the horse-shoes which his uncle, the local blacksmith, makes, but proceeds to observe minor differences. The brief discussion – it must not be protracted, or all work round about ceases – leads to other historical or archaeological points, and the man becomes intelligently interested in his work. But let this discussion be of a casual and particular nature. Don't assume that your workmen are all breathlessly awaiting general instruction in archaeology. I well remember an earnest antiquary inflicting an eloquent address upon the workmen at an excavation (during the lunch-hour) on 'prehistoric man', and turning at last, well pleased with his effort, to a patient member of his audience with the question: 'And now, my man, what interests *you* most in your work here?' – to which the navvy, slowly removing his pipe and meditatively spitting, replied gruffly: 'The five-o'clock whustle.'

CHAPTER 12

Tools

INADEQUATE tools are not an excuse for bad work. No responsible archaeologist will undertake an excavation without adequate staff and equipment save in a rare emergency. The equipment falls into two main categories: that of the directing staff, and that of the labourers.

(a) EQUIPMENT OF THE DIRECTING STAFF

1. Theodolite or simplified equivalent (see p. 168).
2. Plane-table.
3. Reinforced measuring tapes 100 feet (or metric equivalent) long.
4. 2-foot and 5-foot folding rules, or their metric equivalent.
5. Prismatic oil-compass.
6. Drawing-boards, including several light boards of 3-ply wood for work on the site.
7. Plumb-bobs.
8. Bubble-levels.
9. Drawing paper, some of it squared (e.g. in 1-inch squares with eight subdivisions).
10. Architectural scales.
11. Good pencils, and soft erasers.
12. Broad-bladed knives (blade about 7 inches long) and/or pointed masons' trowels.
13. Good string.
14. Indian ink, pens, and paint-brushes.
15. Circular celluloid protractors.
16. Large celluloid set-squares.
17. T-squares.
18. Good drawing-pins.
19. Paper-clips.
20. Small pay-envelopes (for coins, &c.).
21. Small tie-on labels.
22. Notebooks.
23. 3-inch and 6-inch nails.
24. Scales of various kinds for photography, &c.

Some of the above, such as the theodolite, the compass, and the major drawing-instruments, will be stored centrally. But many of them must be in the possession of every site-supervisor, who should keep them in a tin box labelled with the code-name of the area for which he is responsible and preferably also with his own name. This box will contain a measuring-tape, 2-foot rule (or equivalent), plumb-bob, bubble-level, pencil, eraser, string, ink, pens, paint-brushes, paper-clips, envelopes, labels, nails, and, not least, notebook. The knife or trowel should accompany the supervisor everywhere, as an indispensable and inseparable instrument. Indeed, it is almost a badge of rank; without it, the supervisor can scarcely begin upon his task. Its uses in the detailed examination of a section are almost infinite. It is used, for example, for cleaning and checking difficult sections, and for testing by pressure, 'feel', or sound subtle differences in the soil. It is essential in the final preparation of almost every subject for photography. It is a useful marker in survey. It has a hundred uses and should be a treasured personal possession.

(b) THE LABOURERS' EQUIPMENT

This will vary in detail with the locality, and the following is a generalized list.

1. Picks.
2. Small picks or trenching-tools.
3. Large shovels.
4. Small shovels or scoops.
5. Spade.
6. Turf-cutter or trimmer or edging-knife.
7. Baskets or pans (in the East, for the removal of soil).
8. Wheel-barrows (in the West).
9. Knives or trowels.
10. Planks.
11. Crow-bar.
12. Sledge-hammer (particularly for driving in fencing-posts).

Of these, the *pick* is the primary instrument in excavation, not merely for the general loosening of the ground, but also, properly controlled by a good workman, for comparatively delicate work, for which its weight gives it a relatively effortless control. The tool is easily misused, and the pickman requires special watching and training. For example, the tendency to use the broad end must often be checked – the pointed end does less accidental damage. And it is frequently desirable to avoid hammering every scrap of earth with the pick, but rather to use the instrument as a wedge with which to lever off considerable lumps of earth, driving in the point well back from the cutting-face for this purpose. Above all, except in strata known to be of considerable depth, prevent the pickman from driving the pick too deeply into the soil. 'Wholesale' digging obscures the evidence. Lastly, having loosened a reasonable quantity of earth, the pickman should stand aside and leave the spot free for clearance, observation, and detailed work. A good pickman will *think* with the end of his pick, observing not merely with his eyes but also by slight differences in the 'feel' of the earth. The pick should be kept sharp.

The *small pick* or *trenching-tool* is essentially the digging tool of the foreman or supervisor, or of a specially experienced workman. The lightness of this instrument makes it particularly sensitive to slight changes of soil or even of sound – for example in working towards a mud-brick wall (p. 104). With the knife, it is useful for disengaging objects from the soil. It is the normal instrument for the digging of the control-pit, (p. 84), where the supervisor is working in unknown material. A word of warning: a lazy workman (in the East) will always try to exchange his large pick for one of the small ones, so that he may squat and peck idly at the surface with a minimum of effort. The supervisor will soon learn to detect the difference between the escapist and the honest man who is using the small pick for a good and intelligent reason.

The *turf-cutter* or *trimmer* or *edging-knife* is an essential instrument. Its feature is a sharp crescentic blade in the same plane as the handle. It is used for the very important task of trimming the sides of cuttings to a clean, vertical face, without which proper examination and record are difficult or impossible. It should not, however, be used for substantive digging, partly because it is not strong enough for the purpose but partly also because of necessity it cuts clean through any fragile object that comes its way. Upon its proper use in suitable soils depends in no small measure the cleanliness and effectiveness of an excavation in detail.

The *basket* or *iron pan* is used on Eastern sites (*a*) for the removal of spoil-earth, and (*b*), when properly labelled with a tie-on label indicating site and stratum, for collecting pottery in the field. The life of a basket can be extended by reinforcing with wire. For the removal of dusty soil, the inside can be coated with mud or lined with a rag. It should incidentally be a matter of routine to ensure that no clod of unbroken (i.e. unexamined) earth is ever included with the dust.

In Pl. 18 is illustrated a fairly complete set of tools from an Indian excavation. The only notable absentees are a sharp-edged spade and shears or scissors. The objects shown are:

1. 2. Large and small picks.
3. Small pick with shovel-end.
4. Hand-shovel.
5. Shovel.
6. Turf-cutter or trimmer (a much worn example), very useful for trimming down sections.
7. Basket for removing earth, usually carried on the head.
8. Superviser's knife.
9. 2-foot scale.
10. 4-foot pole (6-foot and 8-foot poles should be added).
11. Graduated triangle, with bubble-levels affixed. For use, see p. 89.
12. 2-foot rule.
13. 100-foot reinforced tape.
14. Notebook with alternate pages squared (1-inch squares subdivided into $\frac{1}{8}$-inch squares).
15. Bubble-level.
16. Plumb-bob.
17. Brushes of various sizes and shapes. Brooms, hard and soft, should be added.

CHAPTER 13

The Pottery-Shed [1]

EXCAVATIONS may be expected to produce material which requires to be collected, labelled, stored, and eventually packed and transported from the site. However abundant or restricted this material may be, commensurate arrangements must be made to ensure that it will reach its destination adequately labelled, and so treated and packed that it arrives in at least as good a condition as that in which it was found. These notes are designed as an *aide-mémoire* for pottery- or small-finds assistants (see above, pp. 163–4) or for the student-excavators who may be expected to assist in the work of handling the material. It is assumed throughout this chapter that the pottery-assistant is in supreme charge of the staff detailed for the reception, preliminary classification, and dispatch of all 'finds'.

THE 'FINDS'

The material found will fall roughly into two large classes:

(i) Pottery and bones, which usually form the bulk of the material and are treated mainly as a series of groups of material rather than on an individual basis.

(ii) Other material, which is treated on an individual basis and may be included, whatever its size, under the general term 'small-finds'.

ACCOMMODATION

It is obvious that the amount of storage-space and working space required will be related directly to the type of excavation and its location. For the purposes of the present description, it is proposed to take a moderate-sized excavation on a site producing a fair amount of finds in a country with a rainy climate; but the same basic principles apply to all excavations, whatever their location and problem.

1. I gladly acknowledge the help of Mrs M. Aylwin Cotton, O.B.E., F.S.A., in the preparation of this chapter.

The director (or deputy director) of the expedition will have made arrangements for the necessary accommodation for handling and storage. The pottery-assistant will, however, be expected to utilize these facilities as advantageously as possible, and there is commonly much scope for his initiative in this matter. He (or she) should aim at organizing:

(*a*) A *pottery-shed* in which all the bulky material can be handled and stored.

(*b*) An *office* in which the 'small-finds' can be recorded and stored.

If pottery or objects are to be drawn on the site, a quiet drawing-office is also desirable, and a small field-laboratory will be necessary (p. 195). Locks should be fitted to all these rooms or sheds.

HOURS OF WORK

It is usual for the 'finds' to be transferred from the excavations to the pottery-shed at the end of each working-session. Whatever arrangements are made for working-sessions on the 'dig' itself, the pottery-shed should be open for a reasonable time after the end of each working session to receive and stack the incoming material. As site-supervisors may need at any time to examine the stored material or to obtain supplies or trays, the pottery-shed should also be open as far as possible throughout the day. As it should not be left unsupervised at any time when it is open, the assistant in charge should arrange to 'stagger' the hours of his workers, or, if single-handed, to arrange for a volunteer to take charge during absence.

SITE AND WATER-SUPPLY

The desirable attributes of a pottery-shed are that it shall be spacious and light and equipped either with running water or within easy reach of a water-supply. It should be as close as possible to the areas under excavation, and should have a clear space outside for pottery-washing and drying in fine weather. In wet weather, if sufficiently spacious, it can also be used for washing and drying pottery, but, if space is restricted, the pottery-assistant should try to arrange that shelter elsewhere can be used where volunteers can work on the material. A tent or a marquee is an inadequate substitute for a pottery-shed. A barn, large shed, Nissen hut, empty garage, or bare room serves well. If running water is not at hand but exists in the immediate vicinity, a labour-saving device, well worth consideration, is to run a long hose from the source of supply to a tank or water-butt outside the shed or building. If water has to be carried from a distance, arrangements for local storage are even more necessary.

EQUIPMENT

The minimum furniture required for comfortable working in a pottery-shed is one large trestle-table and a bench or seats. Boxes, ranging in size from tea-chests to match-boxes, are of the first importance. Large storage-boxes can be used both for storage and for the packing and the transport of the heavier finds but, as these are not acquired nowadays easily or cheaply, smaller light wooden crates and strong cardboard boxes should also be collected. Wooden fruit-boxes are very useful for storage and for the transport of lighter materials, and will carry pottery if it is not too heavy. They can often be obtained in the local market from a fruit-merchant or from the head porter at the goods entrance of a large store. They can be stacked in the pottery-shed with their open sides outwards to form racks for the temporary storage of material. Smaller cardboard boxes and tins, of all shapes or sizes, are useful for packing separate pots, small-finds, and earth-samples.

Stationery supplies required are:

> Paper bags of varying sizes.
> Pay-envelopes.
> Tie-on labels and small white tags.
> Paper-clips and balls of string and twine.
> Index-cards and guide-cards.
> Pens, mapping-pens, pencils, chalks, and small paint-brushes.
> Black waterproof Indian, red, and white inks.
> Blotting-paper.

Pottery-washing equipment consists of:

> Trays of various sizes or drying mats.
> Washing-bowls.
> Nail-brushes, soft paint or pottery-brushes, and old tooth-brushes.

POTTERY WASHING

'Finds' from the excavations are received at the pottery-shed in trays, baskets, or bags. Each receptacle will have with it two labels recording its provenance: one loose and one tied on to the receptacle. From the time of its reception until it is dispatched, all or any part of the contents of these receptacles must always have an accompanying label giving this information. In so far as is practicable, the material received at the end of each working-session should be worked over during the succeeding session. If this cannot be done, it should be bagged temporarily and stacked in order of date received. A wet day, with extra assistance, may provide an opportunity for clearing up arrears, the material being dealt with so far as possible in the order of receipt.

The pottery assistant will be expected to instruct volunteers in the details of the handling of the material and will be responsible for seeing that they give it proper treatment and that it is correctly labelled and packed. Although the site-supervisors may have handed in their more important small-finds separately it will be found that the so-called pottery-trays often contain much that is not pottery. On a Roman site a tray may well contain a few bones, oyster-shells, iron slag, brick or tile, tesserae, and perhaps fragments of painted plaster. A preliminary examination should be made, therefore, to see whether there is any material that should either not be washed at all or should be washed with special care. In both cases it is advisable to isolate this material on separate trays, of course with duplicate labels. Soft or fragile pottery should be dried out thoroughly under cover before being washed. If it is still unsuitable for washing, it can be brushed with a soft brush and then impregnated with bedacryl in toluol to consolidate it, or, if bedacryl is unobtainable, a 10 per cent celluloid solution can be substituted.

Each washer, starting with a tray of unwashed pottery and other washable material, requires a clean drying tray or mat, a bowl with washing water, and suitable brushes. The first step is to place one of the two labels in the drying tray. This is essential as it ensures that if the washer is called away and a partly finished tray is moved, the material still retains its identity. Unmarked material isolated from its label cannot be used as dating evidence, and the carelessness of a washer in this respect can destroy the work of a careful excavator. The material is then washed piece by piece and placed on the clean tray to dry. It is not a good thing to empty a number of sherds into the washing bowl. They may not benefit from soaking in the water, they may sink into the muddy sediment which soon collects in the bowl and get thrown away when the water is changed and, in any case, the washing bowl has no label! Hard wheel-turned and well-baked coarse pottery can be scrubbed with a nail-brush or tooth-brush. Hand-made pottery, glazed pottery (e.g. Samian), and badly baked pottery should be washed with a soft pottery-brush. Painted pottery, painted plaster, etc., should not be washed until the director or the site-supervisors have been consulted. The edges of sherds should be brushed as well as the insides and outsides. It will save time in marking and sorting trays if the material is placed on the drying tray in an orderly manner. All rims, bases, and decorated sherds should be placed in the top half, plain sherds at the bottom and sundry objects such as shells, nails, tile, etc., piled in separate small heaps. Finally the washer adds to the finished drying tray the second label from the now empty 'unwashed' tray. Unless the supply of water is restricted, the water in the bowl should be changed frequently. (Pottery washed in muddy water retains a thin coating of mud when dry and may require to be rewashed.) The drying tray is then placed in the open or under shelter until its contents are dry, care being taken to anchor its label firmly.

Washers should be encouraged to take an interest in the material they handle and in its provenance; their memory of where a particular pot can be found has often proved valuable when it has been required quickly for inspection.

Trays of dried material should be shown to the site-supervisors so that they may note the contents in their field notebooks and so that they can reject any material that is not required further. Pottery that has not reacted adequately to simple washing in water can at this stage be segregated and re-treated by further washing in teepol (a detergent) and water, or, if coated in lime which it is desired to remove, treated by soaking in a dilute solution of nitric acid (10 or 20 per cent solution) followed by several rinsings in clean water. Pottery in acid must be kept under observation: often 10 minutes' treatment or until effervescence stops is all that is required. Painted sherds should only be dipped in the solution, and a corner should always be tested first to see if the colour is fugitive.

POTTERY MARKING

The trays are now ready for marking. As a general rule all rims, bases, and decorated sherds are marked. The site-supervisors should be consulted to ascertain whether they require that *all* sherds of a particular group should be marked. The aim in marking is to give each marked piece its provenance in a clearly legible but inconspicuous position so that it can be handled with safety when removed from its label. Rims and sherds are marked on the inside, bases on the underside. For all sherds on which it shows clearly, black waterproof ink is used; black and dark-grey sherds can be marked with white ink. Mapping-pens are used, and, if they are kept clean by wiping, washing, or scraping after use, will write more legibly and will last longer. Markers should remember that sherds may be required for display and that it should be possible to lay them out right side up so that the marking does not show. Some wares, especially Samian, are easily marked on the line of fracture. The exact lettering to be used will be indicated on the labels. As a rule, it consists of a letter or abbreviation to indicate the location of the excavations; a letter or number to indicate the site; the area, square, or trench involved; and the number and perhaps the orientation of the actual layer. Conventionally this last is encircled: e.g. VER/G M II means (14 N) Verulamium, Site G, Area M II, Layer 14 North. 'Group' material does not need any closer identification. If, however, material has been pin-pointed three-dimensionally (p. 87) and given a serial number in the field notebook (a number which is conventionally included in a triangle, e.g. /7\) this may be added. Porous pottery does not take ink readily. The area to be marked should first be varnished and then marked over the dry varnish.

SORTING AND BAGGING

To bundle into a bag the contents of a mixed tray of material is deleterious to the material itself and throws extra work on to the experts who handle the material later. Well-washed pottery if mixed with oyster shells comes out of the bag with a film of shell fragments; large pieces of tile and brick may bruise or break the finer sherds; and iron slag and nails when mixed with the pottery are a constant nuisance. Fresh duplicate labels should be written for each type of material other than pottery in the tray, and these collections with their labels should be placed in separate bags and relegated for further treatment. When the material is reduced to a group of clean, marked pottery only, it is ready for bagging. The site-supervisor should be consulted as to whether special wares or types should be subdivided and bagged separately. If so, further labels will have to be written. The final group of pottery is then placed in a strong paper bag, or, if bulky, in a double bag, together with one of its two labels. The other label is threaded on a suitable length of string. Pottery bags should be treated as small parcels and should be tied up *firmly both along their length and their width*, the string being tied in a single reef-knot or bow and *not* in a multiple knot. Knots are a menace to anyone who may have to open hundreds of bags. Whole pots, or a collection of sherds which may join to form part of a pot, can be bagged or boxed separately. The pottery bags are now ready for storage.

STORAGE OF POTTERY, ETC.

Pottery bags should be sorted into groups from each site, and from each area or trench in that site. They should be stored so that all the bags from any particular area or level can be produced quickly for inspection. Storage-boxes should be labelled clearly with the name of the excavation, the site number or letter, the trench or area number or letter, and the type of object stored in them. If more than one box is required for an area or trench, boxes should be numbered and kept together. They should be packed firmly, but only filled level with the top so that they can be either fitted with lids or slats or piled on top of each other to save space in transport. It is usually convenient to store all bulky material in the pottery-shed, even though it may include sherds which have been indexed separately as 'small-finds'. The boxes used for non-ceramic material should be clearly labelled for each site (e.g. 'bones', 'iron slag', 'architecture', 'earth-samples', 'charcoal', 'shells').

PACKING

At the close of the excavation-season, the material will probably have to be packed for removal from the site. If it is to be sent by rail or by sea, arrangements must be made to pack the boxes securely, to close them with lids or slats and to nail on addressed labels. Whole pots should be filled with wood-shavings or other packing-material. The wedging material in the packing-cases should be rammed in with a wooden rammer to make it so compact that the pots will not work loose and break in transit. Sawdust is not satisfactory as a wedging material. A list of the contents of each case should be included in it and a duplicate list be sent by mail or taken with the excavation-notes.

POTTERY MENDING

If pottery is to be mended on the site, the pottery-shed should be equipped with boxes of sand, plasticine, and jars of cellulose dope, amyl-acetate and acetone. Methods are a matter of demonstration rather than description.

INDEXING 'SMALL-FINDS'

All material treated individually as a 'small-find' will be received by the small-find recorder (p. 163) either direct from the site-supervisor or as bags of material sorted out from the pottery trays and transferred from the pottery-shed. Whether or no this material is to be cleaned and marked on the site, it should always be indexed. 'Small-find' material usually includes the more closely datable evidence and, in addition, tends to be fragile and to require extra care in handling and treatment.

The record falls into two parts: (*a*) the accession-registers, (*b*) the card-indexes.

The most convenient system of registration is to keep a small accession-book for each site (i.e. for each main subdivision of the excavation). Its pages are ruled in columns for entering the accession number, type of object, provenance, finder, date and amount of bonus paid (if any, see p. 176). As each 'find' from a site is received, it is given a serial accession-number which is marked in red ink on its bag and/or labels. The appropriate details are added: e.g. G. 49. 123, Bronze brooch, M II ③ Dark Earth, John Smith, 1.8.49, 6d.

The card index is then prepared in duplicate, for arrangement on the one hand by categories and on the other hand by sites. On the first or 'object' card, the type of object is printed at the top; the accession number is written in red ink on the top right-hand corner; then the provenance and any other useful details follow; and finally a sketch or small photograph is added (if necessary on the back of the card) so that the object can be identified if at any time it should become detached from its label. The second or 'site' card is a duplicate of the first except that the provenance of the object is printed on the top of the card and the type of object below. Two boxes are provided to hold the cards: one for the 'Object Index' and one for the 'Site Index'. The object cards are filed in the Object Index behind guide cards for each type of object. Objects made of the same kind of material should be filed next to each other (e.g. Bronze, Bronze Bracelets, Bronze Brooches). The guide cards should be arranged in alphabetical order. In the Site Index, guide cards are made out for each area or trench (e.g. VER/G M II), and behind these all cards belonging to that area are filled in order of successive layers. The groups of cards for each site should be filed separately so that, for example, all coins from Site A can be looked up easily and are not intermingled with those from Site B. In excavations in which the material has to be left behind, or in which a record of the finds has to be furnished to a local authority, a single card index is inadequate. Arrangements may have to be made to compile a duplicate catalogue in addition. If so, when photographic assistance is available on the site, one drawing of the object may be made, and as many prints of it made as are required. These can then be pasted on to the index cards and in the catalogue in the appropriate places. Often, in this system, type-forms of pottery are drawn and should be treated on a routine 'small-find' basis.

INDEXING COINS

Coins should be identified and fully indexed in both 'object' and 'site' indexes, by reason of their importance as date-indicators.

Beside the record of provenance, the cards should contain the follow-ing information:

1. The obverse legend and type. Breaks in the legend are indicated by a /; illegible letters are enclosed in square brackets [ ].
2. The reverse legend and type.
3. The mint-mark, if present.
4. The condition of the coin, whether it is in mint condition, good condition, worn, corroded, or illegible.
5. If no reference books are available, the date of the emperor's reign should be added. If reference books are available, the coin should be looked up in these and its denomination (e.g. sestertius, antoninianus, etc.) and a more precise dating added.

References for Roman coins down to A.D. 300 can at present be quoted from Mattingly and Sydenham's *Imperial Roman Coinage*: later coins from Cohen's *Monnaies frappées sous l'empire romain*. A specimen card might read as follows:

DUPONDIUS of DOMITIAN   VER/G 49 123
  M II ④⑧ Dark Earth ③ NE S 4′ 1″–2′ 1″–6″
Obv. IMP CAES DOMIT AUG GERM COS XII
    [CENS PER PP] head L.
Rev. MONETA/AUG [USTI] S C Moneta stg. l., hold-
    ing scales and cornucopiae.
      Worn
M. & S.   383   A.D. 86

BONES AND SOILS

Somewhere in this book, and here as well as anywhere, a plea must be put in for a more scholarly collection of biological and botanical material than even our better excavators have normally achieved in the past. For example, animal bones have, it is true, long been the subject of special sections in archaeological reports, but few, very few, of those reports give us the analytical details which, in the present state of knowledge, are urgently required. What usually happens is this: a few bundles of selected bones are sent off to some complaisant biologist, who subsequently reports the presence of *Bos longifrons*, *Ovis aries Studeri*, *Equus agilis*, and *Canis familiaris lacustris*, and receives a fulsome tribute therefor in the published report. Let it be said at once that this sort of thing nowadays gets us almost nowhere. Bones are documents as are potsherds and demand the same scrupulous attention both on the site, in the small-finds shed, and in the laboratory. Consider the information which we may expect from them. If in sufficient quantity (as they not infrequently are) they can give us from phase to phase, not merely a list of the fauna category by category, but also – what is far more important – a hint as to the economic function of that fauna. To what extent do the bones represent food? To what extent do they indicate sheep or cattle killed young, before the winter? Alternatively, what proportion of the sheep or cattle represented were sufficiently aged to prove organized winter-feeding? Were sheep thus maintained more extensively than cattle, implying a dominant importance of wool? Were horses eaten? ridden? driven? (Size and age are here amongst the diagnostic factors.) Were pigs kept in sufficient numbers to imply appreciable exploitation of marginal forest-land? Did the proportion of one category of stock to another vary in the course of the occupation of a site? These are some of the questions on which excavator and biologist must confer after examination of *all* significant bones from a site in their stratigraphical contexts. How often is this done? Of course the quantitative analysis of animal-bones has in it an element of unreality, since a single skeleton is frequently multiplied arbitrarily in its fragments. The same objection applies to the quantitative analysis of potsherds. Nevertheless, exercised with common sense, the counting of bones, as of sherds, may, under normally favourable conditions, be expected to yield usable statistics, and must be attempted.

Similarly with the collection of soil-samples. The preservative capacity of damp soils is truly astonishing. Seeds, leaves, plants, wing-cases of beetles, may be incorporated in a condition that renders recognition easy. At Stanwick in 1951 we found at the bottom of a rock-cut ditch of the first century A.D. a layer of wet clay representing a pool of water which stood there from the earliest days of the cutting. In it, amongst other organic remains, was a puff-ball which the British Museum (Natural History) had no difficulty in recognizing and naming at once after nineteen centuries in the soil. A word of warning may be added: some seeds may be less durable than others, and, whilst positive evidence of an ancient vegetation is satisfactory enough negative evidence may require further thought and consultation.[1]

Finally, whilst on the subject of plant-seeds it may be added that an impressive number of cereal-identifications has been rendered possible by impressions of grains on hand-made pottery. Sherds of little intrinsic significance may in this fashion achieve an accidental importance which justifies and indeed necessitates a careful examination of every scrap, however featureless otherwise, from the moment of discovery onwards.

VARIANT LAYOUT FOR DRY CLIMATES

Where rain is not a factor and work can be carried out for weeks on end in the open, the task of the pottery-assistant can be simplified by the use of a grid outside the pottery-shed.

A reasonable area adjoining the pottery-shed is carefully levelled and smoothed, and a rectangular framework x yards (say, 20 yards) square is marked out by neat lines of stones. Within the frame, subsidiary compartments are formed by similar lines of stones laid down in both directions at 1-yard intervals. These subsidiary squares are then demarcated by flat wooden labels driven in along the margins of the framework and bearing in one direction the denominations of the various excavated sites (square-number or trench-number) and in the other direction the successive numbers of the layers (1, 2, 3, etc.). Thus every subsidiary square is identified with a horizontal and a vertical datum on the excavated site. In the illustration (Pl. 20), taken from the Arikamedu excavations of 1945, the line of labels across the foreground represents the site (A1, A2, A3, etc.) and the line receding from the camera represents the layer or stratum.

The operation of the grid is as follows. As the basket-carriers bring in the labelled baskets of pottery at intervals during the day, the pottery-assistant empties the contents, with their two labels, carefully on to the appropriate square. In the illustration, he is actually emptying a basket on to the square representing stratum 8 on site A4. *This task is never delegated*; it must be remembered that at this stage the

1. For an excellent account of the applications of pollen-analysis, see J. G. D. Clark, *The Mesolithic Settlement of Northern Europe* (Cambridge, 1936), pp. 31 ff.

individual sherds are not marked, and any careless spilling will irreparably transfer a sherd to its wrong stratigraphical position. After being emptied, the basket, no longer labelled, is sent back to the excavation for re-use.

The next stage is to inspect the sherds thus lumped and to transmit all that do not require special treatment to the washers, who in the illustration are seen squatting under the banyan-tree at the back. The contents of *one square only* are washed by each washer or group of washers at any one time, otherwise admixture is inevitable. When dry, the washed sherds are transferred group by group to the table, where they are further examined by the pottery-assistant (and as often as possible by the director) and are marked carefully, sherd by sherd, by the marker under the pottery-assistant's direction, in accordance with the two labels which still, of course, accompany them. Finally, the marked sherds are bagged, group by group, with one label in the bag and the other tied on outside, in accordance with the procedure already described.

CHAPTER 14

The Field-Laboratory

An archaeological chemist must be available to any excavation where friable or perishable materials are likely to be found, and in most parts of the world this means that a small field-laboratory is an integral part of the outfit. It has already been affirmed (above, p. 168) that the primary functions of the field-chemist are to help in the removal of fragile objects from the soil and in their subsequent transportation; to arrest the decay or distortion of objects on exposure; and to clean objects, notably coins, which must be identified as the excavation proceeds. He must also, as a guide to later treatment, keep a log-book of all first-aid administered by him, object by object.

The chemist does not require extravagant accommodation, but he must have a plentiful supply of *salt-free water*. In desert or semi-desert regions, this is not easy. To test for salinity, a silver nitrate solution is recommended. The solution is prepared by dissolving 5 gm. of silver nitrate crystals in 500 c.c. of distilled water, followed by 10 c.c. of strong nitric acid. The test is carried out thus: Two clean test-tubes of the same size are half-filled, one with pure water from the expedition's reserve and the other with the local water. To each of these tubes are added ten drops of the silver nitrate solution, and the tubes are shaken. A white precipitate or milkiness is produced which varies with the amount of the chlorides (which are invariably present with other salts) in the water. The milkiness produced in the pure water will be relatively slight.

The same test can be applied to water in which salt-impregnated objects, such as pottery, have been washed, and the washing should be continued until the wash-water shows no more reaction than the pure water.

Distilled water is also essential, together with the following chemicals, etc.:[1]

1. Miss Ione Gedye, who is in charge of the laboratory of the Archaeological Institute of the University of London, has kindly prepared the list on p. 196, and Dr H. J. Plenderleith has been good enough to read the chapter.

Nitric acid (or hydrochloric acid if nitric is unobtainable).
Acetone.
Amyl-acetate.
Silver nitrate.
Citric acid.
Sulphuric acid.
Acetic acid.
Ammonia.
Caustic soda.
Celluloid cuttings.
Shellac.
Bedacryl 122 x.
Toluol.
Teepol or similar detergent.
Sodium sesquicarbonate.
Polyvinyl acetate.
Methylated spirit or alcohol.
Plaster of Paris.
Granulated zinc.
Graphite slab.
Copper wire.
Copper and brass rods.
Batteries or transformer.
Glass or pottery tank.
Glass or porcelain dishes and beaker.
Saucepans.
Measuring glass.
Test-tubes.
Glass bottles.
Spoons.
Penknives.
Wire brushes (steel and brass).
Nail-brushes.
Tooth-brushes.
Paint-brushes (1 inch and 2 inch).
Emery paper.
Sand-bath.
Wire wool.
Soap.
Wax (to wax labels).
Small tag labels.

Reinforcing material (sacking, iron rods, and wire).
Paraffin wax.
Some source of heat.
Sandpaper.

I do not propose here to present a manual of first-aid: several books are available.[1] But to indicate something of the required scope of this little laboratory, I append a few notes on typical operations.

1. *Metal objects*, particularly ironwork, must be preserved sufficiently to enable them to travel without further damage. Iron objects can often be salved temporarily by covering them with a plaster envelope, a process which must sometimes be done before the removal of the objects from the position in which they are found. After being thus treated, they should be carefully but firmly bound to wooden splints by means of a cloth bandage. (Prior to treatment, however, they should be drawn to scale by the expedition's draftsman, where possible on a glass plate – see p. 171.) Subsequent treatment depends upon circumstances, but should normally be deferred until full laboratory equipment is available. Paraffin wax (with a high melting-point) has frequently been used instead of plaster as a temporary jacket for metal or other fragile objects, but is a last resort. Care must be taken to avoid melting the wax into the objects; the wax is not easy to remove completely for the subsequent treatment, and, if salts are thus imprisoned, disintegration is hastened rather than delayed.

2. *Coins*, if still illegible after drying and brushing, must usually be treated on the spot. The nature of the treatment will depend upon their metal and its condition, and the field-chemist must be fully trained and experienced in this work if he is to do more good than harm. In particular, *it must at the outset be ascertained whether there is a reasonable core of the original metal* – otherwise the washing away of impurities will wash away the coin. (The presence of a metal core in a corroded *iron* object can generally be detected by its being strongly attracted by a magnet.) In a majority of instances, where there is a considerable surviving core, the electrolytic method is the safest for metal, but this is not always feasible. It consists of the suspension of the object (coin, etc.) on a copper wire attached to the negative pole of

1. e.g. H. J. Plenderleith, *The Preservation of Antiquities* (London, 1934); also *Ancient India*, no. 1 (Delhi, 1946), pp. 77-82.

a battery, and immersing it in a $2\frac{1}{2}$ per cent caustic soda solution contained in a glass vessel, in which is immersed a piece of graphite wired to the positive pole of the battery. The electric current passes through the object and the solution and removes impurities from the metal. The difficulty is that the battery needs recharging after 24–48 hours' work, and it is not always possible to sustain the necessary battery service. After treatment, the objects are thoroughly washed in distilled water and are then coated with bedacryl or polyvinyl acetate or some equivalent protective covering; bakelite varnish will serve if nothing better is available. Gold, of course, needs no chemical treatment, unless marred by obstinate stains or incrustations, which can be freed by immersion in a strong hydrochloric acid or by boiling in a detergent solution.

If the electrolytic method is considered unsafe, copper or its alloys may be cleaned in a mixture of 1 part tartaric acid, 1 part of caustic soda, and 10 parts of water. The objects should be kept in the mixture until all the green incrustations have been dissolved away, leaving the liver-red core behind. They are then *thoroughly* washed in water and finally coated with bedacryl or polyvinyl acetate. An alternative treatment is: (i) citric acid, and pickling in 50 per cent sulphuric acid to remove any red oxide; (ii) neutralize with ammonia or any alkali after the acid treatment; (iii) wash in distilled water; (iv) carry out the silver nitrate test with the last wash-water (see above); (v) dry in alcohol; and (vi) coat with bedacryl or polyvinyl acetate. Completely oxidized copper coins should, at the outset, be left in a 10 per cent sodium metaphosphate solution until free from calcareous matter. Sometimes this is sufficient to reveal the inscription; if not, they should be treated with the above-mentioned tartrate mixture diluted to half strength.

Silver coins and other objects, if the metal is debased with copper (as it not infrequently is in the later Roman coinage), can be cleaned with 3 per cent sulphuric acid until free from all red spots of copper oxide. Thereafter, the coins are brushed and well washed in water. Pure silver, if superficially corroded, can be cleaned by immersion in dilute ammonia or dilute formic acid. Or it may be wrapped in zinc sheeting and suspended for a couple of hours in water acidified with a few drops of acetic acid.

Whatever process be adopted, the director must ensure that *at no stage is the object separated from its site-label* (which should be waxed to avoid defacement). The chemist must be sufficiently an archaeologist to appreciate fully the importance of the label. See that he does not undertake too much work at any one time; a crowded laboratory will inevitably lead to confusion of evidence, particularly in the case of coins and other small objects. When a coin is immersed for cleaning, its label must be securely attached to the wire whereby it is suspended.

3. *Tablets or seals of unbaked clay*, such as are found on Mesopotamian and Indian sites, must be baked carefully for handling and preservation. This work should be within the scope of any experienced excavator, but, all things being equal, is a fair charge upon the chemist's time. The method is fully described and illustrated by P. Delougaz, 'The Treatment of Clay Tablets in the Field', *Studies in Ancient Oriental Civilization*, no. 7 (Chicago, 1933), and need not here be repeated. It may be added, however, that the exposure of ornament or script is deferred until after the baking and is most effectively developed, according to modern practice, with the aid of a simple form of sand blast.

4. *Objects of wood* freshly dug from damp soil are liable to split, warp, or be destroyed altogether on drying. The task in the field is to maintain their humidity, for example by embedding them in a thick layer of wet sawdust, moss, or newspaper. Sometimes the wood can be *slowly* dried and the moisture replaced by glycerine, which is retained by a skin of 10 per cent polyvinyl acetate or shellac in alcohol. Wood from saline areas should be washed in salt-free water or treated with applications of liquid paper-pulp for the purpose of drawing out the salt.

An equivalent treatment is necessary for shale and leather.

The working principle should be to keep all such objects damp until they can be handed over to a fully equipped laboratory, and to avoid impregnation with wax or other material liable to make permanent conservation difficult (see p. 197).

5. *Bones* must be carefully and lightly brushed clean, and can be painted or sprayed before removal with polyvinyl acetate diluted with toluene or methylated spirits or shellac diluted with methylated spirits or alcohol. If the bones can be removed but are still fragile, they can be soaked for 3–4 days in a tank containing bedacryl or polyvinyl acetate suitably diluted with toluol with an air-space under the lid. They should then be laid out on a wire grid, otherwise they will stick to everything.

CHAPTER 15

Photography [1]

THE overriding difficulty of the archaeological photographer is to induce his camera to tell the truth. That quality is as much a matter of proper emphasis as of accumulative statement, and not a little of the photographer's time and skill, both in the field and in the studio, are devoted to the rescue of the more from the less significant. The preparation of the subject, the selection of light and angle and lens, the use or non-use of filters, the choice of 'hard', 'soft', or 'medium' printing-paper, the differential printing of portions of the same negative are all matters which extend the photographer's function beyond the limits of mere technical skill. In all of them the director is as busily concerned as is his photographer.

No attempt is made here to interpolate a manual of photography. It is assumed that technical proficiency and good equipment are alike at the director's disposal. They are not difficult to find. On the other hand, their efficient utilization is rare enough to be classed amongst the virtues, and a few notes upon this matter are not out of place.

No amount of mechanical skill is a substitute for the careful preparation of the subject. Clean, sharp angles between the divergent planes of a section, carefully and emphatically cut with trowel, knife, or edging-tool, are essential if the section is to tell its story with the minimum of confusion. Furthermore, a spotlessly clean trench is no mere 'eye-wash', if only because it gives the spectator a justifiable trust in the orderliness and accuracy of the work. Even the top edges of a trench should be neatly trimmed and the grass cut and swept along them; a stray blade of grass in the foreground of the picture may be overlooked by the eye but may loom embarrassingly in the lens. Strata readily distinguishable in nature may merge in the black-and-white of the plate and may, on occasion, have to be emphasized by careful spraying or by additional smoothing or even deliberate

1. Mr M. B. Cookson has been good enough to check the technical points in this chapter.

roughening, though such aids should be used only where all other methods (e.g. the use of a filter) fail. An example is illustrated on Pl. 19. Sometimes, particularly in a dry Eastern climate, a whole section may have to be damped to bring out its texture or colouring. In one way or another must we thus compensate for the absence of photographic colour until such time as colour-photography becomes the normal medium.

Then there is the selection of light. For most archaeological subjects in the open there is one optimum moment during the day, and the day itself may have to be chosen carefully for sun, shadow, or half-light. In the East, where the strong sun usually kills the detail of a subject, most of my photography was done in the fleeting moments between first light and sunrise. The time-margin in these circumstances is a matter of minutes, and everything must be prepared beforehand. In special circumstances reflected sunlight may be employed; thus I photographed the sculptures in the Elephanta caves near Bombay by means of sunlight reflected into the dark recesses by a succession of large mirrors. Whatever the special problem, it may in fact be laid down as a general rule that the preparation of a subject occupies hours, occasionally days, before the brief session with the camera. Innumerable slipshod and uninformative photographs in excavation reports (Pl. 22) prove that this elaborate preparation is not unnecessary.

Every archaeological photograph should include a scale, either in the form of a graduated rule or rod or in that of a human figure. (Adult human skeletons provide their own scale with as much accuracy as may be expected from a photograph.) The scale should normally be parallel with the plane of the camera-plate; if the latter is tilted[1] the graduated scale should be correspondingly tilted, otherwise the graduations are in perspective and of variable length. With very rare exceptions, the scale must be precisely parallel with the side of the plate, and great care should be taken in its placing. Nothing looks worse than a scale unintentionally out of the vertical or horizontal. Incidentally the scale should be clean and unscarred; it is preferable to reserve a graduated pole specially for photography.

1. Note that, however much tilted forward the camera may be, it *must* be level horizontally, if any horizon is visible, and the levelling of the camera with a bubble-level is one of the first acts of the photographer.

Care should also be taken to ensure that the scale is in the same plane as the main feature of the subject. It is surprising how often this obvious precaution is overlooked, a scale, for example, being placed considerably nearer the camera than a small object with which it is supposedly associated. On the other hand, the scale should not monopolize the attention of the spectator. A central scale is, for this reason, usually bad. Where the scale is a human being, as is often desirable in large subjects, the individual thus honoured must remember that he is a mere accessory, just so many feet of bone and muscle. I have in front of me as I write a monumental report on a Palestinian excavation in which a collotype illustration nominally representing a building under excavation shows in the centre the figure of the director facing the camera with a look of smug self-satisfaction, his hat in his hand so that no feature of interest may escape his admirers. Another, even more ludicrous, misuse of the human scale further East is illustrated in Pl. 24b, the sinner again being the director himself. Two axioms of the use of the human scale are (1) that the figure shall not occupy a disproportionately large portion of the picture (if so, a linear scale must be substituted), and (2) that the figure shall not look at the camera but shall be ostensibly employed in as impersonal a manner as possible. On occasion the figure can be something more than a passive scale. For example at Wroxeter, Mr J. P. Bushe Fox was hard put to it to express the placing of a flue in an unspectacular fragment of walling, but eventually lighted upon the successful device of including in his snapshot a workman pouring a bucket of water into the upper end of the flue so that the water, emerging from the lower end, indicated the continuity of the opening through the thickness of the wall.[1]

With panchromatic plates or films a colour-filter is not usually necessary. To emphasize reds and blacks, however, and to eliminate greens and yellows, a green filter may be used with these plates; whilst a yellow filter will produce tone-values more nearly approximating to those observed by the naked eye. The red filter will lighten all reds and yellows, darken all greens and blues (e.g. in the sky, thus emphasizing clouds), and will separate red from black. Variations of exposure for panchromatic plates are as follows:

1. *Wroxeter Report* 1914 (Soc. Ant. Lond. Research Report), pl. x, fig. 1.

With a green filter, an exposure six times as long as normal.
With a yellow filter, an exposure twice as long as normal.
With a red filter, an exposure four times as long as normal.

Orthochromatic or yellow-sensitive plates are not used with a red filter. The yellow filter with these plates will lighten yellow up to light orange and will darken all blues. The variant exposures are as follows:

With a green filter, an exposure nine times as long as normal.
With a yellow filter, an exposure five times as long as normal.

Other matters of importance are the focal length of the lens and the regulation of the lens-aperture or 'stop'. These factors are related to each other and to the size of the camera. Remarkable results can be obtained by very small cameras, and on distant expeditions it may be necessary to adhere to them exclusively. But I have no hesitation in recommending the use of a full-plate (6½ × 8½ inches) camera whenever possible. The main reason for this choice has recently been concisely expressed by Miss Alison Frantz as follows:

Lenses are described and identified by their focal lengths. The focal length, which is fixed for each lens, is approximately the distance between the lens and the image on the film when the lens is focused on a distant point. Lenses of different focal lengths may be used, within reason, on cameras of different sizes. For general use, however, a lens of focal length equal to or slightly greater than the diagonal of the picture-area is customary. Therefore the larger the camera the greater the focal length of its normal lens. The images projected on the film by lenses of the same focal length at a given distance from the object are the same size regardless of the size of the camera, and the image-size increases with the focal length. Therefore a larger camera will take in a greater field than a smaller camera equipped with the same lens.[1]

Lenses with a short focal length and a proportionately wide angle of vision are sometimes necessary, particularly at close range in a confined space. But such a lens exceeds the capacity and expectation of the human eye and reduces the normal visual emphasis of the subject, i.e. flattens it; so that the effect is distortion and falsification.

1. *Archaeology* (Arch. Inst. of America), Dec., 1950, p. 205.

The golden rule is to use as long a focal length (i.e. as narrow a visual angle) as the subject will permit. And since, as explained above, a large plate facilitates this procedure by providing a larger and more inclusive field for any given lens, a large camera is preferable to a small one.

In practice, every archaeological camera requires *three* alternative lenses: a long-focus (narrow angle) lens, a medium-focus lens, and a short-focus (wide angle) lens. Something like a 12-inch lens, a 9-inch lens, and a 6-inch lens, respectively, will suffice in normal usage. To these may be added a telephoto lens, not often used but occasionally of great value.

The use of a large camera with a long-focus lens, however, necessitates a proper understanding of the use of the 'stop', i.e. of the regulation of the aperture in front of the lens. The depth of the field, or in other words the distance between the nearest and the farthest points of sharp focus, *decreases* as the focal length of the lens *increases*. On the other hand, the depth of the field *increases* as the aperture in the diaphragm (or screen in front of the lens) *decreases*. In a subject of any appreciable depth, therefore, the one factor has to be set off against the other. A long or longish lens, desirable to ensure an undistorted perspective, must be given a greater depth of focus by reducing the size of the aperture, i.e. by 'stopping down'. The widest stop is generally f.6·3, the narrowest f.64, the usual series being 6·3, 8, 11, 16, 22, 32, 45, 64. For subjects of average depth, something midway between the two extremes – e.g. f.32 – is commonly adequate. It must be remembered that as the aperture narrows the length of exposure increases because less light penetrates, the rate of increase being $\times 2$ for each successive smaller stop. Thus if f.22 requires an exposure of half a minute, f.32 will require an exposure of a minute.

One further point in connexion with the 'stop'. With any appreciable reduction of the aperture, the lens must be focused on the foreground – say, 15 feet from the camera on the average – and *not* on the middle distance or background.

In the actual exposure, care must be taken to avoid halation. Although modern films are normally 'backed' or 'dyed' to reduce this, the difficulty is not thereby eliminated. Sky seen through trees or over a building or rampart may produce indistinctness or fogging during a long exposure timed to bring out the detail of a dark foreground. When the lens is within 45 degrees of the sun it must be carefully shaded by means of a hat or book or sheet of cardboard.

To the apparatus already indicated for outdoor photography one more item should be added: a mobile tower 10–15 feet high. In the East, where supplies and labour were relatively abundant, I had a wooden tower run up on every major site (Pl. 21). In Britain also towers of various designs have been widely used, though here I generally use trestles borrowed locally – a lazy man's substitute.

So much for out-of-doors. For the indoor photography of individual objects many of the same rules or recommendations apply but a few others may be added. When possible, it is the convention that objects shall be lighted from the top left, but this usage has often to be varied in order to emphasize a design or inscription for which some other angle is more suitable. In any case a proportion of reflected light, transmitted from a white board or a sheet of tin or a board covered with tin-foil, is usually necessary to show up the shadowy side and to lift the object from its background. In a fully equipped studio, artificial lighting may be used throughout, and with experience, undoubtedly yields the most reliable results.

For background I prefer black velvet save when the object itself approximates to that colour. For dark objects, a sheet of glass raised 4 or 5 inches above a sheet of light-coloured (not quite white) paper on four corner-blocks gives a good shadowless background. Pure white paper may produce a slight halation. When, as in the photography of coins, it is desirable to include both sides of an object on the same plate, by interrupting the exposure and turning the object over, a black background is of course essential.

In photographing an object at close range, it is important to ensure that the scale is in or very near the frontal plane. Otherwise, if the object is of any considerable depth and the scale is placed on the background, an appreciable disparity will result. In these circumstances the scale should be raised to the required height on a thin strip of wood or plasticine.

Whatever the subject, the background and lighting should be such that no cutting out is subsequenty necessarily on the film or plate. To have to block out an irrelevant shadow or other feature is a confession of failure and, particularly if the object is a work of art, materially reduces the value of the record.

Lastly, *all field-photographs must be developed immediately*. Many of them cannot be repeated at a later date, and the director must be assured of his results within 20 minutes of the exposure. Rough prints should follow within 12 hours.

ADMINISTRATION AND RECORD KEEPING

The photographer's notebook must contain all details relating to time, position, exposure, and filter used. Thus

Harappā

Site E. Sect. X. South face

11.45 hrs. Strong sunlight

12″ lens. Red filter. F.22. 3 secs.

Ease of access to negatives is essential from the outset of an excavation and, to this end, all negatives made and approved should be numbered with a serial number orientation, the page in the site-supervisor's notebook, and, if possible, the position on the site and the general plan or the drawing number (see below). It is quite simple to do all this in the rebate or margin made by the dark slide, and the work should be carried out with waterproof ink and a mapping pen. If Cellophane envelopes are used for storing negatives, then the same details will be added to the envelope, together with the type of printing paper used in the print produced. Thus, if the Negative Register is ever lost or destroyed, the details would still be available. In the same manner the keeping of a Negative Register is essential, columnized to receive all the foregoing details but with an added 'Remarks' column in which notes can be made of such matters as the existence of lantern-slide negatives of the same subject, or whether the negative has been used for publication, the date and reference of publication being given.

Diagrammatic Examples

Negatives		Negative bag
237. RANCHI. SITE SECT. X.	N.B. 10. P. 41. Drwg. No. 15.	237 RANCHI SITE E. SECT. X SOUTH FACE HUMUS REMOVED NOTEBOOK 10. P.41 DRAWING NO. 15 KODAK BROMIDE GRADE 5 10 SECS.

Negative Register

RANCHI

Neg. serial	Site	Section	Drwg. no.	Sup. note-book	Remarks
237	E	X South face	15	10 p. 41	Humus removed. Interim Report pl. x. Lantern-slide made.

EQUIPMENT

In summary, the archaeological photographer in the field needs the following equipment:

1. A field camera of strong construction, full-plate size ($6\frac{1}{2} \times 8\frac{1}{2}$ inches), with rising and falling lens-panel and swing-back.
   At least six dark slides, each to hold two plates or films, and numbered.
2. Not less than three lenses: a long-focus lens, a medium-focus lens, and a short focus or wide angle. All should be of the best quality and anastigmatic, with a maximum aperture of f.6·3 (most of the exposures will be 'time'). A telephoto lens may usefully be added for occasional use.
3. A set of filters (red, green, and yellow) to fit each lens or adapted to fit the whole series of lenses.

4. A *heavy* tripod, capable of raising the camera to a height of 6 feet, with a 'tilting head' to enable vertical photographs to be taken.

5. A 6-inch bubble-level.

6. A large focusing cloth.

7. A small hand-camera of the Retina Contax or Rollicord type for speed or colour work.

8. A small box which can hold paint-brush, small scales, pins, and plasticine.

9. Tanks or dishes, one for developer, one for fixing, and one for washing. For economy, use packed developer and hypo powder in tins.

10. Printing frame. Check-prints from negatives will have to be made in the field, and, since conditions are likely to be cramped, the printing can be carried out with a printing frame. Bromide paper in three grades (soft, normal, and contrast) is required.

Note. For both negative-development and printing, a small timing clock is an essential, together with a thermometer to ensure that all solutions are at a working temperature. In Great Britain even in summer it is necessary on occasion to bring the developer temperature *up* to 65° F., and in Eastern countries it often becomes essential to bring the solution *down* to a maximum of 75° F. by the use of ice.

CHAPTER 16

Publication and Publicity

'A DISCOVERY dates only from the time of the record of it, and not from the time of its being found in the soil.' This classic sentence of Pitt Rivers proclaims fairly and squarely the ultimate moral and scientific duty of the field-archaeologist. It may be amplified by the familiar corollary that unrecorded excavation is the unforgivable destruction of evidence; and the more complete and scientific the excavation, the greater the measure of destruction. The less persistent methods of an older age may yet leave vital evidence for recovery: for example, in Lydney Park, Gloucestershire, a prehistoric and Romano-British site dug very extensively by an antiquary in 1805 retained all the evidence necessary to reconstruct its character and chronology by re-excavation in 1929. But to-day a site comprehensively excavated by modern methods may be practically gutted of its evidence, and must be written off. The emphasis is on the word 'written'.

The first task in the compilation of an excavation-report is adequate illustration. In this matter there is little to add, in principle, to Sir Flinders Petrie's assertion half a century ago that 'nowadays the main structure of a book on any descriptive science is its plates'. In fact, Petrie's own standards of illustration, genius though he was, generally fell far short of those of his older contemporary, Pitt Rivers, and would not be accepted by the average British excavator of to-day. Nevertheless, his chapter on publication[1] stands as a fair general statement of the theory of the business.

In the matter of literary content it may be said that there are two preliminary problems to consider: those of substance and of form. First, how much detail shall a report contain? The answer is necessarily conditioned in some degree by circumstance. Quantitatively, Pitt Rivers digging a reluctant ditch in Cranborne Chase and Petrie digging a crowded cemetery in Egypt are up against very different propositions. Let us glance at their reactions.

1. *Methods and Aims in Archaeology*, pp. 114–21.

Pitt Rivers approaches the problem with a formidable combination of acute sense and Victorian probity.

The record of an excavator [he says] takes about five times as long as the actual digging. . . . In my fourth volume . . . everything has been recorded, however small and however common. . . . Everything has been drawn, down to the most minute fragment of pottery that had a pattern on it. Common things are of more importance than particular things, because they are more prevalent. I have always remembered a remark of Professor Huxley's in one of his addresses. 'The word "importance",' he said, 'ought to be struck out of scientific dictionaries; that which is important is that which is persistent.' Common things vary in form, as the idea of them passes from place to place, and the date of them and of the places in which they are found may sometimes be determined by gradual variations of form. There is no knowing what may hereafter be found to be most interesting. Things apt to be overlooked may afterwards turn out to be of the greatest value in tracing the distribution of forms. This will be admitted when it is recognized that distribution is a necessary prelude to generalization. I regret to find in endeavouring to trace the distribution of patterns, that archaeological societies illustrate fewer things than formerly. It is thought, perhaps, that when a form has become common, there is no use repeating or even recording it. This is a great mistake in my opinion. . . . The illustrations need not be elaborate, but sufficient to trace the transitions of forms.

The General goes on to describe his *modus operandi*.

The compilation of a work of so much detail necessitates the employment of clerks. I make it a rule that nothing in the letter-press should be issued that is not in my own writing, and of course I am responsible for the whole. But the calculation of the numerous and tedious indices; the compilation of relic tables; the photographs; the identification, measurement and restoration of the skulls, bones and pottery; the surveys, the contouring; careful labelling and correction of proofs; the drawing of the plates; . . . requires the assistance of at least three men of different qualifications. Living in my house [he adds with a delightful Victorian smugness] they must necessarily be men of good character as well as energy. Those who have left me have generally obtained more lucrative employments. . . . As a rule I have been well served by my clerks.[1]

1. *Excavations in Cranborne Chase*, iv (1898), 27–8.

Thus Pitt Rivers. Petrie, overwhelmed by the mass of finds from his Egyptian sites, seeks refuge less in men of good character than in basic index-series or *corpora*, to which newly found material can be briefly and simply related.

The practical utility of such a *corpus* is found at once when excavating. Formerly it was needful to keep dozens of broken specimens, which were of no value except for the fact of being found along with other vases. Now the excavator merely needs to look over the *corpus* of plates, and writes down on the plan of the tomb, say B 23, P 35 b, C 15, F 72, thus the whole record is made, and not a single piece need be kept unless it is a good specimen.

Be it repeated that these two different methods arise from different local problems, and for neither can universal validity be claimed. There cannot be the slightest doubt that the Pitt Rivers system is the ideal aim, but it is only feasible where the material is limited in quantity, or where it does not lend itself to *corpus* classification: that is, where it is too fragmentary or variable for easy systematization. It cannot be disputed that in the more evolved industries, with which Petrie mostly dealt, a useful *corpus*-system can and should be evolved. An obvious example of a ceramic susceptible of *corpus* treatment is Roman *terra sigillata* or Samian ware, which is, or shortly should be, nearly as capable of a detailed standard notation as are Roman coins. These are now becoming a relatively simple matter. Thus in a report of mine some years ago Mr B. H. St J. O'Neil, later Chief Inspector of Ancient Monuments, was able to list the Roman coins with abbreviated references largely to the then new standard works of Mattingly and Sydenham, and thereby compressed his reasoned catalogue of 1,668 coins into eleven pages. This achievement may be contrasted with the allocation of eighty pages to 1,000 coins required in the Wroxeter reports in the same series, issued before the Mattingly-Sydenham *corpus* was published. In other words, publication without the *corpus* occupied twelve times as much space as publication with the *corpus*. The advantages of a scholarly *corpus* or yardstick need no further emphasis in such cases, and the extension of the *corpus*-system is certainly no less urgent now than it was in Petrie's day. But always with the proviso that it presents a very serious danger: it lends itself to loose usage and to the overlooking of those subtle variations of form, the importance of which Pitt Rivers rightly emphasized. Generally speaking, only an evolved and largely mechanized industry offers suitable material for a *corpus*. In practice, particularly in a malleable material such as pottery (unless made in moulds), it will always have to be extensively supplemented by individual illustration.

Whilst on the subject of the illustration of pottery, it may be recalled as a matter of passing interest that 1952 marked the centenary of the systematic sectional illustration of pottery in this country. The method, now standard, whereby a pot is represented wholly or partly in section, although used occasionally by Samuel Lysons early in the nineteenth century, was first formulated by (Sir) John Evans in his report on 'Roman remains found at Box Moor, Herts.', published in *Archaeologia* in 1852. He there shows four Samian vessels in section, and is at pains to describe his *modus operandi*. His description is a curious legacy from a painstaking age, and the description is worth quoting.

As the taking an accurate section of vessels such as those delineated [he writes] at first sight presents some little difficulty, it may not be altogether useless to record the process by which these sections were obtained. The piece of Samian ware after being slightly greased was plunged into fine sand, in a direction perpendicular to the axis of the vessel, to within about a quarter of an inch of the centre, and the surface of the sand was then made level. A thin mixture of plaster of Paris was next poured upon the sand until its upper surface was level with the centre of the vessel. When this was set, the fragment of Samian and the plaster were removed from the sand, and the plaster broken into a sufficient number of pieces to set the fragment free, and these pieces being reunited with their upper side downwards on a piece of paper, gave a section from which the form of the vessel could be accurately traced.

All this is a little reminiscent of the burning-down of the swineherd's cottage to procure roast pig; but in substance the procedure was a cardinal one, and is not the least of the many gifts for which our discipline is indebted to the great Evans clan.

I turn now to the second of our preliminary problems, that of the *form* which the excavation-report should assume. Here there is more room than usual for idiosyncrasy. Certain desiderata can, however, be premised. The report is intended primarily for the specialist-reader, but even the specialist may be accredited with a measure of human frailty. He is not above the appreciation of conciseness, clarity, and ready accessibility – three virtues which are less common than they should be in such literature. The Royal Society, in a pamphlet issued recently on 'The Preparation of Scientific Papers', has clear words upon this matter. 'Most [scientific] journals', it remarks with an amiable cynicism, 'prefer papers written for the moderate specialist, that is to say, an author should write, not for the half-dozen people in the world specially interested in his line of work, but for the hundred or so who may be interested in some aspect of it if the paper is well written.'[1] After all, an excavation-report is a scientific newspaper, with news-paragraphs, leading-articles, stock-market, hatch-match-and-despatch, and even 'small wants'. Let the writer of it study unashamedly the higher forms of journalism, and neither he nor his clientele will lose thereby. And just as, in a newspaper, one does not want or expect to read solidly from front to back in order to discover the salient news and views of the day, so in a well-balanced excavation-report the student may properly expect to discover something of the wood without a prolonged, tedious, and exasperating hunt amongst the trees. Of course the trees must be there, or the wood would not exist. But, alas, how many reports are merely jungle! – *biblia a-biblia*, fit only to be added to Elia's catalogue of *books which are no books.*

A year or two ago, a joint-meeting of three sections of the British Association for the Advancement of Science discussed 'The presentation of technical information', and the primary speaker, Professor R. O. Kapp, had much that was pertinent to say. To-day, he observed, talk and paper were among the more important of the tools with which the scientist and the engineer had to work. Time was just as precious when reading a report as it was when using an instrument, and the worker could not afford to wait while a verbose author was developing an argument at unnecessary length. If one could justify training for research one could justify training in the art of exposition. Let scientists attempt deliberately and systematically to raise the standards of exposition in all its aspects, and try to perfect and teach it. Until that was done, science would continue to be hampered by the bad work of poor expositors. Professor Kapp was followed and

1. *General Notes on the Preparation of Scientific Papers* (London, the Royal Society, 1950), p. 3.

reinforced by the representative of a distinguished firm of publishers, who remarked that in ten years, of over 600 articles of a scientific kind read and checked for publication, only five authors had sent in manuscripts in such a form that they could be forwarded to the printer without delay or query. He might well have added an old dictum of J. M. Barrie's: 'The Man of Science appears to be the only man who has something to say, just now – and the only man who does not know how to say it.' It is but fair, however, to add that our leading scientists are to-day aware of this shortcoming. At the Royal Society's Scientific Information Conference in 1948 considerable concern was expressed about the quality of scientific papers presented for publication, and the pamphlet (already referred to, p. 213) on 'The Preparation of Scientific Papers' was a result. Nor are the disease and its remedies confined to the scientific world. I commend to all and sundry two excellent booklets issued as directives to the Civil Service in an attempt to purge official English. They are entitled *Plain Words* and are from the experienced pen of Sir Ernest Gowers.[1] They are admirable reading and should be in the hand of every archaeologist.

Yet another word may be said upon this matter, for it is near to the heart of the business. I would appeal for a little more artistry in our scholarship. A generation ago, G. M. Trevelyan was inveighing against the dullness of historians, and we archaeologists are certainly in no better case.

The idea that histories [Trevelyan said] which are delightful to read must be the work of superficial temperaments, and that a crabbed style betokens a deep thinker or conscientious worker, is the reverse of truth. What is easy to read has been difficult to write. The labour of writing and rewriting, correcting and recorrecting, is the due exacted by every good book from its author, even if he knows from the beginning exactly what he wants to say. A limpid style is invariably the result of hard labour, and the easily flowing connexion of sentence with sentence and paragraph with paragraph has always been won by the sweat of the brow.[2]

That is, of course, as true to the archaeologist as to the historian.

1. Sir E. Gowers, *Plain Words; A Guide to the Use of English* (H.M. Stationery Office, 1948), and *ABC of Plain Words* (same, 1951).
2. *Clio a Muse and other Essays* (London, 1913), p. 34.

Sweating with the pen is no less important than sweating with the spade. And Trevelyan cannot be bettered when he stresses the *literary* function of the historian,

the exposition of the results of science and imagination in a form that will attract and educate our fellow countrymen. . . . I wish [he adds] to lay greater stress than modern historians are willing to do both on the difficulty and also on the importance of planning and writing a power-ful narrative. . . . Arrangement, composition and style are not as easily acquired as the art of typewriting. Literature never helps any man at his task until, to obtain her services, he is willing to be her faithful appren-tice. Writing is not, therefore, a secondary but one of the primary tasks of the historian.[1]

Of this excessively neglected matter of literary style more will be said later in the chapter. Meanwhile, it is opportune at this point to consider the form and planning of an excavation-report. Plain and effective writing implies a plain and effective structure, and even second-rate expression may sometimes pass if the basic arrangement is sound and simple. At the risk of raising a personal prejudice to a principle, I would lay down certain constituents as a *sine qua non* of every excavation-report. There need be little hesitation in demanding that the report shall begin with a very short summary, giving the main headings of the matter, the plot of the play, so that the reader is at once in possession of the context of all that follows. This summary may usefully be isolated in italics; let there be no mistake as to what and where it is. The nature of the second section of the report is more variable, depending upon the scope and character of the material. Where complex issues are involved, it is useful to have here a reasoned review and interpretation of the new evidence in the light of previous knowledge, recounting the new evidence only in sufficient detail to indicate the nature and degree of its authority. How far interpretation should partake of 'theory' at this stage and in this factual context is matter for judgement and opportunity. But an element of theory there must be if our facts are to mean anything. Julian Huxley well expressed it when he said that 'facts are too bulky to be lugged about conveniently except on wheels of theory'.[2] The facts of to-day are largely the selected and verified theory of yesterday. Once more, it

1. Ibid., p. 31.
2. *Essays of a Biologist* (London, 1926), p. 32.

is all a matter of proportion, and incidentally of a conscientious borderline between fact and theory, in so far as it is humanly possible to distinguish the two. In any case, either succeeding or preceding this section must, of course, come the full statement of structural and stratigraphical evidence which is the hard core of the whole report, followed by description and analysis of the finds. Lastly, it is sometimes useful (before a very full index) to include a short postscript to tie up loose ends and to indicate future needs. Appendices may deal with specially detailed or controversial problems, but it is not usullay advisable to clutter up an already elaborate report with an excessive number of appended essays.

In brief, the nucleus of a report comprises: summary, synthetic review, full statement of evidence, discussion of general context, appendices (if any), index; and, however elaborated, these cardinal features should be clearly defined, immediately obvious and accessible to the reader.

So much for the general shape of the report. Of details I do not propose to say very much, unless to reiterate the plea for brevity. There are reports that are excellent in substance but of such a prolixity as to make them difficult and painful of access. Suitable models are, however, readily available in our own language, and still shining at the head of them is Dr James Curle's monumental work on Newstead, published as long ago as 1908. The importance of a clear exposition of the geographical and physiographical features of the site is now reasonably well understood, thanks largely to the work of O. G. S. Crawford, Cyril Fox, Stuart Piggott, and Grahame Clark in these matters. The 'synthetic section' of the report will deal also with the distribution of forms: we may recall once more the Pitt Rivers axiom – 'distribution is a necessary prelude to generalization' – with the renewed reminder that a secondary function of the field-worker, if he be something more than a mere technician, is to place the evidence which he garners in its general context. Relic-tables, such as those evolved by General Pitt Rivers, have largely been abandoned by his successors in publication (though not in the field), and I am inclined to regret their omission. In suitable circumstances, particularly in dealing with the classification of a new or little-known culture, they serve a useful purpose, provided that they are associated with adequate sectional illustration. Graphs are sometimes a convenient and concise form of record: here again we may easily forget that the General led the way,[1] though in recent years Grahame Clark has developed them effectively for pollen distribution[2] and Christopher Hawkes for pottery.[3] Soil-analysis, where appropriate, is of such importance as to demand a special treatment which lies outside the scope of this book.

But always we come back to the vital and basic problem of illustration. All along the line, the excavator's fundamental function is that of record, primarily pictorial record. And in the preparation of his pictorial record he must clearly understand those technical processes of pictorial reproduction to which his draftsmanship and his photography must be subordinated if his published record is to do justice to his work. Satisfactory presentation is by no means a monopoly of the printer and the blockmaker. Authors and editors must know exactly what they want, and exactly what the technicians and their machines and the kind of paper available may legitimately be expected to achieve. To this chapter are appended brief descriptions of the processes commonly used for archaeological illustration; here I would merely emphasize as an elderly editor that too many authors are insufficiently aware of them. It is indeed highly advisable – one might say *essential* – for the student, as a part of his archaeological training, to visit a blockmaker and to see the processes in operation. Pity the poor blockmaker! His task at the best is no easy one.

A few other elementary exhortations may be added. Let us see to it that our maps, plans, diagrams, photographs state their purpose lucidly and concisely, without excessive margins and other waste space, illegible or untidy figures and lettering, or other irrelevant litter; and let them be printed on the right kind of paper. 'Of course', you will remark; but in self-justification I reproduce here two illustrations from standard archaeological publications as cautionary examples (Pl. 24, a and b). Let us in our line-drawings ensure clean lines, with proper differential emphasis, and simple lettering properly incorporated into the 'picture' with a just sense of balance. And though the artistic appeal of a scientific drawing is of secondary importance, aesthetic quality is not a negligible factor. It is at least as important

1. *Cranborne Chase*, i, following p. 162.
2. *Antiq. Journ.* xvi (1936), 35; xx (1940), 68, &c.
3. *Camulodunum* (London, 1947), p. 175.

as is good literary form in the text. It can help to attract and hold the eye, and so tighten the liaison between author and reader – an eminently desirable objective. In an archaeological photograph, a clear-cut, well-swept subject will tell its story with least effort to the spectator and will, incidentally, carry additional conviction as evidence of deliberation (contrast Pl. 22). It is a sound general rule that untidy work is muddled work. All that I have said in the earlier part of this chapter about the need for clarity of literary style applies to the all-important matter of illustration.

So much for general principle. In practice, as we all well know, archaeological illustrations are normally reproduced in one of three ways: (a) by half-tone block, (b) by line-block, or (c) by lithograph (direct and offset). Collotype and equivalent processes are sometimes used, particularly in foreign publications, with results which may be superficially attractive, even sumptuous; but detail is liable to be lost in inky shadows, and the result does not, as a rule, compete with good half-tone. It should be added, however, that the plates in the present book are reproduced by photogravure. Colour-processes are here omitted, although they have manifest advantages over black-and-white and will in due course become the normal medium. Indeed, they would doubtless already be the standard method, but for the mess which the world has made of its economics during the past dozen years.

*

But it is time to pass on to another aspect of the subject: to turn from the problems attendant upon scientific publication to a related matter which is at the same time easier and more difficult: to the not unimportant question of publicity and vulgarization.

Once more we may begin with Pitt Rivers. Speaking in 1897 he laments the inadequacy (at that period) of archaeological publicity.

If ever a time should come [he observes] when our illustrated newspapers take to recording interesting and sensible things, a new era will have arrived in the usefulness of these journals. The supply, of course, must equal the demand, but the demand shows what intensely stupid people we are. People bowing to one another appears to form the staple of those productions, as if it were not bad enough for those who are compelled actually to take part in such functions. Field sports are no doubt things to be encouraged, but can it be necessary to have a picture of a man running after a ball on every page of every illustrated journal in this country? Let us hope for evolution in this as in all other things.

It is gratifying to observe that, since 1897, evolution has not been idle in this matter. Within the last thirty years, our leading newspaper has seen fit to acquire exclusive rights in the primary publication of an Egyptian tomb. Another daily newspaper has financed the excavation of a Roman amphitheatre in Wales. Yet another has dug for prehistory in the bed of the Thames at Brentford, under arc-lamps at midnight. A well-known illustrated weekly is frequently first in the field in the announcement of archaeological discovery. *Pulvis et umbra* are news-items, and the excavator is perpetually harassed by amiable young men and women with probing pencils and cameras. In such circumstances, whether he wills it or no, it pays the excavator to give his courteous attention. A 'story' is in any case in the making and, if it is to have any sort of authenticity, its fabricator must be led gently up the right sort of path. The press is not always accurate and does not always emphasize those aspects of an excavation which are scientifically the most important; but sympathetic help is the best corrective of these failings, and may be regarded as a scientific no less than a social duty on the part of the modern archaeologist.

Long ago, G. M. Trevelyan remarked that 'if historians neglect to educate the public, if they fail to interest it intelligently in the past, then all their historical learning is valueless except in so far as it educates themselves'.[1] Recently, Mrs Jacquetta Hawkes has been urging much the same thing.

This [she remarks] is the century of the common man. Just as in the eighteenth and nineteenth centuries archaeology was adding to the art collections, the architecture, interior decoration and furniture of the wealthy and aristocratic, so it seems that in the twentieth we must take deliberate pains to make it add something to the life of a democratic society. Our subject has social responsibilities and opportunities which it can fulfil through school education, through museums and books and through all the instruments of what is often rather disagreeably called 'mass communications' – the press; broadcasting, films and now television. If archaeology is to make its contribution to contemporary life and not risk sooner or later being jettisoned by society, all its followers,

1. *Clio*, &c., p. 18.

even the narrowest specialists, should not be too proud to take part in its diffusion. I would go further and say that we should not forget the problems of popular diffusion in planning our research.[1]

Indeed, at the present time the public is prepared, nay eager, to meet the scientist more than half-way. It is now up to the scientist to contribute his share. To do him justice he is not unaware of this duty. There may yet linger in remote cloisters a few pedants of the old school who will have none of this *vulgarization*, but their mortality-rate is happily high. The modern scientist increasingly recognizes the public as his partners. He spreads the empyrean at their feet; he serves up to them the principles of evolution in simple language, sometimes spiced a little with a topical tendentiousness. A monumental work entitled *A Study of History* is a best-seller in ten volumes. *Prehistoric Britain* and *Prehistoric India* are popular Pelican books. A scholarly account of the Pyramids of Egypt finds thousands of readers. Of *Digging up the Past* a quarter of a million copies have, I believe, been sold. And so on. In this welter there is no secret refuge for the field-archaeologist. If he would hide, he must hide in the limelight.

All this is as it should be. A present-day excavation must provide for the General Public as a routine activity. Indirectly at least, that public is paying for a good deal of archaeology, through the national or rate-aided museums, through the Ministry of Works, through various Royal Commissions, through the universities, through archaeological schools overseas in Italy, Greece, Turkey, Iraq, and Jerusalem, through the British Council, and in a variety of other ways. In spite of taxation, it still contributes also a little directly and personally as a testimony of its practical interest. The popes and princes of the Renaissance have in fact been replaced by the British taxpayer. However embarrassing its attentions may be on occasion, the public is now in one way and another our patron, and must be cultivated and suitably rewarded.

On all my major excavations I have accordingly made some special provision for this incidental partner to our work. I may again quote from one of my reports on a site in Dorset.

Under conditions of unobtrusive discipline, the general public were

1. 'Purpose in Prehistory', in *London and Middlesex Arch. Soc. Trans.*, N.S., x (1951), 198.

deliberately encouraged to visit the site. Notices directed the visitor's approach from the nearest main road. He was told (by notices) where to park his car and where to apply for information. Throughout the excavations it was the duty of an official guide-lecturer either to explain the work to visitors or to organize reliefs of student-lecturers who, for regulated periods, undertook this task, which, incidentally, provided for the students in question an admirable training in clear thinking and simple exposition. The public was not charged for these services, but was invited to contribute to the cost of the work – a system which is in practice both more democratic and more productive than a fixed tariff. And, finally, a well-stocked postcard-stall is as popular as it is profitable. Picture-postcards of the site can be produced [or rather, could before 1939] at a cost of little more than a halfpenny each and will sell readily at twopence each. Interim reports of the work, produced at fourpence each, will sell at one shilling each. [Approximately 64,000 postcards and 16,000 interim reports were sold at the site in question.] ... In such multifarious ways can the present-day public be drawn to contribute directly or indirectly to archaeological research.

I would particularly stress the value to the archaeologist himself of speaking to and writing for the General Public. It is not difficult to be a specialist, to write fairly intelligibly for two or three fellow-specialists, to produce 'a preparation of opium distilled by a minority for a minority'.[1] I know a distinguished archaeologist who claims that he writes for five people; most of us are less ambitious. And as specialists we tend to develop a sort of professional jargon which is a deterrent to a wider audience and ultimately a handicap to the specialist himself. I have already in this chapter quoted from the proceedings of the British Association, and I am now reminded of a relevant presidential address at an earlier meeting of the same eminent body. At this meeting attention was drawn to the plague of pedantic verbiage which had infested modern science, and a plea was made for simplification and classification. That plea was a timely one; it might fittingly have been extended from professional science to professional sport, to the cinematograph industry and to professional journalism in general. The danger of all this jargon, at any rate in science, is not merely that it alienates the ordinary educated man but that it is a boomerang liable to fly back and knock the sense out of its users. In the words of

1. R. le Gallienne, *Prose Fancies* (1895), p. 81, speaking of poetry, but singularly appropriate to much archaeology!

the infallible Quiller-Couch, 'If your language is Jargon, your intellect, if not your whole character, will almost certainly correspond. Where your mind should go straight, it will dodge: the difficulties it should approach with a fair front and grip with a firm hand it will seek to evade or circumvent.' I have been turning over the pages of an excellent journal which makes it its business to present the results of scientific archaeology to the general public, and my eye has fallen upon three articles by three of the most eminent archaeologists of the day. On one page I am caught up in the hyphenated tongue-twister 'leaf-shaped-sword-culture-complex'; on another I am invited to consider 'the diagnostic value of negative lynchets'; on a third I am informed that certain place-names 'were left by the equestrian inhumators who brought in the later Hallstatt culture'. (One almost expects to turn the page and find a reference to 'tram-riding cremators'.) An excellent friend of mine, in an attempt to distinguish between the significant and the accidental aspects of megalithic tombs, has recently brought to birth two hideous monstrosities, the twins *genomorph* and *phenomorph*. I pray in all friendliness that they may be short-lived. Yet another of my friends has attempted to make the fairly simple phrase 'historical approach' easy for us by defining it as 'the endeavour to achieve a conceptual integration of individual phenomena in terms of specified time and space'. For a less academic parallel to this sort of thing I need look no further than the newspaper which lies beside me as I write: on its front pages is a quotation from a diplomatic manifesto in which the United States reaffirms 'its stand against unilateral cancellation of contractual relationships and actions of a confiscatory nature' – lovely phrase! Well, well; so one might go on; I have in fact quoted relatively innocuous examples of a widespread and malignant disease – far worse might readily be found. Admittedly, an advancing science is from time to time faced with a genuine and rational need for new nomenclature, new phrasing. But let the need be met with restraint and circumspection. One word is not necessarily more economical than two, whatever may be said elsewhere (in other contexts) to the contrary. On the other hand, one word will suffice to describe the scientific argot of which I am speaking; and that word is Hokum, an alternative to Quiller-Couch's 'Jargon'. Let us purge our writing and our thinking of Hokum. It is an infection to which the over-educated and the under-educated are alike prone. G. M. Trevelyan once lamented a comparable failing amongst historians. 'The substitution of a pseudo-scientific for a literary atmosphere in historical circles', he wrote, 'has not only done much to divorce history from the outside public, but has diminished its humanizing power over its own devotees in school and university.'[1]

A household remedy for this disease is not far to seek. It is to be found in deliberate and periodical *vulgarization*. My advice to the aspiring archaeologist is, Go and explain your ideas, young man, to the Much-binding-on-the-Marsh Antiquarian Society and Field Club. Shun all that is comprised in 'gobbledygook', that wonderful American carpet-bag for wordy and woolly pomposity;[2] use language intelligible to the local bird-scarer. Then at last you will begin to understand yourself if you have aught to say. Let us not scorn the *profanum vulgus*. In fact some of our greatest archaeologists and anthropologists have needed no reminder in this matter. The classic *Romanization of Roman Britain*, by Haverfield, J. G. Frazer's *Golden Bough* (until it became an encyclopaedia), and more recently *Prehistoric Britain*, by Jacquetta and Christopher Hawkes, and *Archaeology and Society* by Grahame Clark, are outstanding examples of the scholarly approach to a wide public, whilst Sir Leonard Woolley is a famous adept at the art. But perhaps for the masterpieces of popular writing in the scientific field as a whole we have still to look to men like J. H. Jeans or J. B. S. Haldane or Julian Huxley, or ultimately to Charles Darwin himself, whose strong, simple prose thrust down all barriers between minds and men. There was no Horatian sniff about Darwin.

Terse, vigorous, direct prose is ultimately a matter of the sensibility of the writer, but the smallest seed of it can be cultivated. I know capable archaeologists who are yet so myopic as scarcely to read a book outside their tiny 'subject'. And I find that Mr St John Ervine has observed the same phenomenon: 'Archaeologists', he remarks, 'are odd fish addicted to periods, and unwilling to take interest in anything outside their own speciality.' They have ceased, or have not begun, to cultivate their garden; at best, they are concerned only with a cabbage-patch. What can they really comprehend of works and

1. *Clio*, p. 25.
2. On gobbledygook see E. Gowers, *ABC of Plain Words* (H.M. Stationery Office, 1951), p. 57.

days, or how express their comprehensions? It is a truism that words create thoughts, only less than thoughts words. And the creation of words is no unskilled job. 'You will not get there,' says the infallible 'Q', 'by hammering away on your own untutored impulse. You must first be your own reader, chiselling out the thought definitely for yourself; and, after that, must carve out the intaglio yet more sharply and neatly, if you would impress its image accurately upon the wax of other men's minds. We found', he adds, 'that even for Men of Science this neat clean carving of words was a very necessary accomplishment.' Yes, words are uncommonly important things, even for Men of Science. And in the end, the *vulgus* is no bad judge. It is the duty of the archaeologist, as of the scientist, to reach and impress the public, and to mould his words in the common clay of its forthright understanding.

POSTSCRIPT TO CHAPTER 16

With reference to pp. 217–18 above, the following notes are added on the three principal processes of pictorial reproduction. By way of preface it may be observed that line blocks, when not exceeding the dimensions of the text-page, are printed with the text and are normally numbered as *text-figures*, with Arabic numerals. Half-tone blocks and lithographs are usually printed separately from the text, on higher-grade paper, and are normally numbered as *plates*, with Roman numerals. Line blocks of larger dimensions than the text-page are also treated as plates.

(a) HALF-TONE BLOCKS

Wash-drawings, photographs, paintings, etc., are 'continuous tone' subjects. For purposes of reproduction, such pictures have to be broken up into half tones (or broken tones), so that the final result is a printing-block made up of a series of dots, varying in size with the relative light and shade of the copy. This necessity arises because half-tone blocks are printed in exactly the same manner as type. A printing-roller charged with printers' ink passes over the surface of the block and by a 'kiss' touch imparts ink to whatever it contacts.

In order to produce these dots for inking, the process includes the re-photographing of the original through a ruled screen interposed in front of the photographic plate. The screen consists of lines ruled on optical glass to form square apertures with opaque dividing lines. These break up the continuity of the subject into dots of varying sizes, the high lights being represented by exceedingly fine dots, the middle tones by larger dots, and the deeper tones by still larger dots. From the negative so obtained a copper plate is made: this is done by coating the copper with bichromated glue and printing it in contact with the negative: the intersections between the dots are eaten away chemically, thus leaving the dots in relief. This copper plate is then mounted on wood and printed just as type is printed in a letterpress machine.

The size of the dots is controlled to meet various conditions of printing. Coarse newspaper-printing calls for a screen-ruling with approximately 60 lines per square inch, ruled at right angles to another 60 lines, giving intersections of $60 \times 60 = 3,600$ dots per square inch. For magazine-printing and such like, a screen-ruling of 100 to 120 is mostly used; for commercial work, 120 to 133 lines per square inch; while for the finest printing, such as that of scientific subjects printed on high-grade art paper, the screen-ruling is generally 133 to 150.

A printer may spcil a good block by bad inking – by the use of too much or too little ink, or by uneven inking. Only an experienced and skilled printer will get the best out of a block, and it is sometimes preferable to have the blocks printed by the blockmaker himself, if he has the necessary trained staff. Again, a block may be spoilt by the use of poor-quality paper. At its best, a half-tone block can be very good, but a second-rate block or the second-rate printing of a good block will very seriously mar any publication, however brilliant its other matter may be. Careful scrutiny in the proof-stage is essential.

There are certain points in which the author must help the blockmaker. First, glazed photographic prints are best for reproduction: matt prints, 'art surfaces', and toned prints should be avoided. Good glossy black-and-white are best. Secondly, the subject must not be overcrowded with detail, having regard to the scale of reduction desired. Remember that, at the best, no half-tone block can be quite as clear as the original photograph, and detail (sometimes essential detail) is liable to be obscured in reproduction. Thirdly, the actual size and shape to which it is required that the original shall be reproduced by the blockmaker should be indicated clearly on the back. Unnecessary margins (e.g. an excess of sky, or of foreground) should not actually be cut off the original, but the required margins should be indicated on the back by *lightly* ruled pencil-lines: care must be taken not to press heavily on the pencil and so to furrow the working-surface. Half-tone blocks, though not normally printed with the text, should not as a rule exceed the dimensions of the text-page, In 'sizing' blocks, do not forget to allow for the titles or 'legends'. Fourthly, avoid, if possible, the preparation of fresh half-tone blocks from existing half-tone illustrations. This involves double-screening and the production of a second-hand doubly obscured version of the original, and is almost always unsatisfactory.

A half-tone block may normally be made up to 15 × 12 inches.

Half-tone blocks, be it repeated, are commonly printed separately from the text and half-tone illustrations are inserted, usually on special paper, as *plates* (not figures). See above.

(b) LINE BLOCKS

Line-drawings in black ink are reproduced by the line-block process: that is to say, they are photographed by the blockmaker in a special camera, and the lines are transferred on to a zinc plate, the 'background' of which is then eaten away in an acid bath, leaving the black lines in relief for subsequent inking and printing. The zinc plate is then nailed or screwed to a wooden block through certain of its recessed portions. The line block, being printed in exactly the same fashion as letterpress, can, as noted above, be reproduced simultaneously with the latter, provided the size permits.

Normally, a one-third (linear) reduction gives satisfactory results, but one-half or one-quarter (rarely smaller) may have to be used. In the case of a one-third reduction (linear) a drawing 12 × 6 inches will come out at 4 × 2 inches and will therefore actually be only one-ninth of the area of the original: hence the use here of the term 'linear' in specifying degree of reduction.

It is essential that the draftsman, in preparing his drawing, shall know the extent of proposed reduction, and shall so be enabled to regulate the thickness of his lines, the size of his lettering, and his general style accordingly. An excessively thin line in the original will become in the zinc-plate an edge of metal so thin as to be liable to flaw in manufacture and damage in the act of printing. Lines drawn excessively close together will tend to merge on reduction: either the metal or the ink, or both, will tend to run from one line to the other, forming an untidy and unexpressive blot. This is particularly prone to happen in the hatching, especially the cross-hatching, of a plan. It is essential that the individual lines of the hatching shall be bold and distinct from one another. And nothing is more unsightly in a plan or diagram than lettering which cannot be easily read. The fullest allowance for reduction must be made in sizing the lettering of the original drawing. Make the lettering rather too large than too small.

In selecting the size, shape, and extent of reduction of a drawing, do not forget to allow space for the necessary title or legend (figure-number, etc.) at the foot. If the illustration is to be printed with the text – a desirable aim, not always feasible – the reduced drawing plus title must not exceed the outside dimensions of the text of a printed page.

A maximum size for a line block may be taken as 26 × 19 inches. Drawings to a scale above that size are reproduced by lithography, and it is better to use this process for all line-illustrations over text-size. A small lithograph is more costly than a small line block, but a large lithograph is less costly than a large line block. Small and simple corrections can be made on a line block but are very undesirable.

(c) LITHOGRAPHS

The old method of lithography – printing from drawings on plane-surface stone – has given way to modern processes of photo-lithography in which the map or plan is reproduced first as a photographic negative and then printed therefrom on to a thin sheet of zinc. By chemical processes the image is made to attract ink and the clean portions of the zinc to repel ink. Such a plate is held taut on a machine printing-cylinder. Ink-rollers charged with litho-ink and damper-rollers charged with water alternately pass over the entire surface of the plate. The inked image is pressed on to another cylinder around which a sheet of special rubber is stretched and therefrom on to the paper, hence the term 'offset' or 'litho-offset' or 'photo-litho-offset'.

The advantage of the 'offset' process is that fine line-work can be printed by the resilient 'kiss' touch of a pliable rubber sheet so that all undue pressure is avoided, and the inked lines are pressed gently into the texture of the paper without any image being visible on the reverse side of the sheet. Corrections, even minor corrections, should be avoided so far as possible.

A lithograph thus requires careful separate printing and cannot be struck off with the text.

Lithographic plates may normally be made up to 40 × 30 inches.

CHAPTER 17

What are we digging up, and why?

'No amount of technical knowledge can replace the comprehension of the humanities or the study of history and philosophy.'
WINSTON S. CHURCHILL, reported in *Københavns Universitets Promotionsfest den 10okt. 1950* (Copenhagen, 1951).

THE previous chapters have touched upon the history of archaeological excavation, upon the search for an absolute chronology as the ultimate basis for the ordering and interrelating of our data, upon the stratigraphical method as a contributory procedure, upon the need for long-term planning if we are to secure the systematic advance of knowledge, and latterly upon the very vital questions of publication and publicity. A little has been said also of the actual technique of digging, of recording in the field, of laboratory-work, and of staff. But there is one overriding aspect of our task which cannot be passed by in a concluding chapter; and that aspect may best be expressed by the question, 'What does it all amount to?' What are we trying to do in this rather complex fashion, and how far can we hope to succeed? Any answer to this question is inevitably subjective and prejudiced, but there is no great harm in a little honest prejudice. It may at least stimulate the wiser judgement of those happy critics who are devoid of bias.

Archaeology is primarily a fact-finding discipline. It has indeed been stated by an American writer that 'Archaeology *per se* is no more than a method and a set of specialized techniques for the gathering of cultural information. The archaeologist, as archaeologist, is really nothing but a technician.'[1] I have no hesitation in denouncing that extreme view as nonsense. A lepidopterist is a great deal more than a butterfly-catcher, and an archaeologist who is not more than a potsherd-catcher is unworthy of his *logos*. He is primarily a fact-finder, but his facts are the material records of human achievement; he is also, by that token, a humanist, and his secondary task is that of

1. W. W. Taylor, as cited, p. 43.

revivifying or humanizing his materials with a controlled imagination that inevitably partakes of the qualities of art and even of philosophy.

But these are after all mere words. What in fact does this thing, Archaeology, really amount to? The question is one which, in our evaluation of evidence, can never be far from our minds. No matter that in a majority of instances we cannot truly know: it is the privilege of the intelligent to ask questions, and the claim of the unintelligent to have all the answers. The state of philosophic doubt is not the least enviable of human conditions. Definition does not necessarily clarify.

Here at the outset we are confronted with elements of conflict. We have on the one hand the technician or, if you will, the 'scientist', busy with inches and analyses and smudges in the soil; busy with the anatomy of history or prehistory. On the other hand we have the humanist busy with its vital interpretation. There is a widespread fashion to-day to incline towards the former trend, to regard archaeology as a natural science and to discount the intervention of 'motive' and 'free will'. 'Motives', says Professor Gordon Childe, 'are in fact hardly capable of genuine historical study.' This trend is a useful reaction from the romanticism of a past century. But it can easily be carried too far. I have remarked elsewhere upon a tendency to devolve archaeology into a sort of dehydrated humanism, to mummify the past, to transform our predecessors into 'battle-axe folk' or 'beaker folk', until, by an instinctive and forgivable reaction, we begin almost to personify battle-axes or beakers with a sort of hungry latter-day animism. Such phraseology represents a tendency that can only be deplored. It runs deeper than its exponents sometimes realize. However broadly we use the words, man is in some sense the casket of a soul as well as five-shillings-worth of chemicals. And the soul or sensibility or mind – whatever we choose to call it – is beyond the reach of finite intelligence, since the mind obviously cannot encompass itself. Within the far-off limit of ultimate causes, the geologist can encompass or objectify the rocks with which he deals; not so the humanist with the intellect. There in the last resort all is subjective, it cannot be otherwise. Archaeology increasingly and very properly adapts and adopts the methods of natural science and unblushingly seeks its aid. It is not on that account itself a science in the class-room meaning of the term. At the best it is a very *inexact* science. But perhaps for that reason its demands upon the constructive imagination are more immediately insistent than are those of some of the more self-explanatory class-room sciences. For that very reason, be it repeated, the archaeologist is a great deal more than a rather superior laboratory-assistant. He is also something of an artist. O. G. S. Crawford was near the mark when he affirmed that 'Archaeology is an art which employs a scientific technique'. Or, as the Oxford historian, Sir Llewellyn Woodward, remarks, 'Historical understanding is more than a series of detective tricks. It requires a mind already attuned to the scale of human action and practised in the subtlest use of language to express the depths and heights.' That is well said. The historian, and with him I group the archaeologist, must have a spark of the intuitive comprehension which inspires the painter or the poet. 'The highest reach of science', proclaimed Matthew Arnold, 'is, one may say, a faculty of divination, akin to the highest power exercised in poetry.' All great historians have something of this power, and owe their greatness no less to it than to their scholarship. They make the past *live* because they are themselves alive and can integrate their reasoned facts with the illogicalities of life. Otherwise they were mere cataloguers, adding dust to dust and ashes to ashes.

As archaeologists, then, we are at the same time collectors and interpreters. The obvious next question is, What do we collect and seek to interpret? The question lands us at the outset in a minor quandary from which escape is urgent. Throughout these chapters the term archaeology has been used in the widest possible sense, including equally the study of eolithic choppers and of Victorian gas-lamps. Others are, I am afraid, sometimes less catholic in their usage. The French appear to have evolved a hierarchical distinction between *l'archéologie* and *la préhistoire* that is subtle enough to escape the average foreigner, but we have our British counterpart. From time to time one hears the terms 'archaeologist' and 'antiquary', or even that hideous and unnecessary pseudo-noun 'antiquarian', used with a sense of divergence significantly akin to that of 'sheep and goats', or 'chalk and cheese'. The antiquary, it seems, is the more genteel of the two; he sits in a chair and uses a quizzing-glass, or in moments of supreme afflatus crashes upon his knees and rubs a brass. The archaeologist, on the other hand, wears corduroy shorts, strides about on draughty landscapes with a shovel and an odorous pipe, and is liable to be an undergraduate. To these divergent types, might be added a third, the anthropologist, vaguely interested in flagrantly un-British 'natives'. Of course all this dichotomy or trichotomy is nonsense; but there does lurk behind it a nucleus of actuality of a not wholly desirable kind. The common tendency to discriminate archaeologists as prehistorians and antiquaries as medievalists does good to nobody. If anything, it attempts on the one hand to rob prehistory of a little of the humanity that comes more easily to the Middle Ages; and on the other hand to deprive medieval studies excessively of the cold and calculating objectivity that is attributed to the prehistorian. Recently, after training the young members of the staff of one of our Historical Monuments Commissions on a typical prehistoric site, I was glad to see them proceed with the excavation of a medieval site by the identical technique, with fruitful results ranging in period from the eleventh to the seventeenth centuries. And yet how rarely has that simple and obvious procedure been attempted! Let it be agreed that the two words 'archaeologist' and 'antiquary' shall in future be exactly synonymous, rooted in a common discipline and striving by the same or closely similar methods to the same end.

But what, when all is said and done, is that end? We have just agreed (I hope) to work as brothers, but what of the nature of our task? Let us for a moment consider its range, with specific examples. In a single year we have had the (former) Disney Professor of Archaeology at Cambridge busily and successfully exploring the Upper Palaeolithic in France and Dr Leakey sweating after his pleistocene industries through tropical Africa. Professor Grahame Clark in Yorkshire was extracting with consummate skill the remarkable relics of as squalid a huddle of marsh-ridden food-gatherers as the imagination could well encompass. Sir Cyril Fox, of science and imagination all compact, was, as recalled in a previous chapter (p. 18), reconstructing the mumbo-jumbo of miserable Bronze Age barrow-burials on the ultimate fringes of the ancient world. The writer was digging into the first foothold of wretched Iron Age immigrants on the English south coast and classifying their incompetent dog-biscuit potsherds. Mrs Stuart Piggott, with an inspiring fortitude, was ransacking the vacant

windswept vestiges of first-century hill-forts in the Scottish Lowlands, buoyed by the thought that it is better to travel hopefully
than to arrive. Professor Ian Richmond, on Hadrian's Wall, was
expending the profoundest learning and an incomparable astuteness
upon the uncovering of a medicine-man's go-down. The list might
easily be extended. But whither is it getting us? One may sometimes
find oneself in two minds about it all. Is all information worth while,
or are we justified in selecting and grading our material on a basis of
priorities? And, if so, what priorities?

This question might easily lead us into a prolonged discussion of a
semi-philosophical nature. The temptation may be resisted without
complete evasion of the issue. At the outset it is sufficiently clear that
no single or simple answer is adequate. Much depends upon the angle
of approach. Man is an animal with a biological tree. He is physically
an unspecialized animal, but with a specialized brain which enables
him to elaborate and amplify his physique by means of an increasing
range of artifacts or artificial limbs. He thus becomes the author of
industries, which accumulate into cultures: until ultimately he is
sufficiently equipped to live in large communities, or in other words
becomes civilized. In a large community the constant clash or col-
laboration of brains leads, under balanced conditions, to a great
civilization; under unbalanced conditions, to a proportionately great
human catastrophe. The period of balance may be brief, as in fifth-
century Greece, or long as in Dynastic Egypt. The period of unbal-
ance may be one of obliteration and oblivion, or it may be one of
patching and reshaping, of constant if unequal striving towards a new
goal. Such sequences and possibilities are sufficiently familiar and
need not be particularized, if only because Mr Arnold Toynbee has
displayed them to a wide public in terms of his own stimulating
philosophy of history.

This elaborate process manifestly offers to the student more than
one line of approach. In fact, modern archaeological research displays
a recurrent duality. The normal approach of archaeology in Great
Britain has in the past been along the lines of the classical tradition.
The Grand Tour and the standard classical education have never, until
recent years, been far from the mind of the British archaeologist; and
names such as those of Stukeley or Sir John Evans or even Pitt Rivers
himself do not outweigh the average truth of that statement. Greece

and Rome were the Mecca of the British student, provincialized a little in latter years by the great influence of Haverfield. For example, the Yates Chair of Archaeology in the University of London, in spite of its generalized designation, has always been interpreted as a chair of *classical* archaeology. And long ago we find the young Arthur Evans inveighing against the same bias at Oxford. Evans in his twenties was urged to apply for an archaeological studentship which had just been established in the University. His immediately reaction was: 'One feels that what is wanted is a student of "Classical Archaeology" and that anyone who wasn't would probably have scant justice done him at Oxford.' He went on to protest that 'the great characteristic of modern Archaeological progress has been the revelations as to periods and races of men about which history is silent. . . . Oxford, however, seems to have set itself to ignore every branch of Archaeology out of its own classical beat.'[1] Evans's youthful protest was in 1879. Four years later his mind was turning once more towards Oxford, and Dr Joan Evans has recorded an entertaining and significant correspondence between him and Freeman which further defines the contemporary attitude towards archaeology in these islands.

There is going to be established a Professorship of Archaeology [wrote Evans], and I have been strongly advised to stand for it. I do not think I shall, unless I see any real prospect of getting it: and to say the truth I see very little. To begin with, it is to be called the Professorship of 'Classical' Archaeology, and . . . to confine a Professorship of Archaeology to classical times seems to me as reasonable as to create a Chair of 'Insular Geography' or 'Mesozoic Geology'. . . . Europe, except of a favoured period and a very limited area (for I take it that neither Gaul, Britain or Illyricum were ever 'classical' in Jowett's sense) is to be rigorously excluded!

Freeman's reply to Evans was,

I think you should stand, if only for a protest. . . . Of course they will have some narrow Balliol fool, suspending all sound learning at the end of his hooked nose, to represent self-satisfied ignorance against you, but I would go in just to tell them a thing or two.[2]

1. Joan Evans, *Time and Chance: the story of Arthur Evans and his Forebears* (London, 1943), pp. 221–2.
2. *Time and Chance*, pp. 261–2.

The upshot was that Arthur Evans went his own way and discovered immortality in Crete. Not indeed until 1926, when the Abercromby Chair was established in Edinburgh, was there a real professorship of prehistoric archaeology in Great Britain; and, if we ignore the purely personal and honorific appointment eventually extended to Arthur Evans (in 1909) as 'Extraordinary Professor of Prehistoric Archaeology', only within the last few years has Oxford so shaken free from the old Jowett tradition as to follow suit with its own substantive chair of European archaeology. This is remarkable, but such is the fact.

In Scandinavia, on the other hand, the situation has been exactly the reverse. There not merely prehistory in general but Scandinavian prehistory in particular, to which much other European prehistory is very greatly indebted, held the field from the beginning of the nineteenth century onwards, and it is only in recent years that classical archaeology has achieved a recognized academic status; for example, by the foundation of classical chairs at Lund and Uppsala about 1910. In Scandinavia the undisguised parish pump has been respectable for a century and a half; in Western Europe as a whole it has, until recent years, been scarcely tolerated save under a classical pavilion.

To-day a great reaction is in progress. Swedes have become classicists and are digging up the Roman Forum; Britons, careless of their classics, are digging up mesolithic forest-scavengers in the mists of their own countryside. Indeed at the present time, save in the dilute form of Romano-British archaeology and apart from some notable work in North Africa by the British School at Rome, classical archaeology is here largely under an eclipse, whilst prehistory flourishes as never before. Even the modern Romans themselves have brazenly uncovered the post-holes of some disreputable prehistoric huts within a few yards of the respectable House of Livia on the Palatine. Old values are being shuffled and new ones are emerging. What is their relative significance? For example, is it really worth our while to expend money and talent upon an entirely empty stone hut on a Welsh mountain, whilst great sites on the arterial routes of human development remain scientifically untouched? True, the one is nearby and costs a few pounds, the other may be thousands of miles away and will cost thousands of pounds; but such opportunist factors are not for the moment at issue. The question is rather one of the principle upon which we are going to work, of our sense of proportion.

Once more, it is, one may suppose, all a matter of our line of approach. Much depends upon whether our starting-point is that of the biologist or that of the humanist. It has been argued by the biologist that human institutions are governed by the same kind of natural laws as is the development of the human body; that humanity and human institutions may properly be studied in much the same way as pigeons or earthworms. It is the developmental process itself that focuses the inquiring mind. Achievement, good or bad, is an element of processional change and is of no special intrinsic interest; it is a register of trial and error in the stumbling progress of evolution. Indeed the words 'good' and 'bad' are subjective misnomers. Who are we to distinguish between them? They are arbitrary grades in our yardstick of change; we might as well say that a fish is 'good' and a jellyfish 'bad'.

Admittedly the biological attitude is here stated crudely and perhaps unfairly. But Oswald Spengler, who has done not a little to lend this attitude the combined prestige of philosophy and history, states the matter in no very different style, and Professor Henri Frankfort has recently commented upon him in terms essentially parallel with my own. Spengler, remarks Frankfort,

actually calls civilizations 'living beings of the highest order', and he undertakes to state with precision which phenomena characterize each stage in their life-circle. For him, an imperialistic and socialistic order follow a traditional and hierarchical society; expanding technique and trade follow greatness in art, music and literature as certainly as the dispersal of the seeds follows the maturing of a plant which will never flower again. But to take the biological metaphor literally, to grant in this manner reality to an image, is not morphology but mythology; and it is belief, not knowledge, which induces Spengler to deny the freedom of the spirit and the impredictability of human behaviour.[1]

I too am of those, then, who, with all proper respect for Spengler and his kind, are not over-readily tempted to equate the development

1. H. Frankfort, *The Birth of Civilization in the Near East* (London, 1951), pp. 18–19.

of human institutions with the normal processes of organic evolution, to Darwinize human 'progress'. As Julian Huxley long ago observed, 'Numerous writers – largely because purely biological are simpler than human phenomena – have been obsessed with the idea that the study of biology as such will teach us principles which can be applied directly and wholesale to human problems.'[1] The tendency is doubtless in part a reaction from the Book of Genesis, but needs a more serious apologia than that. Organic evolution and social evolution are not, in the present or any forseeable stage of research, equivalent processes. Doubtless a remote eye, with a comprehension beyond that of the mere *homunculus*, would integrate organic and intellectual development and see them both as facets of the same crystal, cogs of the same machine. But to the close-up, myopic view with which we must content ourselves, the differences between the two processes are more significant than the resemblances. Professor Gordon Childe has recently had wise words to say on this matter. Speaking of the nature of cultural changes, in fact of 'progress', he remarks:

Inventions can be transmitted from one society to another [by diffusion]. But that is just what is impossible in organic evolution. By no possible means can one species transmit to another the mutation which has proved beneficial, even though both inhabit the same region. All that can happen is that natural selection gradually eliminates the species that lacks the mutation. It is, I suggest, the operation of diffusion more than anything else that distinguishes social from organic evolution and explains the curvatures of the lines in any graphic representation of the process.[2]

No doubt the old postulate of universal and identifiable and even predictable stages in human progress was the wishful thinking of an age which, both in the moral and in the scientific sphere, was strenuously setting its facts in order. Only, in the scientific sphere at any rate, its facts were, of course, inadequate. They constituted a sort of half-knowledge which, as is the way of half-knowledge, has usurped an authority out of all ratio with its intrinsic worth. It is a paradox that in an age when on the one hand the rights and prerogatives of man have been asserted as never before, on the other hand the scientific urge towards system and sequence has tended to put him into a

1. *Essays of a Biologist* (London, 1926), p. 75.
2. *Social Evolution* (London, 1951), p. 170.

queue or 'crocodile'. Must we queue up for everything, even for our humanity? Are we not all, even our scientists, getting excessively queue-minded? I am indeed at one with G. M. Trevelyan when he says that, 'even if cause and effect could be discovered with accuracy, they still would not be the most interesting part of human affairs. It is not man's evolution but his attainment that is the great lesson of the past and the highest theme of history.'[1] There speaks one with a surviving belief in that archaic phrase, the Nobility of Man. We need not close our eyes to Man-the-Jelly-fish or Man-the-Whole-time-Food-gatherer in order to believe in Man-with-Time-to-think-be-tween-Meals, in Civilized Man, but the last is, surely, of overriding importance. Civilization has been defined as 'the aggregation of large populations in cities; the differentiation within these of primary producers (fishers, farmers, etc.), full-time specialist artisans, merchants, officials, priests, and rulers; an effective concentration of economic and political power; the use of conventional symbols for recording and transmitting information (writing), and equally conventional standards of weights and measures of time and space leading to some mathematical and calendrical science.'[2] What a ripeness of human mind and effort all that implies! Man in his most fully expressive phase. As long ago as 1852 the president of the Archaeological Institute could pronounce with some show of reason that in archaeology

it can no longer be assumed that the obscurest periods are the most worthy of investigation. Those, on the contrary, should be preferred which are richest in the materials intrinsically deserving of study; that is, in the visible development of the human intellect, the display of personal character, the creative activity of the arts, the variety of the social relations, and the analogies or contrasts which these may present to life amongst ourselves.[3]

True, a modern supporter of that view lays himself open to an easy charge of atavism, and of choosing as his subject the kind of Man who has had most to say, has expressed it most amply in material things, and is therefore the most susceptible subject for the archaeologist.

1. *Clio*, &c., p. 12.
2. Childe, op. cit., p. 161.
3. E. Oldfield in *Arch. Journ.*, ix (1852), 3.

But I think not. After those words had been written, I heard Sir Llewellyn Woodward, whom I have already quoted, saying much the same thing, though in better shape. He was speaking of certain scholars who had, he said, regained for history a place among the Muses, affirming that they did so 'ultimately because they set a high value upon the dignity of man'. 'I repeat this term deliberately,' he added, 'because one of the signs of disintegration in our own culture is an unwillingness to consider that man has dignity, that his acts may be noble. Once this conception of nobility is lost, history becomes nothing more than a rag-bag, a pawnbroker's catalogue, or at best a psychiatrist's case book.'[1] To this it may be countered that 'nobility' is not of necessity absent from the savage, and that for example a Châtelperront point or a Solutrian lance-head may represent an achievement which partakes of the quality of intellectual nobility. But I am not prepared to admit the Noble Savage within my general definition of the term, for the simple reason that he *is* a savage, suffering from a savage's restricted vision, tangental reasoning and lack of opportunity. I have in mind something far more complex and comprehensive; something in fact which implies the background of civilization or some approximation to it; where the intelligence has been subjected to the widest possible range of stimuli and where its fruits have been most widely, quickly, and intelligently shared.

There may be less hesitation in emphasizing this approach, since there is, it seems, a likelihood that it may receive less than its due patronage from the archaeological student of the future. It seems probable that the humanistic approach to the study of antiquity may from now on give way increasingly to what has above been crudely dubbed the biological approach. That change is due in part to the fault of the humanists themselves. Until the citizens of Minos and of the Indus valley arrived with their unread scripts to complicate the scene, a normal approach to the great civilizations of the ancient world - those of Greece, Rome, the Nile, Palestine, the land of the Twin Rivers - was through the study of language. Archaeology suffered from a linguistic preoccupation, very necessary and valuable in itself but liable to obscure more material and equally valuable aspects. For it would appear to be a truism that the preoccupying study of language is rarely in practice compatible in one and the same

1. *Proc. of the British Academy*, xxxvi (1950), 112.

individual with the scientific, analytic study of phenomena *as they present themselves in the earth*. The linguist is, in my experience, a different sort of man from the excavator or the methodical student of cultural evidence in the wider sense. He is liable to be Little Johnnie Head-in-Air, and we all know what happened to him when he came to a hole in the ground. The consequence of all this has been to isolate certain fields of study, notably the classical civilizations, as preserves of a particular class of humanists, who have tempered their linguistic and historical training with art-criticism but have rarely got down to earth and studied the *stuff* of which their chosen civilizations are composed, or out of which their civilizations have grown. For them, Pitt Rivers has lived in vain. And now their own days appear to be numbered, and with a perverseness which I do not attempt to conceal I begin to lament their passing. To-day the study of Greek is very definitely on the decline and even Latin is under a cloud. We are in a period of speedy transition. The most eminent of our materialistic archaeologists to-day can, and does, read the odes of Pindar after dinner, but he is an elderly gentleman and it may be doubted whether there are more of his kind. The time has come to ask, What is replacing the traditional disciplines? A great variety of skills and techniques, but comparatively little that can educate and stimulate the humanistic imagination. For this vital quality is, it would seem, only in part innate. It is liable in most of us to be a tender growth and needs careful nourishment. It needs the sort of nourishment that reflective literature of the highest quality, with an historical colouring, can best supply. It needs something equivalent to a classical education, and it is difficult to say what the suitable equivalents are. Whatever they be, they are urgently necessary if we are now to save archaeology from an overwhelmingly biological bias.

In the past few moments the argument may seem to have turned a circle. It began with regret for the stranglehold of the linguistic tradition on certain fields of archaeological study, and ended with regret for the decline of that tradition. In actual fact I am once more regretting the prospect of archaeology passing wholly into the hands of the biologist and the technician, just as much as I have been regretting the older and now doomed monopoly of the linguist and historian. There is to-day a genuine risk of a new severance between humanism and science in these matters, just at the time when a closer integration of the two is feasible and necessary. The co-operation of biologists and geologists and botanists and physicists in our research is a welcome portent; there is more cause for doubt when we find our research passing increasingly to those whose main education has been in these fields of natural science. Man, we may be forgiven for recalling, is something a good deal more to us than an ingredient in the chemistry of the cosmos; and a course of poetry or philosophy may properly be regarded as no less needful for the young archaeologist – or the old one for that matter – than a course of pot-making or pollen-analysis.

This part of the present chapter may be closed, then, with the truism that Man is not only the author or vehicle of a culture-trend, he is also a personality. The struggle towards civilization has been the struggle towards the fuller development and the more ample expression of that personality. The corollary is that a fair proportion of our effort should be expended upon the exploration of sites and regions which are likely to reflect the major achievements of civilization. At present we are not doing that. Half a century ago the situation was different. In 1908 Hadrian Allcroft could write: 'Characteristically the English, who have done so much for the Hittite, the Minoan, and the Egyptian, have as yet scarcely concerned themselves to apply the same methods to the secrets of their own soil.' To-day the position is reversed. To-day we are perhaps excessively content with those little domestic secrets: year after year we devote in our island an abounding skill and enthusiasm to the huts or graves of the uttermost rejects of the ancient world. True, we add thereby some particle to the sum-total of human knowledge. But what does it all really amount to? How much does it really *matter*? What of the great world beyond? I was standing not long ago 5,000 miles away from here, in the steppe of Turkestan, upon a tumult of mighty mounds whither age after age came men from China, from the Mediterranean, from Ind, to exchange their goods and fertilize their ideas, to express the ancient world socially and aesthetically in the most complex polity then known to man. Could we but transfer a tithe of our scholarship for a few seasons to this great workshop of civilization – or indeed to many others of the same high potentiality – what should we not gain in our knowledge of human achievement? What could *matter* to us more than that?

This final chapter, therefore, is primarily an appeal for a higher measure of concentration, on the part of British archaeologists, upon the riper achievements of Man as a social animal. It sometimes seems to me that we are liable to start the race in fine form, but to run out halfway down the course. Let us for a change try to come in over the last jump. There is no sort of doubt that we in this United Kingdom can supply an initial field-training of a quality unsurpassed in the world. Here, in Britain, is our training-ground; but where is our ultimate fulfilment? The great adventure still awaits us in a shrinking and increasingly regimented world; and surely adventurers were ever a British export?

The word 'adventure' may be allowed to evoke a tangential sentence or two about a theme which is near my heart. The term 'adventure' is, of course, a relative one. Some, like the late Andrew Lang, are content to find 'Adventures among Books'. Others have to go to the poles or climb Mount Everest to find them. Many so-called adventures are entirely spurious. The other day I was reading a preposterous account by a professional adventurer of a journey through the Khyber Pass to Kabul, such as is made daily by countless greengrocers' vans. It was described as a journey 'through the Pass of Death to the City of Brooding Suspicion'. But, nonsense apart, I am firmly of the opinion that our young men and women will lose nothing by a little real adventuring, and their search as archaeologists for the footsteps of civilized man in Asian or African tracks will add an incidental stimulus of a kind which is otherwise increasingly hard to find. It is now nearly thirty years since John Buchan wrote *The Last Secrets*, heralding the end of discovery in a world which now had nothing more to hide from us. Nevertheless, until a very few years ago the young Briton was still enticed into the paths of adventure by the worldly prospects of governing a tract of Asia many times the size of England, or of trafficking with tribesmen on the roof of the world. Now, in 1952, numbers of these avenues are closed by political change. Much of the potential adventure overseas has suddenly gone out of our life, and, with it, that sharpening and shaping of the character which is a by-product of it. I am speaking soberly, not as a romanticist. Romance is merely adventure remembered in tranquillity, devoid of the ills and anxieties, fleas, fevers, thirst, and toothache, which are liable to be the more instant experience. I am commending first-hand adventure as a necessary medicine to the character of the young, and archaeology of the kind which I have been trailing before the reader is fraught with the right sort of adventure. If ever the student, in the chill recesses of his northern university, feel something of 'that love of the sun, that weariness of the north (*cette fatigue du nord*)' of which Madame de Staël wrote, with Winckelmann in mind, let him indulge it for a while and give him opportunity to do so. It will serve ultimately to enhance his proper patriotism, and meanwhile will harbour him suitably, as an aspiring humanist, in the lands of the south and the sunrise where the humanities and science and civilization were themselves brought to birth. He will gather no harm and possibly much good.

It remains to touch lightly on the large problem of the ultimate potentiality of our archaeological evidence. Whither, at the best, can it lead us? What, after all, matters most in this discipline of ours? If we are, perhaps, to select our objective with a little more thought for essentials than we sometimes do, what shall ultimately govern our choice? Recently, in an after-dinner discussion on relative values, it was rashly suggested to a Palestinian archaeologist that Palestine was rather a backwater. 'Yes,' he replied modestly, 'but, after all, we *did* produce the Trinity.' The conversation then lapsed. I have since been wondering afresh what the value of our archaeological evidence really is. What do our bits and pieces amount to? Listen to the grave words which Dr John Donne uttered on this subject three and a half centuries ago:

The ashes of an Oak in the Chimney are no epitaph of that oak, to tell me how high or how large that was; it tells me not what flocks it sheltered while it stood, nor what men it hurt when it fell. The dust of great persons' graves is speechless, too; it says nothing, it distinguishes nothing. As soon the dust of a wretch whom thou wouldest not, as of a prince whom thou couldest not look upon will trouble thine eyes if the wind blow it thither; and when a whirlewind hath blown the dust of the Churchyard into the Church, and the man sweeps out the dust of the Church into the Churchyard, who will undertake to sift those dusts and to pronounce, this is the Patrician, this is the noble flour, and this the yeomanly, this the Plebeian bran?

Who indeed? Not the poor archaeologist, who may at best bottle the dust and send it hopefully to Professor Zeuner. Dr Donne cannot be gainsaid, but see how he cuts at one of the roots of our study! In a classic sentence it has been observed that a great nation may leave behind it a very poor rubbish-heap. And are we, as practising archaeologists, to award the palm to the unknown Sumerian who was buried at Ur with sixty-three helmeted soldiers, grooms, and gold-garlanded damsels, two chariots and six bullocks, or to the Nazarene in a loin-cloth who was nailed up on Golgotha between two thieves? I merely ask the question, but cannot help feeling that, were archaeology alone the arbiter, the answer would not be in doubt. Give us helmets and gold garlands every time; bread and circuses give us, provided that the bread is carbonized and the circuses well-furnished with good solid bronze and marble. But let us at least, in our gratitude for these things, remember the missing values that cannot be appraised in inches or soil-samples or smudges in the earth.

All this is not very encouraging. The archaeologist may find the tub but altogether miss Diogenes. He may answer with botanical precision Browning's question, 'What porridge had John Keats?' without a passing recognition of the author of *Endymion*. He must accept these risks, consoling himself with the reflection that no single approach to human accomplishment can be other than partial and chancy. The literary historian who overlooks art and craftsmanship and environment may lose as much as the archaeologist who can produce for us a harp without its music or a tub without its philosopher. Let us therefore count our blessings. We cannot fully read the language of the Minoans, but their palaces and frescoes, their wares and jewels, are themselves a pictographic language that tells us not a little of their way of living, and hints, however vaguely, at their way of thinking. We must be content to do what we can with the material vouchsafed to us, in full consciousness of its incompleteness.

Such is the uneven foundation on which the archaeologist is expected to attempt a vital reconstruction of man's past achievement. And in this term 'reconstruction' is included literal, three-dimensional re-creation: the Palace of Minos as rebuilt by Sir Arthur Evans, Little Woodbury as re-created by Mrs Jacquetta Hawkes and her colleagues (Pl. 23), the Celtic chariot as set on its wheels again by Sir Cyril Fox. Whilst lauding such reconstruction, however, we may be well aware of its dangers. In the task of reconstruction it may be suspected that we are safest when we set aside the great civilizations of antiquity and confine ourselves as anthropologists to the less evolved communities, to folk whose anxious existence was concerned mainly with preservation from hunger, gods, and neighbours. Whilst we can never hope to follow in detail the convolutions of that intricate organism called the 'untutored mind' and will tumble inevitably into many gaps in its reasoning, at least its meanderings will lie generally within the horizon of our comprehension. But when, in the security and amplitude of city-life (civilization), men acquired leisure to think between meals, they began also to escape us intellectually, unless they were fully and intelligibly literate. Thus, it is not very difficult for the archaeologist to reconstruct the humanity of Little Woodbury but it is near the limit of his powers to revitalize Mohenjo-daro, for all its astonishing completeness and its admirable plumbing. Mohenjo-daro remains an isolated and petrified complex of another world, a dead city of the *mlechchhas* or aliens whose unintelligible words are not compensated for by any adequate pictorial art. The difference lies not merely in the relative dimensions of the two problems but, above all, in their widely differing quality.

Be it repeated, all this is not very encouraging. But the task of reconstruction, whether three-dimensional or two-dimensional, is one from which the archaeologist must not shrink. It is in a way the crown of his work. And it is surprising and reassuring to find how much good constructive material can in fact be extracted from a rubbish-pit – or lie implicit, for that matter, in the tale of a tub.

That is the end of the present argument, but a postscript may be added. The writer represents the end of an active generation. From his momentary vantage-point, on the one hand he looks back upon the path which he and his colleagues have tried to mark out during the past thirty years, and on the other hand peers hopefully into the mists of the future. Of the past thirty years, it may be averred that we have had to devote a disproportionate share to the invention and elaboration of basic techniques. That process will, of course, continue in the future, but we can perhaps claim – although it is rash to prophesy – to have reached a point from which technical improvement will be incidental and mainly in detail. A good deal of the rough pioneering has been done; it remains to exploit and develop. A second retrospective observation is that we have perforce devoted a great deal of our time to the systematization of cultures. This was inevitable. Thirty years ago we knew all too little where we were, all too little of the extent and direction of our material. We have had to set laboriously about the preparation of a grammar of our subject. Whilst amplifying that grammar, it is for the future to use it constructively and significantly. To change the metaphor, we have, as was remarked in Chapter 10, been preparing time-tables; let us now have some trains. Cultural catalogues are all very well, so far as they go. But they do not, of themselves, go very far. They are a means to an end. An admitted need of the present day is the methodical exploration of the *social unit* on a more expansive scale than has been normal in the past. The phase of the *sondage* or isolated trial-pit, however skilfully executed, is now in large measure past. What we need now is horizontal excavation on an extensive scale. Let us take, as an example, an Anglo-Saxon cemetery. It is not enough to know its general period and character. We now require more precise and ample information. How many graves does it contain in its entirety? What range of time does it cover? What social grades does it indicate? What population-unit does it represent? To answer these questions, we need the careful uncovering of a *whole* cemetery, not merely a few graves here and there. And, in appraising its significance, a suggestion may be offered if only as a *jeu d'esprit*. Let some enterprising investigator make an actuarial and chronological survey of the reasonably modern gravestones of some existing non-industrial village in England or Scotland, and compare its grave-groups with the equivalent periodic census-returns for that village. What ratio does the one bear to the other? A series of such experiments, used with proper care and a good deal of reservation, might introduce a new element of semi-objectivity into the population-problems which are of such vital importance to our understanding of past societies. Indeed, if I were asked to name one problem more than another which demands investigation during the next thirty years, whether here or abroad, I should say, 'the problem of numbers'. It is not an inappropriate exhortation in a census-year, and within a few months of Professor Max Mallowan's great discovery of the census-record of Assyrian Nimrud, to urge that the people of the past be numbered. No light task for the archaeologist, but an essential one if we are to transform dry bones into something approaching live social history. Let us – and by 'us' I mean 'you of the new generation' – get down to this task with steadfastness and determination. Long ago, at Troy, at Silchester, at Mohenjo-daro, at Glastonbury, we learned to hack open the earth and to broadcast its treasures. Later, we learned by careful small-scale dissection how to explore analytically in depth. We now need full-scale three-dimensional excavation, combining the merits of both methods; the total excavation of complete settlements; the provision of reliable data for estimating the density and social structure of population. Up to date, very little of the requisite work has been undertaken and its distribution is very uneven. Indeed, nearly the whole social problem lies before us, and we are now at last fit to tackle it. I envy the new generation its great opportunity, as never before, to dig up people rather than mere things, and to enable us, in the fullness of time, to view the past and the present as a single, continuous and not always unsuccessful battle between Man and his Environment and, above all, between Man and himself.

And from the privilege of the printed page one final challenge may be thrown to the young archaeologist. In years past, Victor Hugo reminded us that we are all under sentence of death.

We have an interval [added Walter Pater] and then our place knows us no more. . . . Our one chance lies in expanding that interval, in getting as many pulsations as possible into the given time. Great passions may give us this quickened sense of life, ecstasy and sorrow of love, the various forms of enthusiastic activity, disinterested or otherwise, which come naturally to many of us. Only be sure it is passion – that it does yield you this fruit of a quickened, multiplied consciousness.

Those are fine words of Walter Pater's, finely thought. They may here serve to remind us, once and for all, that the scientist, the archaeologist, is no mere clerk in a counting-house, no mere draftsman in a drawing-office. Passion, enthusiasm, call it what you will – 'vitality', the overworked *élan vital* will do – that is the basic quality which our discipline exacts from us. And if you who are entering upon it have no vital urge within, turn, I beg of you, to some less human and more finite avocation than the study of mankind. There are enough already of the house-painters who ape the artist.

SELECT BIBLIOGRAPHY

R. J. C. ATKINSON, *Field Archaeology* (London, 1946).

K. M. KENYON, *Beginning in Archaeology* (London, 1952).

GRAHAME CLARK, *Archaeology and Society* (London, 1939).

O. G. S. CRAWFORD, *Archaeology in the Field* (London, 1953).

F. E. ZEUNER, *Dating the Past* (2nd ed., London, 1950).

A. LAMING (editor), *La Découverte du passé* (Paris, 1952).

H. J. PLENDERLEITH, *The Preservation of Antiquities* (London, 1934).

GLYN E. DANIEL, *A Hundred Years of Archaeology* (London, 1950).

M. B. COOKSON, *Photography for Archaeologists* (London, 1954).

INDEX

MORE ABOUT PENGUINS
AND PELICANS

If you have enjoyed reading this book you may wish to know that *Penguin Book News* appears every month. It is an attractively illustrated magazine containing a complete list of books published by Penguins and still in print, together with details of the month's new books. A specimen copy will be sent free on request.

Penguin Book News is obtainable from most bookshops; but you may prefer to become a regular subscriber at 3s. for twelve issues. Just write to Dept EP, Penguin Books Ltd, Harmondsworth, Middlesex, enclosing a cheque or postal order, and you will be put on the mailing list.

Some other books published by Penguins are described on the following pages.

Note: *Penguin Book News* is not
available in the U.S.A.

THE MEGALITH BUILDERS OF
WESTERN EUROPE

GLYN DANIEL

Maes Howe, New Grange, Stonehenge, and the stone rows of Carnac are among the prehistoric wonders of the world. But since the seventeenth century, when they were linked with Druids and giants, a great deal of nonsense has been written about them. A century and a half of excavation and comparative research, however, has told us much about these people who could set up a single standing stone sixty-five feet in height, place a capstone of a hundred tons in position, and build monuments which have lasted for four thousand years and more.

In this study Dr Glyn Daniel, the Cambridge archaeologist who is well known to television viewers, deals principally with the chamber tombs – the most significant element in megalithic constructions. His book provides the only complete and up-to-date introduction to the earliest architecture of Western Europe.

'A landmark in the history of the subject . . . a most concise and readable description of the main types of megalith in Western Europe and an outline of the many controversies . . . which have raged around them' –Prof. R. J. C. Atkinson in the *Sunday Times*

'Unusually clear and sensible conclusions . . . an able survey of the whole subject' *Observer*

DIGGING UP THE PAST

LEONARD WOOLLEY

When archaeology gets into the news it has a habit of making the headlines, for the public imagination is profoundly moved by such discoveries as those of Tutankhamen's Tomb or the Palace of Minos in Crete. But although the men who dig in Egypt or the Middle East often unearth great treasures, they are not engaged on mere treasure-hunts. They are exploring the history of humanity and relating successive cultures to each other. Sir Leonard Woolley begins his fascinating book by explaining what archaeology is about.

In successive chapters he describes how a 'dig' is organized on lines as carefully planned as a military campaign; and how the delicate processes of getting inside a site are carried out. One of the most absorbing sections of his exposition deals with the exact science of 'grave-digging' in the royal cemeteries of antiquity. No less attractive and revealing to the general reader is Sir Leonard Woolley's explanation of how the evidence brought to light by archaeological discovery is analysed, and how it is tested before it is admitted as a link in the endless chain of human history.

Digging Up the Past is illustrated by a fine series of plates covering many of the processes, and the discoveries of archaeology in Ur, Italy, Palestine, Knossos, Egypt, and Scandinavia.